EX LIBRIS

VINTAGE CLASSICS

W Still

WILLIAM STILL

William Still (1821–1902) was an African American abolitionist, writer and historian. As a conductor for the Underground Railroad – the covert resistance network created to aid and protect slaves seeking freedom – William Still helped as many as eight hundred people escape enslavement. He also meticulously collected the letters, biographical sketches, arrival memos, and ransom notes of the escapees. His book, *The Underground Railroad Records* collected an archive of primary documents that traced the narrative arc of the greatest, most successful campaign of civil disobedience in American history.

QUINCY T. MILLS (EDITOR)

Quincy T. Mills, associate professor of history at the University of Maryland, College Park, received his Ph.D. from the University of Chicago in 2006. He was awarded an American Council of Learned Societies Fellowship in 2013. He is the co-editor, with Benjamin Talton, of *Black Subjects in Africa and Its Diasporas: Race and Gender in Research and Writing* (2011) and author of *Cutting Along the Color Line: Black Barbers and Barber Shops in America* (2013).

WILLIAM STILL

Passengers

True Stories of the Underground Railroad

EDITED AND ABRIDGED FROM
THE UNDERGROUND RAILROAD RECORDS BY
Quincy T. Mills

WITH AN INTRODUCTION BY
Ta-Nehisi Coates

VINTAGE

2 4 6 8 10 9 7 5 3 1

Vintage
20 Vauxhall Bridge Road,
London SW1V 2SA

Vintage Classics is part of the Penguin Random House
group of companies whose addresses can be found at
global.penguinrandomhouse.com

Penguin
Random House
UK

Foreword Copyright © Quincy T. Mills 2019
Introduction Copyright © Ta-Nehisi Coates 2019
Map Copyright © Bill Donohoe 2020

This edition published by arrangement with Modern Library, an im-
print of Random House, a division of Penguin Random House LLC

The Underground Railroad Records were first
published in the United States in 1872
This edited and abridged edition first published in
Great Britain by Vintage Classics in 2020

penguin.co.uk/vintage

A CIP catalogue record for this book is available from the British Library

ISBN 9781784876326

Printed and bound in Great Britain by Clays Ltd, Elcograf S.p.A.

CONTENTS

William Still's *The Underground Railroad Records* is a massive testimony of resistance. The "Road," as Still would often refer to it, was paved and rugged, choreographed and improvised. Enslaved people shipped themselves in boxes, stowed away in steamships, and stole away the value placed on their labor and bodies as they dressed as men or passed as free to travel north.

Still stood as a historian of fugitivity. An entrepreneur in Philadelphia and, beginning in 1847, a clerk and corresponding secretary of the Pennsylvania Anti-Slavery Society, he became active in the abolitionist movement. When antislavery activists reorganized the Vigilant Committee into the Vigilance Committee after the Fugitive Slave Act of 1850, Still served as its chairman and coordinated a vast network of antislavery advocates and provided a welcome to many tired souls looking for safe passage anywhere in North America. Still welcomed approximately 649 fugitives and recorded their stories, experiences, and expectations. These records of the Road provide a window onto the paradox of slavery and freedom, and the space between them.

Still first published *The Underground Railroad Records* in 1872. This and subsequent editions included anecdotes, firsthand accounts, and letters from those escaping slavery and those assisting. Still's archival collection amounted to over eight hundred pages. This present edition has been heavily edited to provide readers access to this significant text. While I have omitted approximately two-thirds of the material, I have privileged the experiences of women and families in this edition.

Historians have written extensively about enslaved men who

fled slavery. The assumption was that enslaved women showed up in the advertisements for fugitive slaves less often than men because women were less likely to leave children behind. While this is a misreading of the advertisements, *The Underground Railroad Records* demonstrates that Black women ran away often, with and without children, husbands, and other family members. They were creative and steadfast in their fight and flight.

As much as this text is about slavery and freedom, it is centrally about family. These accounts, and particularly the letters from fugitives to Still, reveal their longing for those left behind. They wanted Still's help in getting wives, husbands, or children out of slavery or help reuniting them with loved ones who left before them and may have been in hiding. They attempted to reconstitute families as a function of how they understood freedom. Indeed, these are love letters, sorrow songs of ingenuity and hope, and records of visibility from people who needed to remain invisible and out of sight.

I have left the letters from enslaved men and women intact, misspellings and all. As Still himself notes, "The originals, however ungrammatically written or erroneously spelt, in their native simplicity possess such beauty and force as corrections and additions could not possibly enhance." While it may take the reader a little time to decipher some words in the text, this minor inconvenience is the least we can endure considering the circumstances and larger historical context in which these letters were written.

Given the time and space constraints, I have omitted a number of accounts and sections of the original text. To be clear, every fugitive, every account, every experience is singularly weighted with the heavy heart and soul of one's journey toward a more free place. In addition to privileging women's experiences, I also sought to include different kinds of journeys from a variety of locations. Although Still's text is also about the work of the Vigilance Committee, I have elected to omit a major section, "Portraits and Sketches," that provides short biographies of some of the most famous and active Black and White abolitionists of the nineteenth century. Many of these names, however, show up in the various accounts of fugitives' journeys. I accept sole responsibility for any errors or shortcomings in this curated edition.

The stories in this book are gripping, heart-wrenching, and telling of the fortitude of those denied liberty. These are stories of the past, but we should not look past their illuminations on our present. Angela Davis's and Assata Shakur's fugitivity could be appended to this text. The stories of unarmed Black men and women could, too, be appended to this text as many have sought spaces something akin to freedom. Their Road was more modern but no more paved. Still's *The Underground Railroad Records* paradoxically hides and unveils the practice of freedom.

—QUINCY T. MILLS

INTRODUCTION

When I was a child one of my favorite field trips was from my Baltimore public school to the National Museum of Natural History at the Smithsonian in Washington. What I remember, and what I loved best, was the life-size dioramas of the past—still dramatizations of Neanderthals or watering holes somewhere on the savannah. Even then I was fascinated by history—a world that shaped my own, but that I could never visit. The dioramas, three-dimensional reconstructions of the past, were as close as I could ever get. The importance of that key word—*reconstructions*—I would not learn until much later. The problems inherent to reconstructing the past, the importing of modern prejudice and expectations, were all there in those dioramas depicting, for instance, the first meetings between the pilgrims and the Native Americans. But the inherent problem of reconstruction isn't simply the importing of prejudice—the problem is in its promise that the past is a fixed entity and can be objectively reconstructed. But the truth is that the past can never be fully captured because the past no longer exists. All we have of it are the dramatizations we conjure, the dioramas we construct, the stories we tell.

For most of American history, this country's historians and mythmakers have favored a particular story of the epic of enslavement and all that came of it. The story comes in two forms. At its most sympathetic, it features heroic whites, joined by pliant and accommodating blacks triumphing over the worst of their bigoted brethren. The recurring vocabulary of this story features a vague "love" and shapeless "hope," which somehow triumphed over a wild and virulent race hatred. In the worse version of the story, these haters are transformed into Arthurian knights, tragically defending an ancient and noble way of life, of which enslavement is but a small part. What each of these stories has in common is the inability to consider the enslaved as the hero of their own epic.

But while these might be the best-known stories, they are not the only ones. From the time of their enslavement to this very day, black people have told different stories—ones that have not enjoyed the glamour and lights of Hollywood. The importance of these stories is not that they present a "different" or "revisionist" story of the past, nor in their lack of embellishment or blind spots. What makes them so vital is that they do not take as their premise an outright lie.

There is no better illustration of this alternative history than William Still's *The Underground Railroad Records*. Still was a conductor for the Underground Railroad, and, of equal importance, he was a lay historian, recording the small daily acts of bravery he witnessed in his work. Still was not burdened with the need to use these stories to exculpate himself from the sins of slavery; nor did he need to establish himself at the center of the story. This allowed him to focus on the people who had the most at stake—the runaways who risked their bodies to escape enslavement. Still simply allows the acts of those he shepherded through to speak for themselves. And those acts of the once enslaved, collected in *The Underground Railroad Records*, offer not just a set of stories that needs no adornment but stories that are ultimately more thrilling than the fabrications that erase them. In a righteous world—one where the dioramas were not fabricated merely to enforce prevailing ideologies—these stories, with their high drama of escape, of freedom, of disguise and espionage, would be the raw material of our national mythmaking. They are as exciting as any Western and as suspenseful as any Mafia movie. But because these stories and their heroes cannot be made to excuse their country's crimes they have mostly existed in the collective memory and history of their descendants.

I think that's changing. It's hard to miss the recent flowering in the world of novels and film of a renewed interest in the story of enslavement told with the enslaved as the central characters. That movement dates back to the fights waged by black historians to see the black past recognized. But, whereas once these stories were told and consumed because it was "the right thing to do," what we now see in the work of a Colson Whitehead or a Yaa Gyasi is black authors drawing from the epic of enslavement and freedom because it makes it our greatest and richest, most heartbreaking and inspiring story.

It is my humble honor to now count myself among the ranks of these storytellers with the publication of *The Water Dancer*, a novel that takes as one of its central inspirations the story of the Still family and their personal struggle against enslavement. William Still tells his story best himself. But what captivated me about the tale was the fact that it centered around something basic and central to human life everywhere—the preservation and protection of family. In this, William Still's struggle is not very different from those he offers up in these pages. Time and time again, when those who escaped enslavement are asked why they fled, their answers turn on the sale or death of a family member. Black people, even in the time of William Still, have long been maligned for their alleged disregard of "family values." And yet it is hard to imagine a greater stand for family than risking all one possesses to preserve family or reconstitute it.

—TA-NEHISI COATES

PASSENGERS

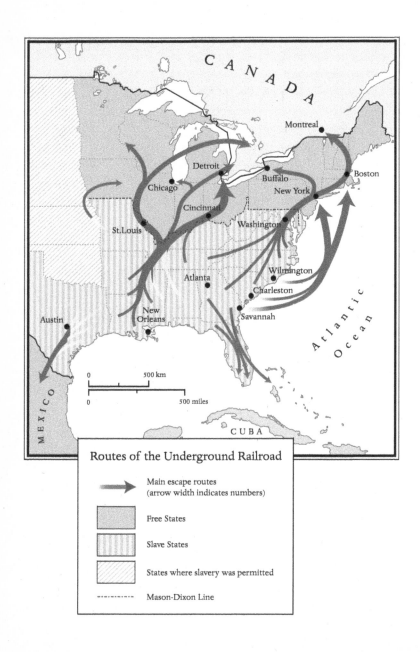

Routes of the Underground Railroad

→ Main escape routes
(arrow width indicates numbers)

Free States

Slave States

States where slavery was permitted

------ Mason-Dixon Line

Preface to Revised Edition

Like millions of my race, my mother and father were born slaves, but were not contented to live and die so. My father purchased himself in early manhood by hard toil. Mother saw no way for herself and children to escape the horrors of bondage but by flight. Bravely, with her four little ones, with firm faith in God and an ardent desire to be free, she forsook the prison-house, and succeeded, through the aid of my father, to reach a free State. Here life had to be begun anew. The old familiar slave names had to be changed, and others, for prudential reasons, had to be found. This was not hard work. However, hardly months had passed ere the keen scent of the slave-hunters had trailed them to where they had fancied themselves secure. In those days all power was in the hands of the oppressor, and the capture of a slave mother and her children was attended with no great difficulty other than the crushing of freedom in the breast of the victims. Without judge or jury, all were hurried back to wear the yoke again. But back this mother was resolved never to stay. She only wanted another opportunity to again strike for freedom. In a few months after being carried back, with only two of her little ones, she took her heart in her hand and her babes in her arms, and this trial was a success. Freedom was gained, although not without the sad loss of her two older children, whom she had to leave behind. Mother and father were again reunited in freedom, while two of their little boys were in slavery. What to do for them other than weep and pray, were questions unanswerable. For over forty years the mother's heart never knew what it was to be free from anxiety about her lost boys. But no tidings came in answer to her many prayers, until one of them, to the great astonishment of his relatives, turned up in Philadelphia, nearly fifty years of age, seeking his long-lost parents. Being directed to the Anti-Slavery Office for instructions as to the best plan to adopt to find out the whereabouts of his parents, fortunately he fell into the hands of his own brother, the writer, whom he had never heard of before, much less seen or known. And here began revelations connected with this marvellous coincidence, which influenced me, for years previous to Emancipation, to preserve the matter found in the pages of this humble volume.

And in looking back now over these strange and eventful Providences, in the light of the wonderful changes wrought by Emancipation, I am more and more constrained to believe that the reasons, which years ago led me to aid the bondman and preserve the records of his sufferings, are to-day quite as potent in convincing me that the necessity of the times requires this testimony.

And since the first advent of my book, wherever reviewed or read by leading friends of freedom, the press, or the race more deeply represented by it, the expressions of approval and encouragement have been hearty and unanimous, and the thousands of volumes which have been sold by me, on the subscription plan, with hardly any facilities for the work, makes it obvious that it would, in the hands of a competent publisher, have a wide circulation.

And here I may frankly state, that but for the hope I have always cherished that this work would encourage the race in efforts for self-elevation, its publication never would have been undertaken by me.

I believe no more strongly at this moment than I have believed ever since the Proclamation of Emancipation was made by Abraham Lincoln, that as a class, in this country, no small exertion will have to be put forth before the blessings of freedom and knowledge can be fairly enjoyed by this people; and until colored men manage by dint of hard acquisition to enter the ranks of skilled industry, very little substantial respect will be shown them, even with the ballot-box and musket in their hands.

Well-conducted shops and stores; lands acquired and good farms managed in a manner to compete with any other; valuable books produced and published on interesting and important subjects—these are some of the fruits which the race are expected to exhibit from their newly gained privileges.

If it is asked "how?" I answer, "through extraordinary determination and endeavor," such as are demonstrated in hundreds of cases in the pages of this book, in the struggles of men and women to obtain their freedom, education and property.

———

These facts must never be lost sight of.

———

The race must not forget the rock from whence they were hewn, nor the pit from whence they were digged.

Like other races, this newly emancipated people will need all the knowledge of their past condition which they can get.

The bondage and deliverance of the children of Israel will never be allowed to sink into oblivion while the world stands.

Those scenes of suffering and martyrdom millions of Christians were called upon to pass through in the days of the Inquisition are still subjects of study, and have unabated interest for all enlightened minds.

The same is true of the history of this country. The struggles of the pioneer fathers are preserved, produced and re-produced, and cherished with undying interest by all Americans, and the day will not arrive while the Republic exists, when these histories will not be found in every library.

While the grand little army of abolitionists was waging its untiring warfare for freedom, prior to the rebellion, no agency encouraged them like the heroism of fugitives. The pulse of the four millions of slaves and their desire for freedom, were better felt through "The Underground Railroad," than through any other channel.

———

Frederick Douglass, Henry Bibb, Wm. Wells Brown, Rev. J.W. Logan, and others, gave unmistakable evidence that the race had no more eloquent advocates than its own self-emancipated champions.

Every step they took to rid themselves of their fetters, or to gain education, or in pleading the cause of their fellow-bondmen in the lecture-room, or with their pens, met with applause on every hand, and the very argument needed was thus furnished in large measure. In those dark days previous to emancipation, such testimony was indispensable.

The free colored men are as imperatively required now to furnish the same manly testimony in support of the ability of the race to surmount the remaining obstacles growing out of oppression, ignorance, and poverty.

In the political struggles, the hopes of the race have been sadly disappointed. From this direction no great advantage is likely to arise very soon.

Only as desert can be proved by the acquisition of knowledge and the exhibition of high moral character, in examples of economy and a disposition to encourage industrial enterprises, conducted by men of their own ranks, will it be possible to make political progress in the face of the present public sentiment.

Here, therefore, in my judgment is the best possible reason for vigorously pushing the circulation of this humble volume—that it may testify for thousands and tens of thousands, as no other work can do.

WILLIAM STILL, Author.
September, 1878. Philadelphia, Pa.

SETH CONCKLIN

In the long list of names who have suffered and died in the cause of freedom, not one, perhaps, could be found whose efforts to redeem a poor family of slaves were more Christlike than Seth Concklin's, whose noble and daring spirit has been so long completely shrouded in mystery. Except John Brown, it is a question, whether his rival could be found with respect to boldness, disinterestedness and willingness to be sacrificed for the deliverance of the oppressed.

By chance one day he came across a copy of the Pennsylvania Freeman, containing the story of Peter Still, "the Kidnapped and the Ransomed,"—how he had been torn away from his mother, when a little boy six years old; how, for forty years and more, he had been compelled to serve under the yoke, totally destitute as to any knowledge of his parents' whereabouts; how the intense love of liberty and desire to get back to his mother had unceasingly absorbed his mind through all these years of bondage; how, amid the most appalling discouragements, prompted alone by his undying determination to be free and be reunited with those from whom he had been sold away, he contrived to buy himself; how, by extreme economy, from doing over-work, he saved up five hundred dollars, the amount of money required for his ransom, which, with his freedom, he, from necessity, placed unreservedly in the confidential keeping of a Jew, named Joseph Friedman, whom he had known for a long time and could venture to trust,—how he had further toiled to save up money to defray his expenses on an expedition in search of his mother and kindred; how, when this end was accomplished, with an earnest purpose he took his carpet-bag in his hand, and his heart throbbing for his old home and people, he turned his mind very privately towards Philadelphia, where he hoped, by having notices read in the colored churches to the effect that "forty-one or forty-two years before two little boys* were kidnapped and carried South"—that the memory of some of the older members might recall the circumstances, and in this way he would be aided in his ardent efforts to become restored to them.

And, furthermore, Seth Concklin had read how, on arriving in Philadelphia, after traveling sixteen hundred miles, that almost the first man whom Peter Still sought advice from was his own unknown brother (whom he had never seen or heard of), who made the discovery that he was the long-lost boy, whose history and fate had been enveloped in sadness so long, and for whom his mother had shed so many tears and offered so many prayers, during the long years of their separation; and, finally, how this self-ransomed and restored captive, notwithstanding his great success, was destined to suffer the keenest pangs of sorrow for his wife and children, whom he had left in Alabama bondage.

Seth Concklin was naturally too singularly sympathetic and humane not to feel now for Peter, and especially for his wife and children left in bonds as bound with them. Hence, as Seth was a man who seemed wholly insensible to fear, and to know no other law of humanity and right, than whenever the claims of the suffering and the wronged appealed to him, to respond unreservedly, whether those thus injured were amongst his nearest kin or the greatest strangers,—it mattered not to what race or clime they might belong,—he, in the spirit of the good Samaritan, owning all such as his neighbors, volunteered his services, without pay or reward, to go and rescue the wife and three children of Peter Still.

The magnitude of this offer can hardly be appreciated. It was literally laying his life on the altar of freedom for the despised and oppressed whom he had never seen, whose kins-folk even he was not acquainted with. At this juncture even Peter was not prepared to accept this proposal. He wanted to secure the freedom of his wife

---

* Sons of Levin and Sidney—the last names of his parents he was too young to remember.

and children as earnestly as he had ever desired to see his mother, yet he could not, at first, hearken to the idea of having them rescued in the way suggested by Concklin, fearing a failure.

To J.M. McKim and the writer, the bold scheme for the deliverance of Peter's family was alone confided. It was never submitted to the Vigilance Committee, for the reason, that it was not considered a matter belonging thereto. On first reflection, the very idea of such an undertaking seemed perfectly appalling. Frankly was he told of the great dangers and difficulties to be encountered through hundreds of miles of slave territory. Seth was told of those who, in attempting to aid slaves to escape had fallen victims to the relentless Slave Power, and had either lost their lives, or been incarcerated for long years in penitentiaries, where no friendly aid could be afforded them; in short, he was plainly told, that without a very great chance, the undertaking would cost him his life. The occasion of this interview and conversation, the seriousness of Concklin and the utter failure in presenting the various obstacles to his plan, to create the slightest apparent misgiving in his mind, or to produce the slightest sense of fear or hesitancy, can never be effaced from the memory of the writer. The plan was, however, allowed to rest for a time.

In the meanwhile, Peter's mind was continually vacillating between Alabama, with his wife and children, and his new-found relatives in the North. Said a brother, "If you cannot get your family, what will you do? Will you come North and live with your relatives?" "I would as soon go out of the world, as not to go back and do all I can for them," was the prompt reply of Peter.

The problem of buying them was seriously considered, but here obstacles quite formidable lay in the way. Alabama laws utterly denied the right of a slave to buy himself, much less his wife and children. The right of slave masters to free their slaves, either by sale or emancipation, was positively prohibited by law. With these reflections weighing upon his mind, having stayed away from his wife as long as he could content himself to do, he took his carpet-bag in his hand, and turned his face toward Alabama, to embrace his family in the prison-house of bondage.

His approach home could only be made stealthily, not daring to breathe to a living soul, save his own family, his nominal Jew master, and one other friend—a slave—where he had been, the prize he had found, or anything in relation to his travels. To his wife and children his return was unspeakably joyous. The situation of his family concerned him with tenfold more weight than ever before.

As the time drew near to make the offer to his wife's master to purchase her with his children, his heart failed him through fear of awakening the ire of slaveholders against him, as he knew that the law and public sentiment were alike deadly opposed to the spirit of freedom in the slave. Indeed, as innocent as a step in this direction might appear, in those days a man would have stood about as good a chance for his life in entering a lair of hungry hyenas, as a slave or free colored man would, in talking about freedom.

He concluded, therefore, to say nothing about buying. The plan proposed by Seth Concklin was told to Vina, his wife; also what he had heard from his brother about the Underground Rail Road,— how, that many who could not get their freedom in any other way, by being aided a little, were daily escaping to Canada. Although the wife and children had never tasted the pleasures of freedom for a single hour in their lives, they hated slavery heartily, and being about to be far separated from husband and father, they were ready to assent to any proposition that looked like deliverance.

So Peter proposed to Vina, that she should give him certain small articles, consisting of a cape, etc., which he would carry with him as memorials, and, in case Concklin or any one else should ever come for her from him, as an unmistakable sign that all was right, he would send back, by whoever was to befriend them, the cape, so that she and the children might not doubt but have faith in the man, when he gave her the sign, (cape).

Again Peter returned to Philadelphia, and was now willing to accept the offer of Concklin. Ere long, the opportunity of an interview was had, and Peter gave Seth a very full description of the country and of his family, and made known to him, that he had very carefully gone over with his wife and children the matter of their freedom. This interview interested Concklin most deeply. If his own wife and children had been in bondage, scarcely could he have manifested greater sympathy for them.

For the hazardous work before him he was at once prepared to make a start. True he had two sisters in Philadelphia for whom he had always cherished the warmest affection, but he conferred not with them on this momentous mission. For full well did he know that it was not in human nature for them to acquiesce in this perilous undertaking, though one of these sisters, Mrs. Supplee, was a most faithful abolitionist.

Having once laid his hand to the plough he was not the man to look back,—not even to bid his sisters good-bye, but he actually left them as though he expected to be home to his dinner as usual. What had become of him during those many weeks of his perilous labors in Alabama to rescue this family was to none a greater mystery than to his sisters. On leaving home he simply took two or three small articles in the way of apparel with one hundred dollars to defray his expenses for a time; this sum he considered ample to start with. Of course he had very safely concealed about him Vina's cape and one or two other articles which he was to use for his identification in meeting her and the children on the plantation.

His first thought was, on reaching his destination, after becoming acquainted with the family, being familiar with Southern manners, to have them all prepared at a given hour for the starting of the steamboat for Cincinnati, and to join him at the wharf, when he would boldly assume the part of a slaveholder, and the family naturally that of slaves, and in this way he hoped to reach Cincinnati direct, before their owner had fairly discovered their escape.

But alas for Southern irregularity, two or three days' delay after being advertised to start, was no uncommon circumstance with steamers; hence this plan was abandoned. What this heroic man endured from severe struggles and unyielding exertions, in traveling thousands of miles on water and on foot, hungry and fatigued, rowing his living freight for seven days and seven nights in a skiff, is hardly to be paralleled in the annals of the Underground Rail Road.

The following interesting letters penned by the hand of Concklin convey minutely his last struggles and characteristically represent the singleness of heart which impelled him to sacrifice his life for the slave—

EASTPORT, MISS., FEB. 3, 1851.

To Wm. Still:—Our friends in Cincinnati have failed finding anybody to assist me on my return. Searching the country opposite Paducah, I find that the whole country fifty miles round is inhabited only by Christian wolves. It is customary, when a strange negro is seen, for any white man to seize the negro and convey such negro through and out of the State of Illinois to Paducah, Ky., and lodge such stranger in Paducah jail, and there claim such reward as may be offered by the master.

There is no regularity by the steamboats on the Tennessee River. I was four days getting to Florence from Paducah. Sometimes they are four days starting, from the time appointed, which alone puts to rest the plan for returning by steamboat. The distance from the mouth of the river to Florence, is from between three hundred and five to three hundred and forty-five miles by the river; by land, two hundred and fifty, or more.

I arrived at the shoe shop on the plantation, one o'clock, Tuesday, 28th. William and two boys were making shoes. I immediately gave the first signal, anxiously waiting thirty minutes for an opportunity to give the second and main signal, during which time I was very sociable. It was rainy and muddy—my pants were rolled up to the knees. I was in the character of a man seeking employment in this country. End of thirty minutes gave the second signal.

William appeared unmoved; soon sent out the boys; instantly sociable; Peter and Levin at the Island; one of the young masters with them; not safe to undertake to see them till Saturday night, when they would be at home; appointed a place to see Vina, in an open field, that night; they to bring me something to eat; our interview only four minutes; I left; appeared by night; dark and cloudy; at ten o'clock appeared William; exchanged signals; led me a few rods to where stood Vina; gave her the signal sent by Peter; our interview ten minutes; she did not call me "master," nor did she say "sir," by which I knew she had confidence in me.

Our situation being dangerous, we decided that I meet Peter and Levin on the bank of the river early dawn of day, Sunday, to establish the laws. During our interview, William prostrated on his knees, and face to the ground; arms sprawling; head cocked back, watching for wolves, by which position a man can see better in the dark. No house to go to safely, traveled round till morning, eating hoe cake which William had given me for supper; next day going around to get employment. I thought of William, who is a Christian preacher, and of the Christian preachers in Pennsylvania. One watching for wolves by night, to rescue Vina and her three children from Christian licentiousness; the other standing erect in open day, seeking the praise of men.

During the four days waiting for the important Sunday morning, I thoroughly surveyed the rocks and shoals of the river from Florence seven miles up, where will be my place of departure. General notice was taken of me as being a stranger, lurking around. Fortunately there are several small grist mills within ten miles around. No taverns here, as in the North; any planter's house entertains travelers occasionally.

One night I stayed at a medical gentleman's, who is not a large planter; another night at an ex-magistrate's house in South Florence—a Virginian by birth—one of the late census takers; told me that many more persons cannot read and write than is reported; one fact, amongst many others, that many persons who do not know the letters of the alphabet, have learned to write their own names; such are generally reported readers and writers.

It being customary for a stranger not to leave the house early in the morning where he has lodged, I was under the necessity of staying out all night Saturday, to be able to meet Peter and Levin, which was accomplished in due time. When we approached, I gave my signal first; immediately they gave theirs. I talked freely. Levin's voice, at first, evidently trembled. No wonder, for my presence universally attracted attention by the lords of the land.

Our interview was less than one hour; the laws were written. I to go to Cincinnati to get a rowing boat and provisions; a first class clipper boat to go with speed. To depart from the place where the laws were written, on Saturday night of the first of March. I to meet one of them at the same place Thursday night, previous to the fourth Saturday from the night previous to the Sunday when the laws were written. We to go down the Tennessee river to some place up the Ohio, not yet decided on, in our row boat. Peter and Levin are good oarsmen. So am I. Telegraph station at Tuscumbia, twelve miles from the plantation, also at Paducah.

Came from Florence to here Sunday night by steamboat. Eastport is in Mississippi. Waiting here for a steamboat to go down; paying one dollar a day for board. Like other taverns here, the wretchedness is indescribable; no pen, ink, paper or newspaper to be had; only one room for everybody, except the gambling rooms. It is difficult for me to write. Vina intends to get a pass for Catharine and herself for the first Sunday in March.

The bank of the river where I met Peter and Levin is two miles from the plantation. I have avoided saying I am from Philadelphia. Also avoided talking about negroes. I never talked so much about milling before. I consider most of the trouble over, till I arrive in a free State with my crew, the first week in March; then will I have to be wiser than Christian serpents, and more cautious than doves. I do not consider it safe to keep this letter in my possession, yet I dare not put it in the post-office here; there is so little business in these post-offices that notice might be taken.

I am evidently watched; everybody knows me to be a miller. I may write again when I get to Cincinnati, if I should have time. The ex-magistrate, with whom I stayed in South Florence, held three hours' talk with me, exclusive of our morning talk. Is a man of good general information; he was exceedingly inquisitive. "I am from Cincinnati, formerly from the *State of New York*." I had no opportunity to get anything to eat from seven o'clock Tuesday morning till six o'clock Wednesday evening, except the hoe cake, and no sleep.

Florence is the head of navigation for small steamboats. Seven miles, all the way up to my place of departure, is swift water, and rocky. Eight hundred miles to Cincinnati. I found all things here as Peter told me, except the distance of the river. South Florence contains twenty white families, three warehouses of considerable business, a post-office, but no school. McKiernon is here waiting for a steamboat to go to New Orleans, so we are in company.

PRINCETON, GIBSON COUNTY, INDIANA, FEB. 18, 1851.

————

To Wm. Still:—The plan is to go to Canada, on the Wabash, opposite Detroit. There are four routes to Canada. One through Illinois, commencing above and below Alton; one through to North Indiana, and the Cincinnati route, being the largest route in the United States.

I intended to have gone through Pennsylvania, but the risk going up the Ohio river has caused me to go to Canada. Steamboat traveling is universally condemned, though many go in boats, consequently many get lost. Going in a skiff is new, and is approved of in my case. After I arrive at the mouth of the Tennessee river, I will go up the Ohio seventy-five miles, to the mouth of the Wabash, then up the Wabash, forty-four miles to New Harmony, where I shall go ashore by night, and go thirteen miles east, to Charles Grier, a farmer, (colored man), who will entertain us, and next night convey us sixteen miles to David Stormon, near Princeton, who will take the command, and I be released.

David Stormon estimates the expenses from his house to Canada, at forty dollars, without which, no sure protection will be given. They might be instructed concerning the course, and beg their way through without money. If you wish to do what should be done, you will send me fifty dollars, in a letter, to Princeton, Gibson county, Inda., so as to arrive there by the 8th of March. Eight days should be estimated for a letter to arrive from Philadelphia.

The money to be State Bank of Ohio, or State Bank, or Northern Bank of Kentucky, or any other Eastern bank. Send no notes larger than twenty dollars.

Levi Coffin had no money for me. I paid twenty dollars for the skiff. No money to get back to Philadelphia. It was not understood that I would have to be at any expense seeking aid.

One half of my time has been used in trying to find persons to assist, when I may arrive on the Ohio river, in which I have failed, except Stormon.

Having no letter of introduction to Stormon from any source, on which I could fully rely, I traveled two hundred miles around, to find out his stability. I have found many Abolitionists, nearly all who have made propositions, which themselves would not comply with, and nobody else would. Already I have traveled over three thousand miles. Two thousand and four hundred by steamboat, two hundred by railroad, one hundred by stage, four hundred on foot, forty-eight in a skiff.

I have yet five hundred miles to go to the plantation, to commence operations. I have been two weeks on the decks of steamboats, three nights out, two of which I got perfectly wet. If I had had paper money, as McKim desired, it would have been destroyed. I have not been entertained gratis at any place except Stormon's. I had one hundred and twenty-six dollars when I left Philadelphia, one hundred from you, twenty-six mine.

Telegraphed to station at Evansville, thirty-three miles from Stormon's, and at Vinclure's, twenty-five miles from Stormon's. The Wabash route is considered the safest route. No one has ever been lost from Stormon's to Canada. Some have been lost between Stormon's and the Ohio. The wolves have never suspected Stormon. Your asking aid in money for a case properly belonging east of Ohio, is detested. If you have sent money to Cincinnati, you should recall it. I will have no opportunity to use it.

Seth Concklin, Princeton, Gibson county, Ind.

P.S. First of April, will be about the time Peter's family will arrive opposite Detroit. You should inform yourself how to find them there. I may have no opportunity.

I will look promptly for your letter at Princeton, till the 10th of
March, and longer if there should have been any delay by the mails.

———

In March, as contemplated, Concklin arrived in Indiana, at the
place designated, with Peter's wife and three children, and sent a
thrilling letter to the writer, portraying in the most vivid light his
adventurous flight from the hour they left Alabama until their arrival in Indiana. In this report he stated, that instead of starting
early in the morning, owing to some unforeseen delay on the part
of the family, they did not reach the designated place till towards
day, which greatly exposed them in passing a certain town which he
had hoped to avoid.

But as his brave heart was bent on prosecuting his journey without further delay, he concluded to start at all hazards, notwithstanding the dangers he apprehended from passing said town by daylight.
For safety he endeavored to hide his freight by having them all lie
flat down on the bottom of the skiff; covered them with blankets,
concealing them from the effulgent beams of the early morning
sun, or rather from the "Christian Wolves" who might perchance
espy him from the shore in passing the town.

The wind blew fearfully. Concklin was rowing heroically when
loud voices from the shore hailed him, but he was utterly deaf to the
sound. Immediately one or two guns were fired in the direction of
the skiff, but he heeded not this significant call; consequently here
ended this difficulty. He supposed, as the wind was blowing so hard,
those on shore who hailed him must have concluded that he did not
hear them and that he meant no disrespect in treating them with
seeming indifference. Whilst many straits and great dangers had to
be passed, this was the greatest before reaching their destination.

But suffice it to say that the glad tidings which this letter contained filled the breast of Peter with unutterable delight and his
friends and relations with wonder beyond degree.* No fond wife

———

* In some unaccountable manner this the last letter Concklin ever penned,
perhaps, has been unfortunately lost.

had ever waited with more longing desire for the return of her husband than Peter had for this blessed news. All doubts had disappeared, and a well grounded hope was cherished that within a few short days Peter and his fond wife and children would be reunited in Freedom on the Canada side, and that Concklin and the friends would be rejoicing with joy unspeakable over this great triumph. But alas, before the few days had expired the subjoined brief paragraph of news was discovered in the morning Ledger.

RUNAWAY NEGROES CAUGHT.—At Vincennes, Indiana, on Saturday last, a white man and four negroes were arrested. The negroes belong to B. McKiernon, of South Florence, Alabama, and the man who was running them off calls himself John H. Miller. The prisoners were taken charge of by the Marshall of Evansville.— April 9th.

How suddenly these sad tidings turned into mourning and gloom the hope and joy of Peter and his relatives no pen could possibly describe; at least the writer will not attempt it here, but will at once introduce a witness who met the noble Concklin and the panting fugitives in Indiana and proffered them sympathy and advice. And it may safely be said from a truer and more devoted friend of the slave they could not have received counsel.

EVANSVILLE, INDIANA, MARCH 31ST, 1851.

————

WM. STILL: *Dear Sir,*—On last Tuesday I mailed a letter to you, written by Seth Concklin. I presume you have received that letter. It gave an account of his rescue of the family of your brother. If that is the last news you have had from them, I have very painful intelligence for you. They passed on from near Princeton, where I saw them and had a lengthy interview with them, up north, I think twenty-three miles above Vincennes, Ind., where they were seized by a party of men, and lodged in jail. Telegraphic dispatches were sent all through the South. I have since learned that the Marshall of Evansville received a dispatch from Tuscumbia, to look out for them. By some means, he and the master, so says report, went to Vincennes and claimed the fugitives, chained Mr. Concklin and hurried all off. Mr. Concklin wrote to Mr. David Stormon, Princeton, as soon as he was cast into prison, to find bail. So soon as we got the letter and could get off, two of us were about setting off to render all possible aid, when we were told they all had passed, a few hours before, through Princeton, Mr. Concklin in chains. What kind of process was had, if any, I know not. I immediately came down to this place, and learned that they had been put on a boat at 3 P.M. I did not arrive until 6. Now all hopes of their recovery are gone. No case ever so enlisted my sympathies. I had seen Mr. Concklin in Cincinnati. I had given him aid and counsel. I happened to see them after they landed in Indiana. I heard Peter and Levin tell their tale of suffering, shed tears of sorrow for them all; but now, since they have fallen a prey to the unmerciful blood-hounds of this state, and have again been dragged back to unrelenting bondage, I am entirely unmanned. And poor Concklin! I fear for him. When he is dragged back to Alabama, I fear they will go far beyond the utmost rigor of the law, and vent their savage cruelty upon him. It is with pain I have to communicate these things. But you may not hear them from him. I could not get to see him or them, as Vincennes is about thirty miles from Princeton, where I was when I heard of the capture.

I take pleasure in stating that, according to the letter he (Concklin) wrote to Mr. D. Stewart, Mr. Concklin did not abandon them, but risked his own liberty to save them. He was not with them when they were taken; but went afterwards to take them out of jail upon a writ of Habeas Corpus, when they seized him too and lodged him in prison.

I write in much haste. If I can learn any more facts of importance, I may write you. If you desire to hear from me again, or if you should learn any thing specific from Mr. Concklin, be pleased to write me at Cincinnati, where I expect to be in a short time. If curious to know your correspondent, I may say I was formerly Editor of the "New Concord Free Press," Ohio. I only add that every case of this kind only tends to make me abhor my (no!) *this* country more and more. It is the Devil's Government, and God will destroy it.

Yours for the slave, N.R. JOHNSTON.

P.S. I broke open this letter to write you some more. The foregoing pages were written at night. I expected to mail it next morning before leaving Evansville; but the boat for which I was waiting came down about three in the morning; so I had to hurry on board, bringing the letter along. As it now is I am not sorry, for coming down, on my way to St. Louis, as far as Paducah, there I learned from a colored man at the wharf that, that same day, in the morning, the master and the family of fugitives arrived off the boat, and had then gone on their journey to Tuscumbia, but that the "white man" (Mr. Concklin) had "got away from them," about twelve miles up the river. It seems he got off the boat some way, near or at Smithland, Ky., a town at the mouth of the Cumberland River. I presume the report is true, and hope he will finally escape, though I was also told that they were in pursuit of him. Would that the others had also escaped. Peter and Levin could have done so, I think, if they had had resolution. One of them rode a horse, he not tied either, behind the coach in which the others were. He followed apparently "contented and happy." From report, they told their master, and even their pursuers, before the master came, that Concklin had decoyed them away, they coming unwillingly. I write on a very unsteady boat.

Yours, N.R. JOHNSTON.

A report found its way into the papers to the effect that "Miller," the white man arrested in connection with the capture of the family, was found drowned, with his hands and feet in chains and his skull fractured. It proved, as his friends feared, to be Seth Concklin. And in irons, upon the river bank, there is no doubt he was buried.

In this dreadful hour one sad duty still remained to be performed. Up to this moment the two sisters were totally ignorant of their brother's whereabouts. Not the first whisper of his death had reached them. But they must now be made acquainted with all the facts in the case. Accordingly an interview was arranged for a meeting, and the duty of conveying this painful intelligence to one of the sisters, Mrs. Supplee, devolved upon Mr. McKim. And most tenderly and considerately did he perform his mournful task.

Although a woman of nerve, and a true friend to the slave, an earnest worker and a liberal giver in the Female Anti-Slavery Society, for a time she was overwhelmed by the intelligence of her brother's death. As soon as possible, however, through very great effort, she controlled her emotions, and calmly expressed herself as being fully resigned to the awful event. Not a word of complaint had she to make because she had not been apprised of his movements; but said repeatedly, that, had she known ever so much of his intentions, she would have been totally powerless in opposing him if she had felt so disposed, and as an illustration of the true character of the man, from his boyhood up to the day he died for his fellow-man, she related his eventful career, and recalled a number of instances of his heroic and daring deeds for others, sacrificing his time and often periling his life in the cause of those who he considered were suffering gross wrongs and oppression. Hence, she concluded, that it was only natural for him in this case to have taken the steps he did. Now and then overflowing tears would obstruct this deeply thrilling and most remarkable story she was telling of her brother, but her memory seemed quickened by the sadness of the occasion, and she was enabled to recall vividly the chief events connected with his past history. Thus his agency in this movement, which cost him his life, could readily enough be accounted for, and the individuals who listened attentively to the story were prepared to fully appreciate his character, for, prior to offering his services in this mission, he had been a stranger to them.

The following extract, taken from a letter of a subsequent date, in addition to the above letter, throws still further light upon the heart-rending affair, and shows Mr. Johnston's deep sympathy with the sufferers and the oppressed generally—

EXTRACT OF A LETTER FROM
REV. N.R. JOHNSTON.

My heart bleeds when I think of those poor, hunted and heart-broken fugitives, though a most interesting family, taken back to bondage ten-fold worse than Egyptian. And then poor Concklin! How my heart expanded in love to him, as he told me his adventures, his trials, his toils, his fears and his hopes! After hearing all, and then seeing and communing with the family, now joyful in hopes of soon seeing their husband and father in the land of freedom; now in terror lest the human blood-hounds should be at their heels, I felt as though I could lay down my life in the cause of the oppressed. In that hour or two of intercourse with Peter's family, my heart warmed with love to them. I never saw more interesting young men. They would make Remonds or Douglasses, if they had the same opportunities.

While I was with them, I was elated with joy at their escape, and yet, when I heard their tale of woe, especially that of the mother, I could not suppress tears of deepest emotion.

My joy was short-lived. Soon I heard of their capture. The telegraph had been the means of their being claimed. I could have torn down all the telegraph wires in the land. It was a strange dispensation of Providence.

On Saturday the sad news of their capture came to my ears. We had resolved to go to their aid on Monday, as the trial was set for Thursday. On Sabbath, I spoke from Psalm xii. 5. "For the oppression of the poor, for the sighing of the needy, now will I arise," saith the Lord: "I will set him in safety from him that puffeth at (from them that would enslave) him." When on Monday morning I learned that the fugitives had passed through the place on Sabbath, and Concklin in chains, probably at the very time I was speaking on the subject referred to, my heart sank within me. And even yet, I cannot but exclaim, when I think of it—O, Father! how long ere Thou wilt arise to avenge the wrongs of the poor slave! Indeed, my dear brother, His ways are very mysterious. We have the consolation, however, to know that all is for the best. Our

Redeemer does all things well. When He hung upon the cross, His poor broken hearted disciples could not understand the providence; it was a dark time to them; and yet that was an event that was fraught with more joy to the world than any that has occurred or could occur. Let us stand at our post and wait God's time. Let us have on the whole armor of God, and fight for the right, knowing, that though we may fall in battle, the victory will be ours, sooner or later.

* * * * *

May God lead you into all truth, and sustain you in your labors, and fulfill your prayers and hopes. Adieu.

N.R. JOHNSTON.

LETTERS FROM LEVI COFFIN.

———

The following letters on the subject were received from the untiring and devoted friend of the slave, Levi Coffin, who for many years had occupied in Cincinnati a similar position to that of Thomas Garrett in Delaware, a sentinel and watchman commissioned of God to succor the fleeing bondman—

CINCINNATI, 4TH MO., 10TH, 1851.

FRIEND WM. STILLL:—We have sorrowful news from our friend Concklin, through the papers and otherwise. I received a letter a few days ago from a friend near Princeton, Ind., stating that Concklin and the four slaves are in prison in Vincennes, and that their trial would come on in a few days. He states that they rowed seven days and nights in the skiff, and got safe to Harmony, Ind., on the Wabash river, thence to Princeton, and were conveyed to Vincennes by friends, where they were taken. The papers state, that they were all given up to the Marshal of Evansville, Indiana.

We have telegraphed to different points, to try to get some information concerning them, but failed. The last information is published in the *Times* of yesterday, though quite incorrect in the particulars of the case. Inclosed is the slip containing it. I fear all is over in regard to the freedom of the slaves. If the last account be true, we have some hope that Concklin will escape from those bloody tyrants. I cannot describe my feelings on hearing this sad intelligence. I feel ashamed to own my country. Oh! what shall I say. Surely a God of justice will avenge the wrongs of the oppressed.

Thine for the poor slave, LEVI COFFIN.
N.B.—If thou hast any information, please write me forthwith.

CINCINNATI, 5TH MO., 11TH, 1851.

WM. STILL:—*Dear Friend*—Thy letter of 1st inst., came duly to hand, but not being able to give any further information concerning our friend, Concklin, I thought best to wait a little before I wrote, still hoping to learn something more definite concerning him. We that became acquainted with Seth Concklin and his hazardous enterprises (here at Cincinnati), who were very few, have felt intense and inexpressible anxiety about them. And particularly about poor Seth, since we heard of his falling into the hands of the tyrants. I fear that he has fallen a victim to their inhuman thirst for blood.

I seriously doubt the rumor, that he had made his escape. I fear that he was sacrificed.

Language would fail to express my feelings; the intense and deep anxiety I felt about them for weeks before I heard of their capture in Indiana, and then it seemed too much to bear. O! my heart almost bleeds when I think of it. The hopes of the dear family all blasted by the wretched blood-hounds in human shape. And poor Seth, after all his toil, and dangerous, shrewd and wise management, and almost unheard of adventures, the many narrow and almost miraculous escapes. Then to be given up to Indianians, to these fiendish tyrants, to be sacrificed. O! Shame, Shame!!

My heart aches, my eyes fill with tears, I cannot write more. I cannot dwell longer on this painful subject now. If you get any intelligence, please inform me. Friend N.R. Johnston, who took so much interest in them, and saw them just before they were taken, has just returned to the city. He is a minister of the Covenanter order. He is truly a lovely man, and his heart is full of the milk of humanity; one of our best Anti-Slavery spirits. I spent last evening with him. He related the whole story to me as he had it from friend Concklin and the mother and children, and then the story of their capture. We wept together. He found thy letter when he got here.

He said he would write the whole history to thee in a few days, as far as he could. He can tell it much better than I can.

Concklin left his carpet sack and clothes here with me, except a shirt or two he took with him. What shall I do with them? For if we do not hear from him soon, we must conclude that he is lost, and the report of his escape all a hoax.

Truly thy friend, LEVI COFFIN.

Stunning and discouraging as this horrible ending was to all concerned, and serious as the matter looked in the eyes of Peter's friends with regard to Peter's family, he could not for a moment abandon the idea of rescuing them from the jaws of the destroyer. But most formidable difficulties stood in the way of opening correspondence with reliable persons in Alabama. Indeed it seemed impossible to find a merchant, lawyer, doctor, planter or minister, who was not too completely interlinked with slavery to be relied upon to manage a negotiation of this nature. Whilst waiting and hoping for something favorable to turn up, the subjoined letter from the owner of Peter's family was received and is here inserted precisely as it was written, spelled and punctuated—

MCKIERNON'S LETTER.

SOUTH FLORENCE ALA 6 August 1851
Mr WILLIAM STILL *No 31 North Fifth street Philadelphia*

Sir a few days sinc mr Lewis Tharenton of Tuscumbia Ala shewed me a letter dated 6 June 51 from Cincinnati signd samuel Lewis in behalf of a Negro man by the name of peter Gist who informed the writer of the Letter that you ware his brother and wished an answer to be directed to you as he peter would be in philadelphi. the object of the letter was to purchis from me 4 Negros that is peters wife & 3 children 2 sons & 1 Girl the Name of said Negres are the woman Viney the (mother) Eldest son peter 21 or 2 years old second son Leven 19 or 20 years 1 Girl about 13 or 14 years old. the Husband & Father of these people once Belonged to a relation of mine by the name of Gist now Decest & some few years since he peter was sold to a man by the Name of Freedman who removed to cincinnati ohio & Tuck peter with him of course peter became free by the volentary act of the master some time last march a white man by the name of Miller apperd in the nabourhood & abducted the bove negroes was caut at vincanes Indi with said negroes & was thare convicted of steling & remanded back to Ala to Abide the penalty of the law & on his return met his Just reward by Getting drownded at the mouth of Cumberland River on the ohio in attempting to make his escape I recovered & Braught Back said 4 negroes or as You would say coulard people under the Belief that peter the Husband was accessory to the offence thareby putting me to much Expense & Truble to the amt $1000 which if he gets them he or his Friends must refund these 4 negroes are worth in the market about 4000 for thea are Extraordinary fine & likely & but for the fact of Elopement I would not take 8000 Dollars for them but as the thing now stands you can say to peter & his new discovered Relations in Philadelphia I will take 5000 for the 4 culerd people & if this will suite him & he can raise the money I will delever to him or his agent at paduca at mouth of Tennessee river said negroes but the money must be Deposeted in the Hands of some respectabl person at paduca before I remove the property it wold not be safe for peter to come to this countery write me a line on recpt of this & let me Know peters views on the above

I am Yours &c B. McKIERNON

N B say to peter to write & let me Know his viewes amediately as I am determined to act in a way if he don't take this offer he will never have an other oppertunity

B McKIERNON

WM. STILL'S ANSWER.

———————

PHILADELPHIA, Aug. 16th, 1851.

To B. McKIERNON, ESQ.: *Sir*—I have received your letter from
South Florence, Ala., under date of the 6th inst. To say that it took
me by surprise, as well as afforded me pleasure, for which I feel to
be very much indebted to you, is no more than true. In regard to
your informants of myself—Mr. Thornton, of Ala., and Mr. Samuel
Lewis, of Cincinnati—to them both I am a stranger. However, I am
the brother of Peter, referred to, and with the fact of his having a
wife and three children in your service I am also familiar. This
brother, Peter, I have only had the pleasure of knowing for the brief
space of one year and thirteen days, although he is now past forty
and I twenty-nine years of age. Time will not allow me at present,
or I should give you a detailed account of how Peter became a
slave, the forty long years which intervened between the time he
was kidnapped, when a boy, being only six years of age, and his
arrival in this city, from Alabama, one year and fourteen days ago,
when he was re-united to his mother, five brothers and three sisters.

None but a father's heart can fathom the anguish and sorrows
felt by Peter during the many vicissitudes through which he has
passed. He looked back to his boyhood and saw himself snatched
from the tender embraces of his parents and home to be made a
slave for life.

During all his prime days he was in the faithful and constant
service of those who had no just claim upon him. In the meanwhile
he married a wife, who bore him eleven children, the greater part of
whom were emancipated from the troubles of life by death, and three
only survived. To them and his wife he was devoted. Indeed I have
never seen attachment between parents and children, or husband and
wife, more entire than was manifested in the case of Peter.

Through these many years of servitude, Peter was sold and
resold, from one State to another, from one owner to another, till
he reached the forty-ninth year of his age, when, in a good
Providence, through the kindness of a friend and the sweat of his
brow, he regained the God-given blessings of liberty. He eagerly

sought his parents and home with all possible speed and pains, when, to his heart's joy, he found his relatives.

Your present humble correspondent is the youngest of Peter's brothers, and the first one of the family he saw after arriving in this part of the country. I think you could not fail to be interested in hearing how we became known to each other, and the proof of our being brothers, etc., all of which I should be most glad to relate, but time will not permit me to do so. The news of this wonderful occurrence, of Peter finding his kindred, was published quite extensively, shortly afterwards, in various newspapers, in this quarter, which may account for the fact of "Miller's" knowledge of the whereabouts of the "fugitives." Let me say, it is my firm conviction that no one had any hand in persuading "Miller" to go down from Cincinnati, or any other place, after the family. As glad as I should be, and as much as I would do for the liberation of Peter's family (now no longer young), and his three "likely" children, in whom he prides himself—how much, if you are a father, you can imagine; yet I would not, and could not, think of persuading any friend to peril his life, as would be the case, in an errand of that kind.

As regards the price fixed upon by you for the family, I must say I do not think it possible to raise half that amount, though Peter authorized me to say he would give you twenty-five hundred for them. Probably he is not as well aware as I am, how difficult it is to raise so large a sum of money from the public. The applications for such objects are so frequent among us in the North, and have always been so liberally met, that it is no wonder if many get tired of being called upon. To be sure some of us brothers own some property, but no great amount; certainly not enough to enable us to bear so great a burden. Mother owns a small farm in New Jersey, on which she has lived for nearly forty years, from which she derives her support in her old age. This small farm contains between forty and fifty acres, and is the fruit of my father's toil. Two of my brothers own small places also, but they have young families, and consequently consume nearly as much as they make, with the exception of adding some improvements to their places.

For my own part, I am employed as a clerk for a living, but my salary is quite too limited to enable me to contribute any great amount towards so large a sum as is demanded. Thus you see how we are situated financially. We have plenty of friends, but little money. Now, sir, allow me to make an appeal to your humanity, although we are aware of your power to hold as property those poor slaves, mother, daughter and two sons,—that in no part of the United States could they escape and be secure from your claim— nevertheless, would your understanding, your heart, or your conscience reprove you, should you restore to them, without price, that dear freedom, which is theirs by right of nature, or would you not feel a satisfaction in so doing which all the wealth of the world could not equal? At all events, could you not so reduce the price as to place it in the power of Peter's relatives and friends to raise the means for their purchase? At first, I doubt not, but that you will think my appeal very unreasonable; but, sir, serious reflection will decide, whether the money demanded by you, after all, will be of as great a benefit to you, as the satisfaction you would find in bestowing so great a favor upon those whose entire happiness in this life depends mainly upon your decision in the matter. If the entire family cannot be purchased or freed, what can Vina and her daughter be purchased for? Hoping, sir, to hear from you, at your earliest convenience, I subscribe myself,

Your obedient servant, WM. STILL.
To B. McKiernon, Esq.

No reply to this letter was ever received from McKiernon. The cause of his reticence can be as well conjectured by the reader as the writer.

Time will not admit of further details kindred to this narrative. The life, struggles, and success of Peter and his family were ably brought before the public in the "Kidnapped and the Ransomed," being the personal recollections of Peter Still and his wife "Vina," after forty years of slavery, by Mrs. Kate E.R. Pickard; with an introduction by Rev. Samuel J. May, and an appendix by William H. Furness, D.D., in 1856. But, of course it was not prudent or safe, in the days of Slavery, to publish such facts as are now brought to light; all such had to be kept concealed in the breasts of the fugitives and their friends.

—

The following brief sketch, touching the separation of Peter and his mother, will fitly illustrate this point, and at the same time explain certain mysteries which have been hitherto kept hidden—

THE SEPARATION.

With regard to Peter's separation from his mother, when a little boy, in few words, the facts were these: His parents, Levin and Sidney, were both slaves on the Eastern Shore of Maryland. "I will die before I submit to the yoke," was the declaration of his father to his young master before either was twenty-one years of age. Consequently he was allowed to buy himself at a very low figure, and he paid the required sum and obtained his "free papers" when quite a young man—the young wife and mother remaining in slavery under Saunders Griffin, as also her children, the latter having increased to the number of four, two little boys and two little girls. But to escape from chains, stripes, and bondage, she took her four little children and fled to a place near Greenwich, New Jersey. Not a great while, however, did she remain there in a state of freedom before the slave-hunters pursued her, and one night they pounced upon the whole family, and, without judge or jury, hurried them all back to slavery. Whether this was kidnapping or not is for the reader to decide for himself.

Safe back in the hands of her owner, to prevent her from escaping a second time, every night for about three months she was cautiously "kept locked up in the garret," until, as they supposed, she was fully "cured of the desire to do so again." But she was incurable. She had been a witness to the fact that her own father's brains had been blown out by the discharge of a heavily loaded gun, deliberately aimed at his head by his drunken master. She only needed half a chance to make still greater struggles than ever for freedom.

She had great faith in God, and found much solace in singing some of the good old Methodist tunes, by day and night. Her owner, observing this apparently tranquil state of mind, indicating that she "seemed better contented than ever," concluded that it was safe to let the garret door remain unlocked at night. Not many weeks were allowed to pass before she resolved to again make a bold strike for freedom. This time she had to leave the two little boys, Levin and Peter, behind.

On the night she started she went to the bed where they were sleeping, kissed them, and, consigning them into the hands of God, bade her mother good-bye, and with her two little girls wended her way again to Burlington County, New Jersey, but to a different neighborhood from that where she had been seized. She changed her name to Charity, and succeeded in again joining her husband, but, alas, with the heart-breaking thought that she had been compelled to leave her two little boys in slavery and one of the little girls on the road for the father to go back after. Thus she began life in freedom anew.

Levin and Peter, eight and six years of age respectively, were now left at the mercy of the enraged owner, and were soon hurried off to a Southern market and sold, while their mother, for whom they were daily weeping, was they knew not where. They were too young to know that they were slaves, or to understand the nature of the afflicting separation. Sixteen years before Peter's return, his older brother (Levin) died a slave in the State of Alabama, and was buried by his surviving brother, Peter.

No idea other than that they had been "kidnapped" from their mother ever entered their minds; nor had they any knowledge of the State from whence they supposed they had been taken, the last names of their mother and father, or where they were born. On the other hand, the mother was aware that the safety of herself and her rescued children depended on keeping the whole transaction a strict family secret. During the forty years of separation, except two or three Quaker friends, including the devoted friend of the slave,

Benjamin Lundy, it is doubtful whether any other individuals were let into the secret of her slave life. And when the account given of Peter's return, etc., was published in 1850, it led some of the family to apprehend serious danger from the partial revelation of the early condition of the mother, especially as it was about the time that the Fugitive Slave law was passed.

Hence, the author of "The Kidnapped and the Ransomed" was compelled to omit these dangerous facts, and had to confine herself strictly to the "personal recollections of Peter Still" with regard to his being "kidnapped." Likewise, in the sketch of Seth Concklin's eventful life, written by Dr. W.H. Furness, for similar reasons he felt obliged to make but bare reference to his wonderful agency in relation to Peter's family, although he was fully aware of all the facts in the case.

WILLIAM PEEL,
ALIAS WILLIAM BOX PEEL JONES.

Arrived Per Erricson Line of Steamers,
Wrapped in Straw and Boxed Up, April, 1859.

William is twenty-five years of age, unmistakably colored, good-looking, rather under the medium size, and of pleasing manners. William had himself boxed up by a near relative and forwarded by the Erricson line of steamers. He gave the slip to Robert H. Carr, his owner (a grocer and commission merchant), after this wise, and for the following reasons: For some time previous his master had been selling off his slaves every now and then, the same as other groceries, and this admonished William that he was liable to be in the market any day; consequently, he preferred the box to the auction-block.

He did not complain of having been treated very badly by Carr, but felt that no man was safe while owned by another. In fact, he "hated the very name of slaveholder." The limit of the box not admitting of straightening himself out he was taken with the cramp on the road, suffered indescribable misery, and had his faith taxed to the utmost,—indeed was brought to the very verge of "screaming aloud" ere relief came. However, he controlled himself, though only for a short season, for before a great while an excessive faintness came over him. Here nature became quite exhausted. He thought he must "die;" but his time had not yet come. After a severe struggle he revived, but only to encounter a third ordeal no less painful than the one through which he had just passed. Next a very "cold chill" came over him, which seemed almost to freeze the very blood in his veins and gave him intense agony, from which he only found relief on awaking, having actually fallen asleep in that condition. Finally, however, he arrived at Philadelphia, on a steamer, Sabbath morning. A devoted friend of his, expecting him, engaged a carriage and repaired to the wharf for the box. The bill of lading and the receipt he had with him, and likewise knew where the box was located on the boat. Although he well knew freight was not usually delivered on Sunday, yet his deep solicitude for the safety of his friend determined him to do all that lay in his power to rescue him from his perilous situation. Handing his bill of lading to the proper officer of the boat, he asked if he could get the freight that it called for. The officer looked at the bill and said, "No, we do not deliver freight on Sunday;" but, noticing the anxiety of the man, he asked him if he would know it if he were to see it. Slowly—fearing that too much interest manifested might excite suspicion—he replied: "I think I should." Deliberately looking around amongst all the "freight," he discovered the box, and said, "I think that is it there." Said officer stepped to it, looked at the directions on it, then at the bill of lading, and said, "That is right, take it along." Here the interest in these two bosoms was thrilling in the highest degree. But the size of the box was too large for the carriage, and the driver refused to take it. Nearly an hour and a half was spent in looking for a furniture car. Finally one was procured, and again the box was laid hold of by the occupant's particular friend, when, to his dread alarm, the poor fellow within gave a sudden cough. At this startling circumstance he dropped the box; equally as quick, although dreadfully frightened, and, as if helped by some invisible agency, he commenced singing, "Hush, my babe, lie still and slumber," with the most apparent indifference, at the same time slowly making his way from the box. Soon his fears subsided, and it was presumed that no one was any the wiser on account of the accident, or coughing. Thus, after summoning courage, he laid hold of the box a third time, and the Rubicon was passed. The car driver, totally ignorant of the contents of the box, drove to the number to which he was directed to take it—left it and went about his business. Now is a moment of intense interest—now of inexpressible delight. The box is opened, the straw removed, and the poor fellow is loosed; and is rejoicing, I will venture to say, as mortal never did rejoice, who had not been in similar peril. This particular friend was scarcely less overjoyed, however, and their joy did not abate for several hours;

nor was it confined to themselves, for two invited members of the Vigilance Committee also partook of a full share. This box man was named Wm. Jones. He was boxed up in Baltimore by the friend who received him at the wharf, who did not come in the boat with him, but came in the cars and met him at the wharf.

The trial in the box lasted just seventeen hours before victory was achieved. Jones was well cared for by the Vigilance Committee and sent on his way rejoicing, feeling that Resolution, Underground Rail Road, and Liberty were invaluable.

On his way to Canada, he stopped at Albany, and the subjoined letter gives his view of things from that stand-point—

MR. STILL:—I take this opportunity of writing a few lines to you hoping that tha may find you in good health and femaly. i am well at present and doing well at present i am now in a store and getting sixteen dollars á month at the present. i feel very much o blige to you and your family for your kindnes to me while i was with you i have got a long without any trub le a tal. i am now in albany City. give my lov to mrs and mr miller and tel them i am very much a blige to them for there kind ns. give my lov to my Brother nore Jones tel him i should like to here from him very much and he must write. tel him to give my love to all of my perticnlar frends and tel them i should like to see them very much. tel him that he must come to see me for i want to see him for sum thing very perticler. please ansure this letter as soon as posabul and excuse me for not writting sooner as i don't write myself. no more at the present. WILLIAM JONES.

derect to one hundred 125 lydus. Stt

His good friend returned to Baltimore the same day the box man started for the North, and immediately dispatched through the post the following brief letter, worded in Underground Rail Road parables:

BALTIMO APRIL 16, 1859.

W. STILL:—Dear brother i have taken the opportunity of writing you these few lines to inform you that i am well an hoping these few lines may find you enjoying the same good blessing please to write me word at what time was it when isreal went to Jerico i am very anxious to hear for thare is a mighty host will pass over and you and i my brother will sing hally luja i shall notify you when the great catastrophe shal take place No more at the present but remain your brother N.L.J.

WESLEY HARRIS,* ALIAS ROBERT JACKSON, AND THE MATTERSON BROTHERS.

In setting out for freedom, Wesley was the leader of this party. After two nights of fatiguing travel at a distance of about sixty miles from home, the young aspirants for liberty were betrayed, and in an attempt made to capture them a most bloody conflict ensued. Both fugitives and pursuers were the recipients of severe wounds from gun shots, and other weapons used in the contest.

Wesley bravely used his fire arms until almost fatally wounded by one of the pursuers, who with a heavily loaded gun discharged the contents with deadly aim in his left arm, which raked the flesh from the bone for a space of about six inches in length. One of Wesley's companions also fought heroically and only yielded when badly wounded and quite overpowered. The two younger (brothers of C. Matterson) it seemed made no resistance.

In order to recall the adventures of this struggle, and the success of Wesley Harris, it is only necessary to copy the report as then penned from the lips of this young hero, while on the Underground Rail Road, even then in a very critical state. Most fearful indeed was his condition when he was brought to the Vigilance Committee in this City.

UNDERGROUND RAIL ROAD RECORD.

————

November 2d, 1853.—Arrived: Robert Jackson (shot man), *alias* Wesley Harris; age twenty-two years; dark color; medium height, and of slender stature.

* Shot by slave-hunters.

Robert was born in Martinsburg, Va., and was owned by Philip Pendleton. From a boy he had always been hired out. At the first of this year he commenced services with Mrs. Carroll, proprietress of the United States Hotel at Harper's Ferry. Of Mrs. Carroll he speaks in very grateful terms, saying that she was kind to him and all the servants, and promised them their freedom at her death. She excused herself for not giving them their freedom on the ground that her husband died insolvent, leaving her the responsibility of settling his debts.

But while Mrs. Carroll was very kind to her servants, her manager was equally as cruel. About a month before Wesley left, the overseer, for some trifling cause, attempted to flog him, but was resisted, and himself flogged. This resistance of the slave was regarded by the overseer as an unpardonable offence; consequently he communicated the intelligence to his owner, which had the desired effect on his mind as appeared from his answer to the overseer, which was nothing less than instructions that if he should again attempt to correct Wesley and he should repel the wholesome treatment, the overseer was to put him in prison and sell him. Whether he offended again or not, the following Christmas he was to be sold without fail.

Wesley's mistress was kind enough to apprise him of the intention of his owner and the overseer, and told him that if he could help himself he had better do so. So from that time Wesley began to contemplate how he should escape the doom which had been planned for him.

"A friend," says he, "by the name of C. Matterson, told me that he was going off. Then I told him of my master's writing to Mrs. Carroll concerning selling, etc., and that I was going off too. We then concluded to go together. There were two others—brothers of Matterson—who were told of our plan to escape, and readily joined with us in the undertaking. So one Saturday night, at twelve o'clock, we set out for the North. After traveling upwards of two days and over sixty miles, we found ourselves unexpectedly in Terrytown, Md. There we were informed by a friendly colored man of the danger we were in and of the bad character of the place towards colored people, especially those who were escaping to freedom; and he advised us to hide as quickly as we could. We at once went to the woods and hid. Soon after we had secreted ourselves a man came near by and commenced splitting wood, or rails, which alarmed us. We then moved to another hiding-place in a thicket near a farmer's barn, where we were soon startled again by a dog approaching and barking at us. The attention of the owner of the dog was drawn to his barking and to where we were. The owner of the dog was a farmer. He asked us where we were going. We replied to Gettysburg—to visit some relatives, etc. He told us that we were running off. He then offered friendly advice, talked like a Quaker, and urged us to go with him to his barn for protection. After much persuasion, we consented to go with him.

"Soon after putting us in his barn, himself and daughter prepared us a nice breakfast, which cheered our spirits, as we were hungry. For this kindness we paid him one dollar. He next told us to hide on the mow till eve, when he would safely direct us on our road to Gettysburg. All, very much fatigued from traveling, fell asleep, excepting myself; I could not sleep; I felt as if all was not right.

"About noon men were heard talking around the barn. I woke my companions up and told them that that man had betrayed us. At first they did not believe me. In a moment afterwards the barn door was opened, and in came the men, eight in number. One of the men asked the owner of the barn if he had any long straw. 'Yes,' was the answer. So up on the mow came three of the men, when, to their great surprise, as they pretended, we were discovered. The question was then asked the owner of the barn by one of the men, if he harbored runaway negroes in his barn? He answered, 'No,' and pretended to be entirely ignorant of their being in his barn. One of the men replied that four negroes were on the mow, and he knew of it. The men then asked us where we were, going. We told them to Gettysburg, that we had aunts and a mother there. Also we spoke of a Mr. Houghman, a gentleman we happened to have some knowledge of, having seen him in Virginia. We were next asked for our passes. We told them that we hadn't any, that we had not been required to carry them where we came from. They then said that we would have to go before a magistrate, and if he allowed us to go on, well and good. The men all being armed and furnished with ropes, we were ordered to be tied. I told them if they took me they would have to take me dead or crippled. At that instant one of my friends cried out—'Where is the man that betrayed us?' Spying him at the same moment, he shot him (badly wounding him). Then the conflict fairly began. The constable seized me by the collar, or rather behind my shoulder. I at once shot him with my pistol, but in consequence of his throwing up his arm, which hit mine as I fired, the effect of the load of my pistol was much turned aside; his face, however, was badly burned, besides his shoulder being wounded. I again fired on the pursuers, but do not know whether I hit anybody or not. I then drew a sword, I had brought with me, and was about cutting my way to the door, when I was shot by one of the men, receiving the entire contents of one load of a double barreled gun in my left arm, that being the arm with which I was defending myself. The load brought me to the ground, and I was unable to make further struggle for myself. I was then badly beaten with guns, &c. In the meantime, my friend Craven, who was defending himself, was shot badly in the face, and most violently beaten until he was conquered and tied. The two young brothers of Craven stood still, without making the least resistance. After we were fairly captured, we were taken to Terrytown, which was in sight of where we were betrayed. By this time I had lost so much blood from my wounds, that they concluded my situation was too dangerous to admit of being taken further; so I was made a prisoner at a tavern, kept by a man named Fisher. There my wounds were dressed, and thirty-two shot were taken from my arm. For three days I was crazy, and they thought I would die. During the first two weeks, while I was a prisoner at the tavern, I raised a great deal of blood, and was considered in a very dangerous condition—so much so that persons desiring to see me were not permitted. Afterwards I began to get better, and was then kept privately—was strictly watched day and night. Occasionally, however, the cook, a colored woman (Mrs. Smith), would manage to get to see me. Also James Matthews succeeded in getting to see me; consequently, as my wounds healed, and my senses came to me, I began to plan how to make another effort to escape. I asked one of the friends, alluded to above, to get me a rope. He got it. I kept it about me four days in my pocket; in the meantime I procured three nails. On Friday night, October 14th, I fastened my nails in under the window sill; tied my rope to the nails, threw my shoes out of the window, put the rope in my mouth, then took hold of it with my well hand, clambered into the window, very weak, but I managed to let myself down to the ground. I was so weak, that I could scarcely walk, but I managed to hobble off to a place three quarters of a mile from the tavern, where a friend had fixed upon for me to go, if I succeeded in making my escape. There I was found by my friend, who kept me secure till Saturday eve, when a swift horse was furnished by James Rogers, and a colored man found to conduct me to Gettysburg. Instead of going direct to Gettysburg, we took a different road, in order to shun our pursuers, as the news of my escape had created general excitement. My three other companions, who were captured, were sent to Westminster jail, where they were kept three weeks, and afterwards sent to Baltimore and sold for twelve hundred dollars a piece, as I was informed while at the tavern in Terrytown."

The Vigilance Committee procured good medical attention and afforded the fugitive time for recuperation, furnished him with clothing and a free ticket, and sent him on his way greatly improved in health, and strong in the faith that, "He who would be free, himself must strike the blow." His safe arrival in Canada, with his thanks, were duly announced. And some time after becoming naturalized, in one of his letters, he wrote that he was a brakesman on the Great Western R.R., (in Canada—promoted from the U.G.R.R.,) the result of being under the protection of the British Lion.

CLARISSA DAVIS.

Arrived Dressed in Male Attire.

Clarissa fled from Portsmouth, Va., in May, 1854, with two of her brothers. Two months and a half before she succeeded in getting off, Clarissa had made a desperate effort, but failed. The brothers succeeded, but she was left. She had not given up all hope of escape, however, and therefore sought "a safe hiding-place until an opportunity might offer," by which she could follow her brothers on the U.G.R.R. Clarissa was owned by Mrs. Brown and Mrs. Burkley, of Portsmouth, under whom she had always served.

Of them she spoke favorably, saying that she "had not been used as hard as many others were." At this period, Clarissa was about twenty-two years of age, of a bright brown complexion, with handsome features, exceedingly respectful and modest, and possessed all the characteristics of a well-bred young lady. For one so little acquainted with books as she was, the correctness of her speech was perfectly astonishing.

For Clarissa and her two brothers a "reward of one thousand dollars" was kept standing in the papers for a length of time, as these (articles) were considered very rare and valuable; the best that could be produced in Virginia.

In the meanwhile the brothers had passed safely on to New Bedford, but Clarissa remained secluded, "waiting for the storm to subside." Keeping up courage day by day, for seventy-five days, with the fear of being detected and severely punished, and then sold, after all her hopes and struggles, required the faith of a martyr. Time after time, when she hoped to succeed in making her escape, ill luck seemed to disappoint her, and nothing but intense suffering appeared to be in store. Like many others, under the crushing weight of oppression, she thought she "should have to die" ere she tasted liberty. In this state of mind, one day, word was conveyed to her that the steamship, City of Richmond, had arrived from Philadelphia, and that the steward on board (with whom she was acquainted), had consented to secrete her this trip, if she could manage to reach the ship safely, which was to start the next day. This news to Clarissa was both cheering and painful. She had been "praying all the time while waiting," but now she felt "that if it would only rain right hard the next morning about three o'clock, to drive the police officers off the street, then she could safely make her way to the boat." Therefore she prayed anxiously all that day that it would rain, "but no sign of rain appeared till towards midnight." The prospect looked horribly discouraging; but she prayed on, and at the appointed hour (three o'clock—before day), the rain descended in torrents. Dressed in male attire, Clarissa left the miserable coop where she had been almost without light or air for two and a half months, and unmolested, reached the boat safely, and was secreted in a box by Wm. Bagnal, a clever young man who sincerely sympathized with the slave, having a wife in slavery himself; and by him she was safely delivered into the hands of the Vigilance Committee.

Clarissa Davis here, by advice of the Committee, dropped her old name, and was straightway christened "Mary D. Armstead." Desiring to join her brothers and sister in New Bedford, she was duly furnished with her U.G.R.R. passport and directed thitherward. Her father, who was left behind when she got off, soon after made his way on North, and joined his children. He was too old and infirm probably to be worth anything, and had been allowed to go free, or to purchase himself for a mere nominal sum. Slaveholders would, on some such occasions, show wonderful liberality in letting their old slaves go free, when they could work no more. After reaching New Bedford, Clarissa manifested her gratitude in writing to her friends in Philadelphia repeatedly, and evinced a very lively interest in the U.G.R.R. The appended letter indicates her sincere feelings of gratitude and deep interest in the cause—

NEW BEDFORD, August 26, 1855.

MR. STILL:—I avail my self to write you thes few lines hopeing they may find you and your family well as they leaves me very well and all the family well except my father he seams to be improveing with his shoulder he has been able to work a little I received the papers I was highly delighted to receive them I was very glad to hear from you in the wheler case I was very glad to hear that the persons ware safe I was very sory to hear that mr Williamson was put in prison but I know if the praying part of the people will pray for him and if he will put his trust in the lord he will bring him out more than conquer please remember my Dear old farther and sisters and brothers to your family kiss the children for me I hear that the yellow fever is very bad down south now if the underground railroad could have free course the emergrant would cross the river of gordan rapidly I hope it may continue to run and I hope the wheels of the car may be greesed with more substantial greese so they may run over swiftly I would have wrote before but circumstances would not permit me Miss Sanders and all the friends desired to be remembered to you and your family I shall be pleased to hear from the underground rail road often.

Yours respectfully, MARY D. ARMSTEAD.

ISAAC FORMAN, WILLIAM DAVIS,
AND WILLIS REDICK.

Hearts Full of Joy for Freedom—Very anxious for Wives in Slavery.

These passengers all arrived together, concealed, per steamship City of Richmond, December, 1853. Isaac Forman, the youngest of the party—twenty-three years of age and a dark mulatto—would be considered by a Southerner capable of judging as "very likely." He fled from a widow by the name of Mrs. Sanders, who had been in the habit of hiring him out for "one hundred and twenty dollars a year." She belonged in Norfolk, Va.; so did Isaac. For four years Isaac had served in the capacity of steward on the steamship Augusta. He stated that he had a wife living in Richmond, and that she was confined the morning he took the U.G.R.R. Of course he could not see her. The privilege of living in Richmond with his wife "had been denied him." Thus, fearing to render her unhappy, he was obliged to conceal from her his intention to escape. "Once or twice in the year was all the privilege allowed" him to visit her. This only added "insult to injury," in Isaac's opinion; wherefore he concluded that he would make one less to have to suffer thus, and common sense said he was wise in the matter. No particular charges are found recorded on the U.G.R.R. books against the mistress. He went to Canada.

In the subjoined letters (about his wife) is clearly revealed the sincere gratitude he felt towards those who aided him: at the same time it may be seen how the thought of his wife being in bondage grieved his heart. It would have required men with stone hearts to have turned deaf ears to such appeals. Extract from letter soon after reaching Canada—hopeful and happy—

EXTRACT OF LETTER FROM ISAAC FORMAN.

TORONTO, Feb. 20th, 1854.

MR. WILLIAM STILL:—*Sir*—Your kind letter arrived safe at
hand on the 18th, and I was very happy to receive it. I now feel that
I should return you some thanks for your kindness. Dear sir I do
pray from the bottom of my heart, that the high heavens may bless
you for your kindness; give my love to Mr. Bagnel and Mr.
Minkins, ask them if they have heard anything from my brother,
tell Mr. Bagnel to give my love to my sister-in-law and mother and
all the family. I am now living at Russell's Hotel; it is the first
situation I have had since I have been here and I like it very well.
Sir you would oblige me by letting me know if Mr. Minkins has
seen my wife; you will please let me know as soon as possible. I
wonder if Mr. Minkins has thought of any way that he can get my
wife away. I should like to know in a few days. Your well wisher,
ISAAC FORMAN.

Another letter from Isaac. He is very gloomy and his heart is almost
breaking about his wife.

SECOND LETTER.

TORONTO, May 7, 1854.

MR. W. STILL:—*Dear Sir*—I take this opportunity of writing you
these few lines and hope when they reach you they will find you
well. I would have written you before, but I was waiting to hear
from my friend, Mr. Brown. I judge his business has been of
importance as the occasion why he has not written before. Dear sir,
nothing would have prevented me from writing, in a case of this
kind, except death.

My soul is vexed, my troubles are inexpressible. I often feel as if I were willing to die. I must see my wife in short, if not, I will die. What would I not give no tongue can utter. Just to gaze on her sweet lips one moment I would be willing to die the next. I am determined to see her some time or other. The thought of being a slave again is miserable. I hope heaven will smile upon me again, before I am one again. I will leave Canada again shortly, but I don't name the place that I go, it may be in the bottom of the ocean. If I had known as much before I left, as I do now, I would never have left until I could have found means to have brought her with me. You have never suffered from being absent from a wife, as I have. I consider that to be nearly superior to death, and hope you will do all you can for me, and inquire from your friends if nothing can be done for me. Please write to me immediately on receipt of this, and say something that will cheer up my drooping spirits. You will oblige me by seeing Mr. Brown and ask him if he would oblige me by going to Richmond and see my wife, and see what arrangements he could make with her, and I would be willing to pay all his expenses there and back. Please to see both Mr. Bagnel and Mr. Minkins, and ask them if they have seen my wife. I am determined to see her, if I die the next moment. I can say I was once happy, but never will be again, until I see her; because what is freedom to me, when I know that my wife is in slavery? Those persons that you shipped a few weeks ago, remained at St. Catherine, instead of coming over to Toronto. I sent you two letters last week and I hope you will please attend to them. The post-office is shut, so I enclose the money to pay the post, and please write me in haste.

I remain evermore your obedient servant, I. FORMAN.

WILLIS REDICK.

He was owned by S.J. Wilson, a merchant, living in Portsmouth, Va. Willis was of a very dark hue, thick set, thirty-two years of age, and possessed of a fair share of mind. The owner had been accustomed to hire Willis out for "one hundred dollars a year." Willis thought his lot "pretty hard," and his master rather increased this notion by his severity, and especially by "threatening" to sell him. He had enjoyed, as far as it was expected for a slave to do, "five months of married life," but he loved slavery no less on this account. In fact he had just begun to consider what it was to have a wife and children that he "could not own or protect," and who were claimed as another's property. Consequently he became quite restive under these reflections and his master's ill-usage, and concluded to "look out," without consulting either the master or the young wife.

This step looked exceedingly hard, but what else could the poor fellow do? Slavery existed expressly for the purpose of crushing souls and breaking tender hearts.

WILLIAM DAVIS.

William might be described as a good-looking mulatto, thirty-one years of age, and capable of thinking for himself. He made no grave complaints of ill-usage under his master, "Joseph Reynolds," who lived at Newton, Portsmouth, Va. However, his owner had occasionally "threatened to sell him." As this was too much for William's sensitive feelings, he took umbrage at it and made a hasty and hazardous move, which resulted in finding himself on the U.G.R.R. The most serious regret William had to report to the Committee was, that he was compelled to "leave" his "wife," Catharine, and his little daughter, Louisa, two years and one month, and an infant son seven months old. He evidently loved them very tenderly, but saw no way by which he could aid them, as long as he was daily liable to be put on the auction block and sold far South. This argument was regarded by the Committee as logical and unanswerable; consequently they readily endorsed his course, while they deeply sympathized with his poor wife and little ones. "Before escaping," he "dared not" even apprise his wife and child, whom he had to leave behind in the prison house.

EX-PRESIDENT TYLER'S HOUSEHOLD LOSES
AN ARISTOCRATIC "ARTICLE."

James Hambleton Christian is a remarkable specimen of the "well fed, &c." In talking with him relative to his life as a slave, he said very promptly, "I have always been treated well; if I only have half as good times in the North as I have had in the South, I shall be perfectly satisfied. Any time I desired spending money, five or ten dollars were no object." At times, James had borrowed of his master, one, two, and three hundred dollars, to loan out to some of his friends. With regard to apparel and jewelry, he had worn the best, as an every-day adornment. With regard to food also, he had fared as well as heart could wish, with abundance of leisure time at his command. His deportment was certainly very refined and gentlemanly. About fifty per cent. of Anglo-Saxon blood was visible in his features and his hair, which gave him no inconsiderable claim to sympathy and care. He had been to William and Mary's College in his younger days, to wait on young master James B.C., where, through the kindness of some of the students he had picked up a trifling amount of book learning. To be brief, this man was born the slave of old Major Christian, on the Glen Plantation, Charles City county, Va. The Christians were wealthy and owned many slaves, and belonged in reality to the F.F.V's. On the death of the old Major, James fell into the hands of his son, Judge Christian, who was executor to his father's estate. Subsequently he fell into the hands of one of the Judge's sisters, Mrs. John Tyler (wife of Ex-President Tyler), and then he became a member of the President's domestic household, was at the White House, under the President, from 1841 to 1845. Though but very young at that time, James was only fit for training in the arts, science, and mystery of waiting, in which profession, much pains were taken to qualify him completely for his calling.

After a lapse of time; his mistress died. According to her request, after this event, James and his old mother were handed over to her nephew, William H. Christian, Esq., a merchant of Richmond. From this gentleman, James had the folly to flee.

Passing hurriedly over interesting details, received from him respecting his remarkable history, two or three more incidents too good to omit must suffice.

"How did you like Mr. Tyler?" said an inquisitive member of the Vigilance Committee. "I didn't like Mr. Tyler much," was the reply. "Why?" again inquired the member of the Committee. "Because Mr. Tyler was a poor man. I never did like poor people. I didn't like his marrying into our family, who were considered very far Tyler's superiors." "On the plantation," he said, "Tyler was a very cross man, and treated the servants very cruelly; but the house servants were treated much better, owing to their having belonged to his wife, who protected them from persecution, as they had been favorite servants in her father's family." James estimated that "Tyler got about thirty-five thousand dollars and twenty-nine slaves, young and old, by his wife."

What prompted James to leave such pleasant quarters? It was this: He had become enamored of a young and respectable free girl in Richmond, with whom he could not be united in marriage solely because he was a slave, and did not own himself. The frequent sad separations of such married couples (where one or the other was a slave) could not be overlooked; consequently, the poor fellow concluded that he would stand a better chance of gaining his object in Canada than by remaining in Virginia. So he began to feel that he might himself be sold some day, and thus the resolution came home to him very forcibly to make tracks for Canada.

In speaking of the good treatment he had always met with, a member of the Committee remarked, "You must be akin to some one of your master's family?" To which he replied, "I am Christian's son." Unquestionably this passenger was one of that happy class so commonly referred to by apologists for the "Patriarchal Institution." The Committee, feeling a deep interest in his story, and desiring great success to him in his Underground efforts to get rid of slavery, and at the same time possess himself of his affianced, made him heartily welcome, feeling assured that the struggles and hardships he had submitted to in escaping, as well as the luxuries he was leaving behind, were nothing to be compared with the blessings of liberty and a free wife in Canada.

EDWARD MORGAN, HENRY JOHNSON, JAMES AND STEPHEN BUTLER.

"TWO THOUSAND DOLLARS REWARD.—The above Reward will be paid for the apprehension of two blacks, who escaped on Sunday last. It is supposed they have made their way to Pennsylvania. $500 will be paid for the apprehension of either, so that we can get them again. The oldest is named Edward Morgan, about five feet six or seven inches, heavily made—is a dark black, has rather a down look when spoken to, and is about 21 years of age.

"Henry Johnson is a colored negro, about five feet seven or eight inches, heavily made, aged nineteen years, has a pleasant countenance, and has a mark on his neck below the ear.

"Stephen Butler is a dark-complexioned negro, about five feet seven inches; has a pleasant countenance, with a scar above his eye; plays on the violin; about twenty-two years old.

"Jim Butler is a dark-complexioned negro, five feet eight or nine inches; is rather sullen when spoken to; face rough; aged about twenty-one years. The clothing not recollected. They had black frock coats and slouch hats with them. Any information of them address Elizabeth Brown, Sandy Hook P.O., or of Thomas Johnson, Abingdon P.O., Harford county, Md.

"ELIZABETH BROWN.
"THOMAS JOHNSON."

FROM THE UNDERGROUND RAIL ROAD RECORDS.

————

The following memorandum is made, which, if not too late, may afford some light to "Elizabeth Brown and Thomas Johnson," if they have not already gone the way of the "lost cause"—

June 4, 1857.—Edward is a hardy and firm-looking young man of twenty-four years of age, chestnut color, medium size, and "likely,"—would doubtless bring $1,400 in the market. He had been held as the property of the widow, "Betsy Brown," who resided near Mill Green P.O., in Harford county, Md. "She was a very bad woman; would go to church every Sunday, come home and go to fighting amongst the colored people; was never satisfied; she treated my mother very hard, (said Ed.); would beat her with a walking-stick, &c. She was an old woman and belonged to the Catholic Church. Over her slaves she kept an overseer, who was a very wicked man; very bad on colored people; his name was 'Bill Eddy;' Elizabeth Brown owned twelve head."

Henry is of a brown skin, a good-looking young man, only nineteen years of age, whose prepossessing appearance would insure a high price for him in the market—perhaps $1,700. With Edward, he testifies to the meanness of Mrs. Betsy Brown, as well as to his own longing desire for freedom. Being a fellow-servant with Edward, Henry was a party to the plan of escape. In slavery he left his mother and three sisters, owned by the "old woman" from whom he escaped.

James is about twenty-one years of age, full black, and medium size. As he had been worked hard on poor fare, he concluded to leave, in company with his brother and two cousins, leaving his parents in slavery, owned by the "Widow Pyle," who was also the owner of himself. "She was upwards of eighty, very passionate and ill-natured, although a member of the Presbyterian Church." James may be worth $1,400.

Stephen is a brother of James', and is about the same size, though a year older. His experience differed in no material respect from his brother's; was owned by the same woman, whom he "hated for her bad treatment" of him. Would bring $1,400, perhaps.

In substance, and to a considerable extent in the exact words, these facts are given as they came from the lips of the passengers, who, though having been kept in ignorance and bondage, seemed to have their eyes fully open to the wrongs that had been heaped upon them, and were singularly determined to reach free soil at all hazards. The Committee willingly attended to their financial and other wants, and cheered them on with encouraging advice.

They were indebted to "The Baltimore Sun" for the advertisement information. And here it may be further added, that the "Sun" was quite famous for this kind of U.G.R.R. literature, and on that account alone the Committee subscribed for it daily, and never failed to scan closely certain columns, illustrated with a black man running away with a bundle on his back. Many of these popular illustrations and advertisements were preserved, many others were sent away to friends at a distance, who took a special interest in the U.G.R.R. matters. Friends and stockholders in England used to take a great interest in seeing how the fine arts, in these particulars, were encouraged in the South ("the land of chivalry").

HENRY PREDO.

Broke Jail, Jumped out of the Window and Made His Escape.

Henry fled from Buckstown, Dorchester Co., Md., March, 1857. Physically he is a giant. About 27 years of age, stout and well-made, quite black, and no fool, as will appear presently. Only a short time before he escaped, his master threatened to sell him south. To avoid that fate, therefore, he concluded to try his luck on the Underground Rail Road, and, in company with seven others—two of them females—he started for Canada. For two or three days and nights they managed to outgeneral all their adversaries, and succeeded bravely in making the best of their way to a Free State.

In the meantime, however, a reward of $3,000 was offered for their arrest. This temptation was too great to be resisted, even by the man who had been intrusted with the care of them, and who had faithfully promised to pilot them to a safe place. One night, through the treachery of their pretended conductor, they were all taken into Dover Jail, where the Sheriff and several others, who had been notified beforehand by the betrayer, were in readiness to receive them. Up stairs they were taken, the betrayer remarking as they were going up, that they were "cold, but would soon have a good warming." On a light being lit they discovered the iron bars and the fact that they had been betrayed. Their liberty-loving spirits and purposes, however, did not quail. Though resisted brutally by the sheriff with revolver in hand, they made their way down one flight of stairs, and in the moment of excitement, as good luck would have it, plunged into the sheriff's private apartment, where his wife and children were sleeping. The wife cried murder lustily. A shovel full of fire, to the great danger of burning the premises, was scattered over the room; out of the window jumped two of the female fugitives. Our hero Henry, seizing a heavy andiron, smashed out the window entire, through which the others leaped a distance of twelve feet. The railing or wall around the jail, though at first it looked forbidding, was soon surmounted by a desperate effort. At this stage of the proceedings, Henry found himself without the walls, and also lost sight of his comrades at the same time. The last enemy he spied was the sheriff in his stockings without his shoes. He snapped his pistol at him, but it did not go off. Six of the others, however, marvellously got off safely together; where the eighth went, or how he got off, was not known.

DANIEL HUGHES.

————

Daniel fled from Buckstown, Dorchester Co., also. His owner's name was Richard Meredith, a farmer. Daniel is one of the eight alluded to above. In features he is well made, dark chestnut color, and intelligent, possessing an ardent thirst for liberty. The cause of his escape was: "Worked hard in all sorts of weather—in rain and snow," so he thought he would "go where colored men are free." His master was considered the hardest man around. His mistress was "eighty-three years of age," "drank hard," was "very stormy," and a "member of the Methodist Church" (Airy's meeting-house). He left brothers and sisters, and uncles and aunts behind. In the combat at the prison he played his part manfully.

THOMAS ELLIOTT.

————

Thomas is also one of the brave eight who broke out of Dover Jail. He was about twenty-three years of age, well made, wide awake, and of a superb black complexion. He too had been owned by Richard Meredith. Against the betrayer, who was a black man, he had vengeance in store if the opportunity should ever offer. Thomas left only one brother living; his "father and mother were dead."

The excitement over the escape spread very rapidly next morning, and desperate efforts were made to recapture the fugitives, but a few friends there were who had sympathy and immediately rendered them the needed assistance.

The appended note from the faithful Garrett to Samuel Rhoads, may throw light upon the occurrence to some extent.

WILMINGTON, 3d mo. 13th, 1857.

DEAR COUSIN, SAMUEL RHOADS:—I have a letter this day from an agent of the Underground Rail Road, near Dover, in this state, saying I must be on the look out for six brothers and two sisters, they were decoyed and betrayed, he says by a colored man named Thomas Otwell, who pretended to be their friend, and sent a *white scamp* ahead to wait for them at Dover till they arrived; they were arrested and put in Jail there, with Tom's assistance, and some officers. On third day morning about four o'clock, they broke jail; six of them are secreted in the neighborhood, and the writer has not known what became of the other two. The six were to start last night for this place. I hear that their owners have persons stationed at several places on the road watching. I fear they will be taken. If they could lay quiet for ten days or two weeks, they might then get up safe. I shall have two men sent this evening some four or five miles below to keep them away from this town, and send them (if found to Chester County). Thee may show this to Still and McKim, and oblige thy cousin, THOMAS GARRETT.

———

Further light about this exciting contest, may be gathered from a colored conductor on the Road, in Delaware, who wrote as follows to a member of the Vigilance Committee at Philadelphia.

CAMDEN, DEL., March 23d, 1857.

DEAR SIR;—I tak my pen in hand to write to you, to inform you what we have had to go throw for the last two weaks. Thir wir six men and two woman was betraid on the tenth of this month, thea had them in prison but thea got out was conveyed by a black man, he told them he wood bring them to my hows, as he wos told, he had ben ther Befor, he has com with Harrett, a woman that stops at my hous when she pases tow and throw yau. You don't no me I supos, the Rev. Thomas H. Kennard dos, or Peter Lowis. He Road Camden Circuit, this man led them in dover prisin and left them with a whit man; but tha tour out the winders and jump out, so cum back to camden. We put them throug, we hav to carry them 19 mils and cum back the sam night wich maks 38 mils. It is tou much for our littel horses. We must do the bes we can, ther is much Bisness dun on this Road. We hay to go throw dover and smerny, the two wors places this sid of mary land lin. If you have herd or sean them ples let me no. I will Com to Phila be for long and then I will call and se you. There is much to do her. Ples to wright, I Remain your frend,

WILLIAM BRINKLY.
Remember me to Thom. Kennard.

The balance of these brave fugitives, although not named in this connection, succeeded in getting off safely. But how the betrayer, sheriff and hunters got out of their dilemma, the Committee was never fully posted.

The Committee found great pleasure in assisting these passengers, for they had the true grit. Such were always doubly welcome.

MARY EPPS, ALIAS EMMA BROWN—JOSEPH AND ROBERT ROBINSON.

A Slave Mother Loses her Speech at the Sale of her Child—Bob Escapes from his Master, a Trader, with $1500 in North Carolina Money.

Mary fled from Petersburg and the Robinsons from Richmond. A fugitive slave law-breaking captain by the name of B., who owned a schooner, and would bring any kind of freight that would pay the most, was the conductor in this instance. Quite a number of passengers at different times availed themselves of his accommodations and thus succeeded in reaching Canada.

His risk was very great. On this account he claimed, as did certain others, that it was no more than fair to charge for his services— indeed he did not profess to bring persons for nothing, except in rare instances. In this matter the Committee did not feel disposed to interfere directly in any way, further than to suggest that whatever understanding was agreed upon by the parties themselves should be faithfully adhered to.

Many slaves in cities could raise, "by hook or by crook," fifty or one hundred dollars to pay for a passage, providing they could find one who was willing to risk aiding them. Thus, while the Vigilance Committee of Philadelphia especially neither charged nor accepted anything for their services, it was not to be expected that any of the Southern agents could afford to do likewise.

The husband of Mary had for a long time wanted his own freedom, but did not feel that he could go without his wife; in fact, he resolved to get her off first, then to try and escape himself, if possible. The first essential step towards success, he considered, was to save his money and make it an object to the captain to help him. So when he had managed to lay by one hundred dollars, he willingly offered this sum to Captain B., if he would engage to deliver his wife into the hands of the Vigilance Committee of Philadelphia. The captain agreed to the terms and fulfilled his engagement to the letter. About the 1st of March, 1855, Mary was presented to the Vigilance Committee. She was of agreeable manners, about forty-five years of age, dark complexion, round built, and intelligent. She had been the mother of fifteen children, four of whom had been sold away from her; one was still held in slavery in Petersburg; the others were all dead.

At the sale of one of her children she was so affected with grief that she was thrown into violent convulsions, which caused the loss of her speech for one entire month. But this little episode was not a matter to excite sympathy in the breasts of the highly refined and tender-hearted Christian mothers of Petersburg. In the mercy of Providence, however, her reason and strength returned.

She had formerly belonged to the late Littleton Reeves, whom she represented as having been "kind" to her, much more so than her mistress (Mrs. Reeves). Said Mary, "She being of a jealous disposition, caused me to be hired out with a hard family, where I was much abused, frequently flogged, and stinted for food," etc.

But the sweets of freedom in the care of the Vigilance Committee now delighted her mind, and the hope that her husband would soon follow her to Canada, inspired her with expectations that she would one day "sit under her own vine and fig tree where none dared to molest or make her afraid."

The Committee rendered her the usual assistance, and in due time, forwarded her on to Queen Victoria's free land in Canada. On her arrival she wrote back as follows—

TORONTO, March 14th, 1855.

DEAR MR. STILL:—I take this opportunity of addressing you with these few lines to inform you that I arrived here to-day, and hope that this may find yourself and Mrs. Still well, as this leaves me at the present. I will also say to you, that I had no difficulty in getting along. the two young men that was with me left me at Suspension Bridge. they went another way.

I cannot say much about the place as I have ben here but a short time but so far as I have seen I like very well. you will give my

Respect to your lady, & Mr & Mrs Brown. If you have not written
to Petersburg you will please to write as soon as can I have nothing
More to Write at present but yours Respectfully
EMMA BROWN (old name MARY EPPS).

Now, Joseph and Robert (Mary's associate passengers from Richmond) must here be noticed. Joseph was of a dark orange color,
medium size, very active and intelligent, and doubtless, well understood the art of behaving himself. He was well acquainted with
the auction block—having been sold three times, and had had the
misfortune to fall into the hands of a cruel master each time. Under
these circumstances he had had but few privileges. Sundays and
week days alike he was kept pretty severely bent down to duty. He
had been beaten and knocked around shamefully. He had a wife,
and spoke of her in most endearing language, although, on leaving,
he did not feel at liberty to apprise her of his movements, "fearing
that it would not be safe so to do." His four little children, to whom
he appeared warmly attached, he left as he did his wife—in Slavery.
He declared that he "stuck to them as long as he could." George E.
Sadler, the keeper of an oyster house, held the deed for "Joe," and a
most heartless wretch he was in Joe's estimation. The truth was, Joe
could not stand the burdens and abuses which Sadler was inclined
to heap upon him. So he concluded to join his brother and go off on
the U.G.R.R.

Robert, his younger brother, was owned by Robert Slater, Esq., a
regular negro trader. Eight years this slave's duties had been at the
slave prison, and among other daily offices he had to attend to, was
to lock up the prison, prepare the slaves for sale, etc. Robert was a
very intelligent young man, and from long and daily experience
with the customs and usages of the slave prison, he was as familiar
with the business as a Pennsylvania farmer with his barn-yard
stock. His account of things was too harrowing for detail here, except in the briefest manner, and that only with reference to a few
particulars. In order to prepare slaves for the market, it was usual
to have them greased and rubbed to make them look bright and
shining. And he went on further to state, that "females as well as

males were not uncommonly stripped naked, lashed flat to a bench, and then held by two men, sometimes four, while the brutal trader would strap them with a broad leather strap." The strap being preferred to the cow-hide, as it would not break the skin, and damage the sale. "One hundred lashes would only be a common flogging." The separation of families was thought nothing of. "Often I have been flogged for refusing to flog others." While not yet twenty-three years of age, Robert expressed himself as having become so daily sick of the brutality and suffering he could not help witnessing, that he felt he could not possibly stand it any longer, let the cost be what it might. In this state of mind he met with Captain B. Only one obstacle stood in his way—material aid. It occurred to Robert that he had frequent access to the money drawer, and often it contained the proceeds of fresh sales of flesh and blood; and he reasoned that if some of that would help him and his brother to freedom, there could be no harm in helping himself the first opportunity.

The captain was all ready, and provided he could get three passengers at $100 each he would set sail without much other freight. Of course he was too shrewd to get out papers for Philadelphia. That would betray him at once. Washington or Baltimore, or even Wilmington, Del., were names which stood fair in the eyes of Virginia. Consequently, being able to pack the fugitives away in a very private hole of his boat, and being only bound for a Southern port, the captain was willing to risk his share of the danger. "Very well," said Robert, "to-day I will please my master so well, that I will catch him at an unguarded moment, and will ask him for a pass to go to a ball to-night (slave-holders love to see their slaves fiddling and dancing of nights), and as I shall be leaving in a hurry, I will take a grab from the day's sale, and when Slater hears of me again, I will be in Canada." So after having attended to all his disagreeable duties, he made his "grab," and got a hand full. He did not know, however, how it would hold out. That evening, instead of participating with the gay dancers, he was just one degree lower down than the regular bottom of Captain B's. deck, with several hundred dollars in his pocket, after paying the worthy captain one hundred each for himself and his brother, besides making the captain an additional present of nearly one hundred. Wind and tide were now what they prayed for to speed on the U.G.R.R. schooner, until they might reach the depot at Philadelphia.

The Richmond *Dispatch*, an enterprising paper in the interest of slaveholders, which came daily to the Committee, was received in advance of the passengers, when lo! and behold, in turning to the interesting column containing the elegant illustrations of "runaway negroes," it was seen that the unfortunate Slater had "lost $1500 in North Carolina money, and also his dark orange-colored, intelligent, and good-looking turnkey, Bob." "Served him right, it is no stealing for one piece of property to go off with another piece," reasoned a member of the Committee.

In a couple of days after the Dispatch brought the news, the three U.G.R.R. passengers were safely landed at the usual place, and so accurate were the descriptions in the paper, that, on first seeing them, the Committee recognized them instantly, and, without any previous ceremonies, read to them the advertisement relative to the "$1500 in N.C. money, &c.," and put the question to them direct: "Are you the ones?" "We are," they owned up without hesitation. The Committee did not see a dollar of their money, but understood they had about $900, after paying the captain; while Bob considered he made a "very good grab," he did not admit that the amount advertised was correct. After a reasonable time for recruiting, having been so long in the hole of the vessel, they took their departure for Canada.

From Joseph, the elder brother, is appended a short letter, announcing their arrival and condition under the British Lion—

SAINT CATHARINE, April 16, 1855.

MR. WILLIAM STILL, DEAR SIR:—Your letter of date April 7th I have just got, it had been opened before it came to me. I have not received any other letter from you and can get no account of them in the Post Office in this place, I am well and have got a good situation in this city and intend staying here. I should be very glad to hear from you as soon as convenient and also from all of my friends near you. My Brother is also at work with me and doing well.

There is nothing here that would interest you in the way of news. There is a Masonic Lodge of our people and two churches and societys here and some other institutions for our benefit. Be kind enough to send a few lines to the Lady spoken of for that mocking bird and much oblige me. Write me soon and believe me your obedient Serv't

Love & respects to Lady and daughter JOSEPH ROBINSON.

As well as writing to a member of the Committee, Joe and Bob had the assurance to write back to the trader and oyster-house keeper. In their letter they stated that they had arrived safely in Canada, and were having good times,—in the eating line had an abundance of the best,—also had very choice wines and brandies, which they supposed that they (trader and oyster-house keeper) would give a great deal to have a "smack at." And then they gave them a very cordial invitation to make them a visit, and suggested that the quickest way they could come, would be by telegraph, which they admitted was slightly dangerous, and without first greasing themselves, and then hanging on very fast, the journey might not prove altogether advantageous to them. This was worm-wood and gall to the trader and oyster-house man. A most remarkable coincidence was that, about the time this letter was received in Richmond, the captain who brought away the three passengers, made it his business for some reason or other, to call at the oyster-house kept by the owner of Joe, and while there, this letter was read and commented on in torrents of Billingsgate phrases; and the trader told the captain that he would give him "two thousand dollars if he would get them;" finally he told him he would "give every cent they would bring, which would be much over $2000," as they were "so very likely." How far the captain talked approvingly, he did not exactly tell the Committee, but they guessed he talked strong Democratic doctrine to them under the frightful circumstances. But he was good at concealing his feelings, and obviously managed to avoid suspicion.

HENRY BOX BROWN.

Arrived by Adams Express.

Although the name of Henry Box Brown has been echoed over the land for a number of years, and the simple facts connected with his marvelous escape from slavery in a box published widely through the medium of anti-slavery papers, nevertheless it is not unreasonable to suppose that very little is generally known in relation to this case.

Briefly, the facts are these, which doubtless have never before been fully published—

Brown was a man of invention as well as a hero. In point of interest, however, his case is no more remarkable than many others. Indeed, neither before nor after escaping did he suffer one-half what many others have experienced.

He was decidedly an unhappy piece of property in the city of Richmond, Va. In the condition of a slave he felt that it would be impossible for him to remain. Full well did he know, however, that it was no holiday task to escape the vigilance of Virginia slave-hunters, or the wrath of an enraged master for committing the unpardonable sin of attempting to escape to a land of liberty. So Brown counted well the cost before venturing upon this hazardous undertaking. Ordinary modes of travel he concluded might prove disastrous to his hopes; he, therefore, hit upon a new invention altogether, which was to have himself boxed up and forwarded to Philadelphia direct by express. The size of the box and how it was to be made to fit him most comfortably, was of his own ordering. Two feet eight inches deep, two feet wide, and three feet long were the exact dimensions of the box, lined with baize. His resources with regard to food and water consisted of the following: One bladder of water and a few small biscuits. His mechanical implement to meet the death-struggle for fresh air, all told, was one large gimlet. Satisfied that it would be far better to peril his life for freedom in this way than to remain under the galling yoke of Slavery, he entered his box, which was safely nailed up and hooped with five hickory hoops, and was then addressed by his next friend, James A. Smith, a shoe dealer, to Wm. H. Johnson, Arch street, Philadelphia, marked, "This side up with care." In this condition he was sent to Adams' Express office in a dray, and thence by overland express to Philadelphia. It was twenty-six hours from the time he left Richmond until his arrival in the City of Brotherly Love. The notice, "This side up, &c.," did not avail with the different expressmen, who hesitated not to handle the box in the usual rough manner common to this class of men. For a while they actually had the box upside down, and had him on his head for miles. A few days before he was expected, certain intimation was conveyed to a member of the Vigilance Committee that a box might be expected by the three o'clock morning train from the South, which might contain a man. One of the most serious walks he ever took—and they had not been a few—to meet and accompany passengers, he took at half past two o'clock that morning to the depot. Not once, but for more than a score of times, he fancied the slave would be dead. He anxiously looked while the freight was being unloaded from the cars, to see if he could recognize a box that might contain a man; one alone had that appearance, and he confessed it really seemed as if there was the scent of death about it. But on inquiry, he soon learned that it was not the one he was looking after, and he was free to say he experienced a marked sense of relief. That same afternoon, however, he received from Richmond a telegram, which read thus, "Your case of goods is shipped and will arrive to-morrow morning."

At this exciting juncture of affairs, Mr. McKim, who had been engineering this important undertaking, deemed it expedient to change the programme slightly in one particular at least to insure greater safety. Instead of having a member of the Committee go again to the depot for the box, which might excite suspicion, it was decided that it would be safest to have the express bring it direct to the Anti-Slavery Office.

But all apprehension of danger did not now disappear, for there was no room to suppose that Adams' Express office had any sympathy with the Abolitionist or the fugitive, consequently for Mr. McKim to appear personally at the express office to give directions with reference to the coming of a box from Richmond which would be directed to Arch street, and yet not intended for that street, but for the Anti-Slavery office at 107 North Fifth street, it needed of course no great discernment to foresee that a step of this kind was wholly impracticable and that a more indirect and covert method would have to be adopted. In this dreadful crisis Mr. McKim, with his usual good judgment and remarkably quick, strategical mind, especially in matters pertaining to the U.G.R.R., hit upon the following plan, namely, to go to his friend, E.M. Davis,* who was then extensively engaged in mercantile business, and relate the circumstances. Having daily intercourse with said Adams' Express office, and being well acquainted with the firm and some of the drivers, Mr. Davis could, as Mr. McKim thought, talk about "boxes, freight, etc.," from any part of the country without risk. Mr. Davis heard Mr. McKim's plan and instantly approved of it, and was heartily at his service.

"Dan, an Irishman, one of Adams' Express drivers, is just the fellow to go to the depot after the box," said Davis. "He drinks a little too much whiskey sometimes, but he will do anything I ask him to do, promptly and obligingly. I'll trust Dan, for I believe he is the very man." The difficulty which Mr. McKim had been so anxious to overcome was thus pretty well settled. It was agreed that Dan should go after the box next morning before daylight and bring it to the Anti-Slavery office direct, and to make it all the more agreeable for Dan to get up out of his warm bed and go on this errand before day, it was decided that he should have a five dollar gold piece for himself. Thus these preliminaries having been satisfactorily arranged, it only remained for Mr. Davis to see Dan and give him instructions accordingly, etc.

---

* E. M. Davis was a member of the Executive Committee of the Pennsylvania Anti-Slavery Society and a long-tried Abolitionist, son-in-law of James and Lucretia Mott.

Next morning, according to arrangement, the box was at the Anti-Slavery office in due time. The witnesses present to behold the resurrection were J.M. McKim, Professor C.D. Cleveland, Lewis Thompson, and the writer.

Mr. McKim was deeply interested; but having been long identified with the Anti-Slavery cause as one of its oldest and ablest advocates in the darkest days of slavery and mobs, and always found by the side of the fugitive to counsel and succor, he was on this occasion perfectly composed.

Professor Cleveland, however, was greatly moved. His zeal and earnestness in the cause of freedom, especially in rendering aid to passengers, knew no limit. Ordinarily he could not too often visit these travelers, shake them too warmly by the hand, or impart to them too freely of his substance to aid them on their journey. But now his emotion was overpowering.

Mr. Thompson, of the firm of Merrihew & Thompson—about the only printers in the city who for many years dared to print such incendiary documents as anti-slavery papers and pamphlets—one of the truest friends of the slave, was composed and prepared to witness the scene.

All was quiet. The door had been safely locked. The proceedings commenced. Mr. McKim rapped quietly on the lid of the box and called out, "All right!" Instantly came the answer from within, "All right, sir!"

The witnesses will never forget that moment. Saw and hatchet quickly had the five hickory hoops cut and the lid off, and the marvellous resurrection of Brown ensued. Rising up in his box, he reached out his hand, saying, "How do you do, gentlemen?" The little assemblage hardly knew what to think or do at the moment. He was about as wet as if he had come up out of the Delaware. Very soon he remarked that, before leaving Richmond he had selected for his arrival-hymn (if he lived) the Psalm beginning with these words: *"I waited patiently for the Lord, and He heard my prayer."* And most touchingly did he sing the psalm, much to his own relief, as well as to the delight of his small audience.

He was then christened Henry Box Brown, and soon afterwards was sent to the hospitable residence of James Mott and E.M. Davis, on Ninth street, where, it is needless to say, he met a most cordial reception from Mrs. Lucretia Mott and her household. Clothing and creature comforts were furnished in abundance, and delight and joy filled all hearts in that stronghold of philanthropy.

As he had been so long doubled up in the box he needed to promenade considerably in the fresh air, so James Mott put one of his broad-brim hats on his head and tendered him the hospitalities of his yard as well as his house, and while Brown promenaded the yard flushed with victory, great was the joy of his friends.

After his visit at Mr. Mott's, he spent two days with the writer, and then took his departure for Boston, evidently feeling quite conscious of the wonderful feat he had performed, and at the same time it may be safely said that those who witnessed this strange resurrection were not only elated at his success, but were made to sympathize more deeply than ever before with the slave. Also the noble-hearted Smith who boxed him up was made to rejoice over Brown's victory, and was thereby encouraged to render similar service to two other young bondmen, who appealed to him for deliverance. But, unfortunately, in this attempt the undertaking proved a failure. Two boxes containing the young men alluded to above, after having been duly expressed and some distance on the road, were, through the agency of the telegraph, betrayed, and the heroic young fugitives were captured in their boxes and dragged back to hopeless bondage. Consequently, through this deplorable failure, Samuel A. Smith was arrested, imprisoned, and was called upon to suffer severely, as may be seen from the subjoined correspondence, taken from the New York Tribune soon after his release from the penitentiary.

THE DELIVERER OF BOX BROWN—MEETING OF THE COLORED CITIZENS OF PHILADELPHIA.

[Correspondence of the N.Y. Tribune.]
PHILADELPHIA, Saturday, July 5, 1856.

Samuel A. Smith, who boxed up Henry Box Brown in Richmond, Va., and forwarded him by overland express to Philadelphia, and who was arrested and convicted, eight years ago, for boxing up two other slaves, also directed to Philadelphia, having served out his imprisonment in the Penitentiary, was released on the 18th ultimo, and arrived in this city on the 21st.

Though he lost all his property; though he was refused witnesses on his trial (no officer could be found, who would serve a summons on a witness); though for five long months, in hot weather, he was kept heavily chained in a cell four by eight feet in dimensions; though he received five dreadful stabs, aimed at his heart, by a bribed assassin, nevertheless he still rejoices in the motives which prompted him to "undo the heavy burdens, and let the oppressed go free." Having resided nearly all his life in the South, where he had traveled and seen much of the "peculiar institution," and had witnessed the most horrid enormities inflicted upon the slave, whose cries were ever ringing in his ears, and for whom he had the warmest sympathy, Mr. Smith could not refrain from believing that the black man, as well as the white, had God-given rights. Consequently, he was not accustomed to shed tears when a poor creature escaped from his "kind master;" nor was he willing to turn a deaf ear to his appeals and groans, when he knew he was thirsting for freedom. From 1828 up to the day he was incarcerated, many had sought his aid and counsel, nor had they sought in vain. In various places he operated with success. In Richmond, however, it seemed expedient to invent a new plan for certain emergencies, hence the Box and Express plan was devised, at the instance of a few heroic slaves, who had manifested their willingness to die in a box, on the road to liberty, rather than continue longer under the yoke. But these heroes fell into the power of their enemies. Mr. Smith had not been long in the Penitentiary before he had fully gained the esteem and confidence of the Superintendent and other officers. Finding him to be humane and generous-hearted—showing kindness toward all, especially in buying bread, &c., for the starving prisoners, and by a timely note of warning, which had saved the life of one of the keepers, for whose destruction a bold plot had been arranged—the officers felt disposed to show him such favors as the law would allow. But their good intentions were soon frustrated. The Inquisition (commonly called the Legislature), being in session in Richmond, hearing that the Superintendent had been speaking well of Smith, and circulating a petition for his pardon, indignantly demanded to know if the rumor was well founded. Two weeks were spent by the Inquisition, and many witnesses were placed upon oath, to solemnly testify in the matter. One of the keepers swore that his life had been saved by Smith. Col. Morgan, the Superintendent, frequently testified in writing and verbally to Smith's good deportment; acknowledging that he had circulated petitions, &c.; and took the position, that he sincerely believed, that it would be to the interest of the institution to pardon him; calling the attention of the Inquisition, at the same time, to the fact, that not unfrequently pardons had been granted to criminals, under sentence of death, for the most cold-blooded murder, to say nothing of other gross crimes. The effort for pardon was soon abandoned, for the following reason given by the Governor: "I can't, and I won't pardon him!"

In view of the unparalleled injustice which Mr. S. had suffered, as well as on account of the aid he had rendered to the slaves, on his arrival in this city the colored citizens of Philadelphia felt that he was entitled to sympathy and aid, and straightway invited him to remain a few days, until arrangements could be made for a mass meeting to receive him. Accordingly, on last Monday evening, a mass meeting convened in the Israel church, and the Rev. Wm. T. Catto was called to the chair, and Wm. Still was appointed secretary. The chairman briefly stated the object of the meeting. Having lived in the South, he claimed to know something of the workings of the oppressive system of slavery generally, and declared that, notwithstanding the many exposures of the evil which came under his own observation, the most vivid descriptions fell far short of the realities his own eyes had witnessed. He then introduced Mr. Smith, who arose and in a plain manner briefly told his story, assuring the audience that he had always hated slavery,

and had taken great pleasure in helping many out of it, and though
he had suffered much physically and pecuniarily for the cause'
sake, yet he murmured not, but rejoiced in what he had done. After
taking his seat, addresses were made by the Rev. S. Smith, Messrs.
Kinnard, Brunner, Bradway, and others. The following preamble
and resolutions were adopted—

WHEREAS, We, the colored citizens of Philadelphia, have among
us Samuel A. Smith, who was incarcerated over seven years in the
Richmond Penitentiary, for doing an act that was honorable to his
feelings and his sense of justice and humanity, therefore,

Resolved, That we welcome him to this city as a martyr to the
cause of Freedom.

Resolved, That we heartily tender him our gratitude for the good
he has done to our suffering race.

Resolved, That we sympathize with him in his losses and
sufferings in the cause of the poor, down-trodden slave.

W.S.

During his stay in Philadelphia, on this occasion, he stopped for
about a fortnight with the writer, and it was most gratifying to learn
from him that he was no new worker on the U.G.R.R. But that he
had long hated slavery thoroughly, and although surrounded with
perils on every side, he had not failed to help a poor slave whenever
the opportunity was presented.

Pecuniary aid, to some extent, was rendered him in this city, for
which he was grateful, and after being united in marriage, by
Wm. H. Furness, D.D., to a lady who had remained faithful to him
through all his sore trials and sufferings, he took his departure for
Western New York, with a good conscience and an unshaken faith
in the belief that in aiding his fellow-man to freedom he had but
simply obeyed the word of Him who taught man to do unto others
as he would be done by.

TRIAL OF THE EMANCIPATORS OF COL. J.H. WHEELER'S SLAVES, JANE JOHNSON AND HER TWO LITTLE BOYS.

Among other duties devolving on the Vigilance Committee when hearing of slaves brought into the State by their owners, was immediately to inform such persons that as they were not fugitives, but were brought into the State by their masters, they were entitled to their freedom without another moment's service, and that they could have the assistance of the Committee and the advice of counsel without charge, by simply availing themselves of these proffered favors.

Many slave-holders fully understood the law in this particular, and were also equally posted with regard to the vigilance of abolitionists. Consequently they avoided bringing slaves beyond Mason and Dixon's Line in traveling North. But some slave-holders were not thus mindful of the laws, or were too arrogant to take heed, as may be seen in the case of Colonel John H. Wheeler, of North Carolina, the United States Minister to Nicaragua. In passing through Philadelphia from Washington, one very warm July day in 1855, accompanied by three of his slaves, his high official equilibrium, as well as his assumed rights under the Constitution, received a terrible shock at the hands of the Committee. Therefore, for the readers of these pages, and in order to completely illustrate the various phases of the work of the Committee in the days of Slavery, this case, selected from many others, is a fitting one. However, for more than a brief recital of some of the more prominent incidents, it will not be possible to find room in this volume. And, indeed, the necessity of so doing is precluded by the fact that Mr. Williamson in justice to himself and the cause of freedom, with great pains and singular ability, gathered the most important facts bearing on his memorable trial and imprisonment, and published them in a neat volume for historical reference.

In order to bring fully before the reader the beginning of this interesting and exciting case, it seems only necessary to publish the subjoined letter, written by one of the actors in the drama, and addressed to the New York Tribune, and an additional paragraph which may be requisite to throw light on a special point, which Judge Kane decided was concealed in the "obstinate" breast of Passmore Williamson, as said Williamson persistently refused before the said Judge's court, to own that he had a knowledge of the mystery in question. After which, a brief glance at some of the more important points of the case must suffice.

LETTER COPIED FROM THE NEW YORK TRIBUNE.

[Correspondence of The N.Y. Tribune.]
PHILADELPHIA, Monday, July 30, 1855.

As the public have not been made acquainted with the facts and particulars respecting the agency of Mr. Passmore Williamson and others, in relation to the slave case now agitating this city, and especially as the poor slave mother and her two sons have been so grossly misrepresented, I deem it my duty to lay the facts before you, for publication or otherwise, as you may think proper.

On Wednesday afternoon, week, at 4-½ o'clock, the following note was placed in my hands by a colored boy whom I had never before seen, to my recollection:

"MR. STILL—*Sir:* Will you come down to Bloodgood's Hotel as soon as possible—as there are three fugitive slaves here and they want liberty. Their master is here with them, on his way to New York."

The note was without date, and the signature so indistinctly written as not to be understood by me, having evidently been penned in a moment of haste.

Without delay I ran with the note to Mr. P. Williamson's office, Seventh and Arch, found him at his desk, and gave it to him, and after reading it, he remarked that he could not go down, as he had to go to Harrisburg that night on business—but he advised me to go, and to get the names of the slave-holder and the slaves, in order to telegraph to New York to have them arrested there, as no time remained to procure a writ of habeas corpus here.

I could not have been two minutes in Mr. W.'s office before starting in haste for the wharf. To my surprise, however, when I reached the wharf, there I found Mr. W., his mind having undergone a sudden change; he was soon on the spot.

I saw three or four colored persons in the hall at Bloodgood's, none of whom I recognized except the boy who brought me the note. Before having time for making inquiry some one said they had gone on board the boat. "Get their description," said Mr. W. I instantly inquired of one of the colored persons for the desired description, and was told that she was "a tall, dark woman, with two little boys."

Mr. W. and myself ran on board of the boat, looked among the passengers on the first deck, but saw them not. "They are up on the second deck," an unknown voice uttered. In a second we were in their presence. We approached the anxious-looking slave-mother with her two boys on her left-hand; close on her right sat an ill-favored white man having a cane in his hand which I took to be a sword-cane. (As to its being a sword-cane, however, I might have been mistaken.)

The first words to the mother were: "Are you traveling?" "Yes," was the prompt answer. "With whom?" She nodded her head toward the ill-favored man, signifying with him. Fidgeting on his seat, he said something, exactly what I do not now recollect. In reply I remarked: "Do they belong to you, Sir?" "Yes, they are in my charge," was his answer. Turning from him to the mother and her sons, in substance, and word for word, as near as I can remember, the following remarks were earnestly though calmly addressed by the individuals who rejoiced to meet them on free soil, and who felt unmistakably assured that they were justified by the laws of Pennsylvania as well as the Law of God, in informing them of their rights:

"You are entitled to your freedom according to the laws of Pennsylvania, having been brought into the State by your owner. If you prefer freedom to slavery, as we suppose everybody does, you have the chance to accept it now. Act calmly—don't be frightened by your master—you are as much entitled to your freedom as we are, or as he is—be determined and you need have no fears but that you will be protected by the law. Judges have time and again decided cases in this city and State similar to yours in favor of freedom! Of course, if you want to remain a slave with your master, we cannot force you to leave; we only want to make you sensible of your rights. *Remember, if you lose this chance you may never get such another,"* etc.

This advice to the woman was made in the hearing of a number of persons present, white and colored; and one elderly white gentleman of genteel address, who seemed to take much interest in what was going on, remarked that they would have the same chance for their freedom in New Jersey and New York as they then had—seeming to sympathize with the woman, etc.

During the few moments in which the above remarks were made, the slaveholder frequently interrupted—said she understood all about the laws making her free, and her right to leave if she wanted to; but contended that she did not want to leave—that she was on a visit to New York to see her friends—afterward *wished to return to her three children whom she left in Virginia, from whom it would be* HARD *to separate her.* Furthermore, he diligently tried to constrain her to say that she did not want to be interfered with—that she wanted to go with him—that she was on a visit to New York— had children in the South, etc.; but the woman's desire to be free was altogether too strong to allow her to make a Single acknowledgment favorable to his wishes in the matter. On the contrary, she repeatedly said, distinctly and firmly, "*I am not free, but I want my freedom*—ALWAYS *wanted to be free!! but he holds me.*"

While the slaveholder claimed that she belonged to him, he said *that she was free*! Again he said that he was *going to give her her freedom,* etc. When his eyes would be off of hers, such eagerness as her looks expressed, indicative of her entreaty that we would not forsake her and her little ones in their weakness, it had never been my lot to witness before, under any circumstances.

The last bell tolled! The last moment for further delay passed! The arm of the woman being slightly touched, accompanied with the word, "Come!" she instantly arose. "Go along—go along!" said some, who sympathized, to the boys, at the same time taking hold of their arms. By this time the parties were fairly moving toward the stairway leading to the deck below. Instantly on their starting, the slave-holder rushed at the woman and her children, to prevent their leaving; and, if I am not mistaken, he simultaneously took hold of the woman and Mr. Williamson, which resistance on his part caused Mr. W. to take hold of him and set him aside quickly.

The passengers were looking on all around, but none interfered in behalf of the slaveholder except one man, whom I took to be another slaveholder. He said harshly, "Let them alone; they are his *property*!" The youngest boy, about 7 years of age—too young to know what these things meant—cried "Massa John! Massa John!" The elder boy, 11 years of age, took the matter more dispassionately, and the mother *quite calmly*. The mother and her sympathizers all moved down the stairs together in the presence of quite a number of spectators on the first deck and on the wharf, all of whom, as far as I was able to discern, seemed to look upon the whole affair with the greatest indifference. The woman and children were assisted, but not forced to leave. Nor were there any violence or threatenings as I saw or heard. The only words that I heard from any one of an objectionable character, were: "Knock him down; knock him down!" but who uttered it or who was meant I knew not, nor have I since been informed. However, if it was uttered by a colored man, I regret it, as there was not the slightest cause for such language, especially as the sympathies of the spectators and citizens seemed to justify the course pursued.

While passing off of the wharf and down Delaware-avenue to Dock st., and up Dock to Front, where a carriage was procured, the slaveholder and one police officer were of the party, if no more. The youngest boy on being put in the carriage was told that he was "a fool for crying so after 'Massa John,' who would sell him if he ever caught him." Not another whine was heard on the subject.

The carriage drove down town slowly, the horses being fatigued and the weather intensely hot; the inmates were put out on Tenth street—not at any house—after which they soon found hospitable friends and quietude. The excitement of the moment having passed by, the mother *seemed very cheerful, and rejoiced greatly that herself and boys had been, as she thought, so "providentially delivered from the house of bondage!"* For the first time in her life she could look upon herself and children and feel free!

Having felt the iron in her heart for the best half of her days— having been sold with her children on the auction block—having had one of her children sold far away from her without hope of her seeing him again—she very naturally and wisely concluded to go to Canada, fearing if she remained in this city—as some assured her she could do with entire safety—that she might again find herself in the clutches of the tyrant from whom she had fled.

A few items of what she related concerning the character of her master may be interesting to the reader—

Within the last two years he had sold all his slaves—between thirty and forty in number—having purchased the present ones in that space of time. She said that before leaving Washington, coming on the cars, and at his father-in-law's in this city, a number of persons had told him that in bringing his slaves into Pennsylvania they would be free. When told at his father-in-law's, as she overheard it, that he "could not have done a worse thing," &c., he replied that "Jane would not leave him."

As much, however, as he affected to have such implicit confidence in Jane, he scarcely allowed her to be out of his presence a moment while in this city. To use Jane's own language, he was "on her heels every minute," fearing that some one might get to her ears the sweet music of freedom. By the way, Jane had it deep in her heart before leaving the South, and was bent on succeeding in New York, if disappointed in Philadelphia.

At Bloodgood's, after having been belated and left by the 2 o'clock train, while waiting for the 5 o'clock line, his appetite tempted her "master" to take a hasty dinner. So after placing Jane where he thought she would be pretty secure from "evil communications" from the colored waiters, and after giving her a double counselling, he made his way to the table; remained but a little while, however, before leaving to look after Jane; finding her composed, looking over a bannister near where he left her, he returned to the table again and finished his meal.

But, alas, for the slave-holder! Jane had her "top eye open," and in that brief space had appealed to the sympathies of a person whom she ventured to trust, saying, "I and my children are slaves, and we want liberty!" I am not certain, but suppose that person, in the goodness of his heart, was the cause of the note being sent to the Anti-Slavery office, and hence the result.

As to her going on to New York to see her friends, and wishing to return to her three children in the South, and his going to free her, &c., Jane declared repeatedly and very positively, that there was not a particle of truth in what her master said on these points. The truth is she had not the slightest hope of freedom through any act of his. She had only left one boy in the South, who had been sold far away, where she scarcely ever heard from him, indeed never expected to see him any more.

In appearance Jane is tall and well formed, high and large forehead, of genteel manners, chestnut color, and seems to possess, naturally, uncommon good sense, though of course she has never been allowed to read.

Thus I have given as truthful a report as I am capable of doing, of Jane and the circumstances connected with her deliverance.

W. STILL.

P.S.—Of the five colored porters who promptly appeared, with warm hearts throbbing in sympathy with the mother and her children, too much cannot be said in commendation. In the present case they acted nobly, whatever may be said of their general character, of which I know nothing. How human beings, who have ever tasted oppression, could have acted differently under the circumstances I cannot conceive.

The mystery alluded to, which the above letter did not contain, and which the court failed to make Mr. Williamson reveal, might have been truthfully explained in these words. The carriage was procured at the wharf, while Col. Wheeler and Mr. Williamson were debating the question relative to the action of the Committee, and at that instant, Jane and her two boys were invited into it and accompanied by the writer, who procured it, were driven down town, and on Tenth Street, below Lombard, the inmates were invited out of it, and the said conductor paid the driver and discharged him. For prudential reasons he took them to a temporary resting-place, where they could tarry until after dark; then they were invited to his own residence, where they were made welcome, and in due time forwarded East. Now, what disposition was made of them after they had left the wharf, while Williamson and Wheeler were discussing matters—(as was clearly sworn to by Passmore, in his answer to the writ of Habeas Corpus)—he Williamson did not know. That evening, before seeing the member of the Committee, with whom he acted in concert on the boat, and who had entire charge of Jane and her boys, he left for Harrisburg, to fulfill business engagements. The next morning his father (Thomas Williamson) brought the writ of Habeas Corpus (which had been served at Passmore's office after he left) to the Anti-Slavery Office. In his calm manner he handed it to the writer, at the same time remarking that "Passmore had gone to Harrisburg," and added, "thee had better attend to it" (the writ). Edward Hopper, Esq., was applied to with the writ, and in the absence of Mr. Williamson, appeared before the court, and stated "that the writ had not been served, as Mr. W. was out of town," etc.

After this statement, the Judge postponed further action until the next day. In the meanwhile, Mr. Williamson returned and found the writ awaiting him, and an agitated state of feeling throughout the city besides. Now it is very certain, that he did not seek to know from those in the secret, where Jane Johnson and her boys were taken after they left the wharf, or as to what disposition had been made of them, in any way; except to ask simply, "are they safe?" (and when told "yes," he smiled) consequently, he might have been examined for a week, by the most skillful lawyer, at the Philadelphia bar, but he could not have answered other than he did in making his return to the writ, before Judge Kane, namely: *"That the persons named in the writ, nor either of them, are now nor was at the time of issuing of the writ, or the original writ, or at any other time in the custody, power, or possession of the respondent, nor by him confined or restrained; wherefore he cannot have the bodies,"* etc.

Thus, while Mr. W. was subjected to the severest trial of his devotion to Freedom, his noble bearing throughout, won for him the admiration and sympathy of the friends of humanity and liberty throughout the entire land, and in proof of his fidelity, he most cheerfully submitted to imprisonment rather than desert his principles. But the truth was not wanted in this instance by the enemies of Freedom; obedience to Slavery was demanded to satisfy the South. The opportunity seemed favorable for teaching abolitionists and negroes, that they had no right to interfere with a "chivalrous southern gentleman," while passing through Philadelphia with his slaves. Thus, to make an effective blow, all the pro-slavery elements of Philadelphia were brought into action, and matters looked for a time as though Slavery in this instance would have everything its own way. Passmore was locked up in prison on the flimsy pretext of contempt of court, and true bills were found against him and half a dozen colored men, charging them with "riot," "forcible abduction," and "assault and battery," and there was no lack of hard swearing on the part of Col. Wheeler and his pro-slavery sympathizers in substantiation of these grave charges. But the pro-slaveryites had counted without their host—Passmore would not yield an inch, but stood as firmly by his principles in prison, as he did on the boat. Indeed, it was soon evident, that his resolute course was bringing floods of sympathy from the ablest and best minds throughout the North. On the other hand, the occasion was rapidly awakening thousands daily, who had hitherto manifested little or no interest at all on the subject, to the wrongs of the slave.

It was soon discovered by the "chivalry" that keeping Mr. Williamson in prison would indirectly greatly aid the cause of

Freedom—that every day he remained would make numerous con-
verts to the cause of liberty; that Mr. Williamson was doing ten-fold
more in prison for the cause of universal liberty than he could possibly do while pursuing his ordinary vocation.

With regard to the colored men under bonds, Col. Wheeler and
his satellites felt very confident that there was no room for them to
escape. They must have had reason so to think, judging from the
hard swearing they did, before the committing magistrate. Consequently, in the order of events, while Passmore was still in prison,
receiving visits from hosts of friends, and letters of sympathy from
all parts of the North, William Still, William Curtis, James P. Brad-
dock, John Ballard, James Martin and Isaiah Moore, were brought
into court for trial. The first name on the list in the proceedings of
the court was called up first.

Against this individual, it was pretty well understood by the
friends of the slave, that no lack of pains and false swearing would
be resorted to on the part of Wheeler and his witnesses, to gain a
verdict.

Mr. McKim and other noted abolitionists managing the defense,
were equally alive to the importance of overwhelming the enemy in
this particular issue. The Hon. Charles Gibbons, was engaged to
defend William Still, and William S. Pierce, Esq., and William B.
Birney, Esq., the other five colored defendants.

In order to make the victory complete, the anti-slavery friends
deemed it of the highest importance to have Jane Johnson in court,
to face her master, and under oath to sweep away his "refuge of
lies," with regard to her being "abducted," and her unwillingness to
"leave her master," etc. So Mr. McKim and the friends very privately arranged to have Jane Johnson on hand at the opening of the
defense.

Mrs. Lucretia Mott, Mrs. McKim, Miss Sarah Pugh and Mrs.
Plumly, volunteered to accompany this poor slave mother to the
court-house and to occupy seats by her side, while she should face
her master, and boldly, on oath, contradict all his hard swearing. A
better subject for the occasion than Jane, could not have been desired. She entered the court room veiled, and of course was not

known by the crowd, as pains had been taken to keep the public in ignorance of the fact, that she was to be brought on to bear witness. So that, at the conclusion of the second witness on the part of the defense, "Jane Johnson" was called for, in a shrill voice. Deliberately, Jane arose and answered, in a lady-like manner to her name, and was then the observed of all observers. Never before had such a scene been witnessed in Philadelphia. It was indescribable. Substantially, her testimony on this occasion, was in keeping with the subjoined affidavit, which was as follows—

"*State of New York, City and County of New York.*

"Jane Johnson being sworn, makes oath and says—
    "My name is Jane—Jane Johnson; I was the slave of Mr. Wheeler of Washington; he bought me and my two children, about two years ago, of Mr. Cornelius Crew, of Richmond, Va.; my youngest child is between six and seven years old, the other between ten and eleven; I have one other child only, and he is in Richmond; I have not seen him for about two years; never expect to see him again; Mr. Wheeler brought me and my two children to Philadelphia, on the way to Nicaragua, to wait on his wife; I didn't want to go without my two children, and he consented to take them; we came to Philadelphia by the cars; stopped at Mr. Sully's, Mr. Wheeler's father-in-law, a few moments; then went to the steamboat for New York at 2 o'clock, but were too late; we went into Bloodgood's Hotel; Mr. Wheeler went to dinner; Mr. Wheeler had told me in Washington to have nothing to say to colored persons, and if any of them spoke to me, to say I was a free woman traveling with a minister; we staid at Bloodgood's till 5 o'clock; Mr. Wheeler kept his eye on me all the time except when he was at dinner; he left his dinner to come and see if I was safe, and then went back again; while he was at dinner, I saw a colored woman and told her I was a slave woman, that my master had told me not to speak to colored people, and that if any of them spoke to me to say that I was free; but I am not free; but I want to be free; she said: 'poor thing, I pity you;' after that I saw a colored man and said the same thing to him, he said he would telegraph to New York, and

two men would meet me at 9 o'clock and take me with them; after that we went on board the boat, Mr. Wheeler sat beside me on the deck; I saw a colored gentleman come on board, he beckoned to me; I nodded my head, and could not go; Mr. Wheeler was beside me and I was afraid; a white gentleman then came and said to Mr. Wheeler, 'I want to speak to your servant, and tell her of her rights;' Mr. Wheeler rose and said, 'If you have anything to say, say it to me—she knows her rights;' the white gentleman asked me if I wanted to be free; I said 'I do, but I belong to this gentleman and I can't have it;' he replied, 'Yes, you can, come with us, you are as free as your master, if you want your freedom come now; if you go back to Washington you may never get it;' I rose to go, Mr. Wheeler spoke, and said, 'I will give you your freedom,' but he had never promised it before, and I knew he would never give it to me; the white gentleman held out his hand and I went toward him; I was ready for the word before it was given me; I took the children by the hands, who both cried, for they were frightened, but both stopped when they got on shore; a colored man carried the little one, I led the other by the hand. We walked down the street till we got to a hack; nobody forced me away; nobody pulled me, and nobody led me; I went away of my own free will; I always wished to be free and meant to be free when I came North; I hardly expected it in Philadelphia, but I thought I should get free in New York; I have been comfortable and happy since I left Mr. Wheeler, and so are the children; I don't want to go back; I could have gone in Philadelphia if I had wanted to; I could go now; but I had rather die than go back. I wish to make this statement before a magistrate, because I understand that Mr. Williamson is in prison on my account, and I hope the truth may be of benefit to him."

JANE [her X mark.] JOHNSON.

It might have been supposed that her honest and straightforward testimony would have been sufficient to cause even the most relentless slaveholder to abandon at once a pursuit so monstrous and utterly hopeless as Wheeler's was. But although he was sadly confused and put to shame, he hung on to the "lost cause" tenaciously. And

his counsel, David Webster, Esq., and the United States District Attorney, Vandyke, completely imbued with the pro-slavery spirit,
were equally as unyielding. And thus, with a zeal befitting the most
worthy object imaginable, they labored with untiring effort to convict the colored men.

By this policy, however, the counsel for the defense was doubly
aroused. Mr. Gibbons, in the most eloquent and indignant strains,
perfectly annihilated the "distinguished Colonel John H. Wheeler,
United States Minister Plenipotentiary near the Island of Nicaragua," taking special pains to ring the changes repeatedly on his long
appellations. Mr. Gibbons appeared to be precisely in the right
mood to make himself surpassingly forcible and eloquent, on whatever point of law he chose to touch bearing on the case; or in whatever direction he chose to glance at the injustice and cruelty of the
South. Most vividly did he draw the contrast between the States of
"Georgia" and "Pennsylvania," with regard to the atrocious laws of
Georgia. Scarcely less vivid is the impression after a lapse of sixteen
years, than when this eloquent speech was made. With the District
Attorney, Wm. B. Mann, Esq., and his Honor, Judge Kelley, the defendants had no cause to complain. Throughout the entire proceedings, they had reason to feel, that neither of these officials
sympathized in the least with Wheeler or Slavery. Indeed in the
Judge's charge and also in the District Attorney's closing speech the
ring of freedom could be distinctly heard—much more so than was
agreeable to Wheeler and his Pro-Slavery sympathizers. The case
of Wm. Still ended in his acquittal; the other five colored men were
taken up in order. And it is scarcely necessary to say that Messrs.
Peirce and Birney did full justice to all concerned. Mr. Peirce, especially, was one of the oldest, ablest and most faithful lawyers to the
slave of the Philadelphia Bar. He never was known, it may safely be
said, to hesitate in the darkest days of Slavery to give his time and
talents to the fugitive, even in the most hopeless cases, and when,
from the unpopularity of such a course, serious sacrifices would be
likely to result. Consequently he was but at home in this case, and
most nobly did he defend his clients, with the same earnestness that
a man would defend his fireside against the approach of burglars. At

the conclusion of the trial, the jury returned a verdict of "not guilty," as to all the persons in the first count, charging them with riot. In the second count, charging them with "Assault and Battery" (on Col. Wheeler) Ballard and Curtis were found "guilty," the rest "not guilty." The guilty were given about a week in jail. Thus ended this act in the Wheeler drama.

The following extract is taken from the correspondence of the New York Tribune touching Jane Johnson's presence in the court, and will be interesting on that account:

"But it was a bold and perilous move on the part of her friends, and the deepest apprehensions were felt for a while, for the result. The United States Marshal was there with his warrant and an extra force to execute it. The officers of the court and other State officers were there to protect the witness and vindicate the laws of the State. Vandyke, the United States District Attorney, swore he would take her. The State officers swore he should not, and for a while it seemed that nothing could avert a bloody scene. It was expected that the conflict would take place at the door, when she should leave the room, so that when she and her friends went out, and for some time after, the most intense suspense pervaded the court-room. She was, however, allowed to enter the carriage that awaited her without disturbance. She was accompanied by Mr. McKim, Secretary of the Pennsylvania Anti-Slavery Society, Lucretia Mott and George Corson, one of our most manly and intrepid police officers. The carriage was followed by another filled with officers as a guard; and thus escorted she was taken back in safety to the house from which she had been brought. Her title to Freedom under the laws of the State will hardly again be brought into question."

Mr. Williamson was committed to prison by Judge Kane for contempt of Court, on the 27th day of July, 1855, and was released on the 3d day of November the same year, having gained, in the estimation of the friends of Freedom every where, a triumph and a fame which but few men in the great moral battle for Freedom could claim.

A SLAVE GIRL'S NARRATIVE.

Cordelia Loney, Slave of Mrs. Joseph Cahell (Widow of the Late Hon. Joseph Cahell, of Va.), of Fredericksburg, Va.—Cordelia's Escape from Her Mistress in Philadelphia.

Rarely did the peculiar institution present the relations of mistress and maid-servant in a light so apparently favorable as in the case of Mrs. Joseph Cahell (widow of the late Hon. Jos Cahell, of Va.), and her slave, Cordelia. The Vigilance Committee's first knowledge of either of these memorable personages was brought about in the following manner.

About the 30th of March, in the year 1859, a member of the Vigilance Committee was notified by a colored servant, living at a fashionable boarding-house on Chestnut street that a lady with a slave woman from Fredericksburg, Va., was boarding at said house, and, that said slave woman desired to receive counsel and aid from the Committee, as she was anxious to secure her freedom, before her mistress returned to the South. On further consultation about the matter, a suitable hour was named for the meeting of the Committee and the Slave at the above named boarding-house. Finding that the woman was thoroughly reliable, the Committee told her "that two modes of deliverance were open before her. One was to take her trunk and all her clothing and quietly retire." The other was to "sue out a writ of habeas corpus; and bring the mistress before the Court, where she would be required, under the laws of Pennsylvania, to show cause why she restrained this woman of her freedom." Cordelia concluded to adopt the former expedient, provided the Committee would protect her. Without hesitation the Committee answered her, that to the extent of their ability, she should have their aid with pleasure, without delay. Consequently a member of the Committee was directed to be on hand at a given hour that evening, as Cordelia would certainly be ready to leave her mistress to take care of herself. Thus, at the appointed hour, Cordelia, very deliberately, accompanied the Committee away from her "kind hearted old mistress."

In the quiet and security of the Vigilance Committee Room, Cordelia related substantially the following brief story touching her relationship as a slave to Mrs. Joseph Cahell. In this case, as with thousands and tens of thousands of others, as the old adage fitly expresses it, "All is not gold that glitters." Under this apparently pious and noble-minded lady, it will be seen, that Cordelia had known naught but misery and sorrow.

Mrs. Cahell, having engaged board for a month at a fashionable private boarding-house on Chestnut street, took an early opportunity to caution Cordelia against going into the streets, and against having anything to say or do with "free niggers in particular"; withal, she appeared unusually kind, so much so, that before retiring to bed in the evening, she would call Cordelia to her chamber, and by her side would take her Prayer-book and Bible, and go through the forms of devotional service. She stood very high both as a church communicant and a lady in society.

For a fortnight it seemed as though her prayers were to be answered, for Cordelia apparently bore herself as submissively as ever, and Madame received calls and accepted invitations from some of the *elite* of the city, without suspecting any intention on the part of Cordelia to escape. But Cordelia could not forget how her children had all been sold by her mistress!

Cordelia was about fifty-seven years of age, with about an equal proportion of colored and white blood in her veins; very neat, respectful and prepossessing in manner.

From her birth to the hour of her escape she had worn the yoke under Mrs. C., as her most efficient and reliable maid-servant. She had been at her mistress' beck and call as seamstress, dressing-maid, nurse in the sickroom, etc., etc., under circumstances that might appear to the casual observer uncommonly favorable for a slave. Indeed, on his first interview with her, the Committee man was so forcibly impressed with the belief, that her condition in Virginia had been favorable, that he hesitated to ask her if she did not desire her liberty. A few moments' conversation with her, however, convinced him of her good sense and decision of purpose with regard to this matter. For, in answer to the first question he put to her, she answered, that, "As many creature comforts and religious privileges as she had been the recipient of under her 'kind mistress,' still she 'wanted to be free,' and 'was bound to leave,' that she had been 'treated very cruelly,' that her children had 'all been sold away' from her; that she had been threatened with sale herself 'on the first insult,'" etc.

She was willing to take the entire responsibility of taking care of herself. On the suggestion of a friend, before leaving her mistress, she was disposed to sue for her freedom, but, upon a reconsideration of the matter, she chose rather to accept the hospitality of the Underground Rail Road, and leave in a quiet way and go to Canada, where she would be free indeed. Accordingly she left her mistress and was soon a free woman.

The following sad experience she related calmly, in the presence of several friends, an evening or two after she left her mistress:

Two sons and two daughters had been sold from her by her mistress, within the last three years, since the death of her master. Three of her children had been sold to the Richmond market and the other in Nelson county.

Paulina was the first sold, two years ago last May. Nat was the next; he was sold to Abram Warrick, of Richmond. Paulina was sold before it was named to her mother that it had entered her mistress's mind to dispose of her. Nancy, from infancy, had been in poor health. Nevertheless, she had been obliged to take her place in the field with the rest of the slaves, of more rugged constitution, until she had passed her twentieth year, and had become a mother. Under these circumstances, the overseer and his wife complained to the mistress that her health was really too bad for a field hand and begged that she might be taken where her duties would be less oppressive. Accordingly, she was withdrawn from the field, and was set to spinning and weaving. When too sick to work her mistress invariably took the ground, that "nothing was the matter," notwithstanding the fact, that her family physician, Dr. Ellsom, had pronounced her "quite weakly and sick."

In an angry mood one day, Mrs. Cahell declared she would cure her; and again sent her to the field, "with orders to the overseer, to whip her every day, and make her work or kill her." Again the overseer said it was "no use to try, for her health would not stand it," and she was forthwith returned. The mistress then concluded to sell her.

One Sabbath evening a nephew of hers, who resided in New Orleans, happened to be on a visit to his aunt, when it occurred to her, that she had "better get Nancy off if possible." Accordingly, Nancy was called in for examination. Being dressed in her "Sunday best" and "before a poor candle-light," she appeared to good advantage; and the nephew concluded to start with her on the following Tuesday morning. However, the next morning, he happened to see her by the light of the sun, and in her working garments, which satisfied him that he had been grossly deceived; that she would barely live to reach New Orleans; he positively refused to carry out the previous evening's contract, thus leaving her in the hands of her mistress, with the advice, that she should "doctor her up."

The mistress, not disposed to be defeated, obviated the difficulty by selecting a little boy, made a lot of the two, and thus made it an inducement to a purchaser to buy the sick woman; the boy and the woman brought $700.

In the sale of her children, Cordelia was as little regarded as if she had been a cow.

"I felt wretched," she said, with emphasis, "when I heard that Nancy had been sold," which was not until after she had been removed. "But," she continued, "I was not at liberty to make my grief known to a single white soul. I wept and couldn't help it." But remembering that she was liable, "on the first insult," to be sold herself, she sought no sympathy from her mistress, whom she describes as "a woman who shows as little kindness towards her servants as any woman in the States of America. She neither likes to feed nor clothe well."

With regard to flogging, however, in days past, she had been up to the mark. "A many a slap and blow" had Cordelia received since she arrived at womanhood, directly from the madam's own hand.

One day smarting under cruel treatment, she appealed to her mistress in the following strain: "I stood by your mother in all her sickness and nursed her till she died!" "I waited on your niece, night and day for months, till she died." "I waited upon your husband all my life—in his sickness especially, and shrouded him in death, etc., yet I am treated cruelly." It was of no avail.

Her mistress, at one time, was the owner of about five hundred slaves, but within the last few years she had greatly lessened the number by sales.

She stood very high as a lady, and was a member of the Episcopal Church.

To punish Cordelia, on several occasions, she had been sent to one of the plantations to work as a field hand. Fortunately, however, she found the overseers more compassionate than her mistress, though she received no particular favors from any of them.

Asking her to name the overseers, etc., she did so. The first was "Marks, a thin-visaged, poor-looking man, great for swearing." The second was "Gilbert Brower, a very rash, portly man." The third was "Buck Young, a stout man, and very sharp." The fourth was "Lynn Powell, a tall man with red whiskers, very contrary and spiteful." There was also a fifth one, but his name was lost.

Thus Cordelia's experience, though chiefly confined to the "great house," extended occasionally over the corn and tobacco fields, among the overseers and field hands generally. But under no circumstances could she find it in her heart to be thankful for the privileges of Slavery.

After leaving her mistress she learned, with no little degree of pleasure, that a perplexed state of things existed at the boarding-house; that her mistress was seriously puzzled to imagine how she would get her shoes and stockings on and off; how she would get her head combed, get dressed, be attended to in sickness, etc., as she (Cordelia), had been compelled to discharge these offices all her life.

Most of the boarders, being slave-holders, naturally sympathized in her affliction; and some of them went so far as to offer a reward to some of the colored servants to gain a knowledge of her where-abouts. Some charged the servants with having a hand in her leaving, but all agreed that "she had left a very kind and indulgent mistress," and had acted very foolishly in running out of Slavery into Freedom.

A certain Doctor of Divinity, the pastor of an Episcopal church in this city and a friend of the mistress, hearing of her distress, by request or voluntarily, undertook to find out Cordelia's place of seclusion. Hailing on the street a certain colored man with a familiar face, who he thought knew nearly all the colored people about town, he related to him the predicament of his lady friend from the South, remarked how kindly she had always treated her servants, signified that Cordelia would rue the change, and be left to suffer among the "miserable blacks down town," that she would not be able to take care of herself; quoted Scripture justifying Slavery, and finally suggested that he (the colored man) would be doing a duty and a kindness to the fugitive by using his influence to "find her and prevail upon her to return."

It so happened that the colored man thus addressed, was Thomas Dorsey, the well-known fashionable caterer of Philadelphia, who had had the experience of quite a number of years as a slave at the South,—had himself once been pursued as a fugitive, and having, by his industry in the condition of Freedom, acquired a handsome estate, he felt entirely qualified to reply to the reverend gentleman, which he did, though in not very respectful phrases, telling him that Cordelia had as good a right to her liberty as he had, or her mistress either; that God had never intended one man to be the slave of another; that it was all false about the slaves being better off than the free colored people; that he would find as many "poor, miserably degraded," of his own color "down-town," as among the "degraded blacks"; and concluded by telling him that he would "rather give her a hundred dollars to help her off, than to do aught to make known her whereabouts, if he knew ever so much about her."

What further steps were taken by the discomfited divine, the mistress, or her boarding-house sympathizers, the Committee was not informed.

But with regard to Cordelia: she took her departure for Canada, in the midst of the Daniel Webster (fugitive) trial, with the hope of being permitted to enjoy the remainder of her life in Freedom and peace. Being a member of the Baptist Church, and professing to be a Christian, she was persuaded that, by industry and assistance of the Lord, a way would be opened to the seeker of Freedom even in a strange land and among strangers.

This story appeared in part in the *N.Y. Evening Post*, having been furnished by the writer, without his name to it. It is certainly none the less interesting now, as it may be read in the light of Universal Emancipation.

ARRIVAL OF JACKSON, ISAAC AND
EDMONDSON TURNER FROM PETERSBURG.

Touching Scene on Meeting Their Old Blind Father at the U.G.R.R. Depot. Letters and Warning to Slaveholders.

About the latter part of December, 1857, Isaac and Edmondson, brothers, succeeded in making their escape together from Petersburg, Va. They barely escaped the auction block, as their mistress, Mrs. Ann Colley, a widow, had just completed arrangements for their sale on the coming first day of January. In this kind of property, however, Mrs. Colley had not largely invested. In the days of her prosperity, while all was happy and contented, she could only boast of "four head:" these brothers, Jackson, Isaac and Edmondson and one other. In May, 1857, Jackson had fled and was received by the Vigilance Committee, who placed him upon their books briefly in the following light:

"RUNAWAY—*Fifty Dollars Reward,*—Ran away some time in May last, my *Servant-man*, who calls himself *Jackson Turner.* He is about 27 years of age, and has one of his front teeth out. He is quite black, with thick lips, a little bow-legged, and looks down when spoken to. I will give a reward of Fifty dollars if taken out of the city, and twenty five Dollars if taken within the city. I forewarn all masters of vessels from harboring or employing the said slave; all persons who disregard this Notice will be punished as the law directs. ANN COLLEY. Petersburg, June 8th, 1857."

JACKSON is quite dark, medium size, and well informed for one in his condition. In Slavery, he had been "pressed hard." His hire, "ten dollars per month" he was obliged to produce at the end of each month, no matter how much he had been called upon to expend for "doctor bills, &c." The woman he called mistress went by the name of Ann Colley, a widow, living near Petersburg. "She was

very quarrelsome," although a "member of the Methodist Church."
Jackson seeing that his mistress was yearly growing "harder and
harder," concluded to try and better his condition "if possible."
Having a free wife in the North, who was in the habit of communi-
cating with him, he was kept fully awake to the love of Freedom.
The Underground Rail Road expense the Committee gladly bore.
No further record of Jackson was made. Jackson found his poor old
father here, where he had resided for a number of years in a state of
almost total blindness, and of course in much parental anxiety
about his boys in chains. On the arrival of Jackson, his heart over-
flowed with joy and gratitude not easily described, as the old man
had hardly been able to muster faith enough to believe that he
should ever look with his dim eyes upon one of his sons in Freedom.
After a day or two's tarrying, Jackson took his departure for safer
and more healthful localities,—her "British Majesty's possessions."
The old man remained only to feel more keenly than ever, the pang
of having sons still toiling in hopeless servitude.

In less than seven months after Jackson had shaken off the yoke,
to the unspeakable joy of the father, Isaac and Edmondson succeeded in following their brother's example, and were made happy
partakers of the benefits and blessings of the Vigilance Committee
of Philadelphia. On first meeting his two boys, at the Underground
Rail Road Depot, the old man took each one in his arms, and as
looking through a glass darkly, straining every nerve of his almost
lost sight, exclaiming, whilst hugging them closer and closer to his
bosom for some minutes, in tears of joy and wonder, "My son Isaac,
is this you? my son Isaac, is this you, &c.?" The scene was calculated
to awaken the deepest emotion and to bring tears to eyes not accustomed to weep. Little had the old man dreamed in his days of sadness, that he should share such a feast of joy over the deliverance of
his sons. But it is in vain to attempt to picture the affecting scene at
this reunion, for that would be impossible. Of their slave life, the
records contain but a short notice, simply as follows:

"Isaac is twenty-eight years of age, hearty-looking, well made,
dark color and intelligent. He was owned by Mrs. Ann Colley, a
widow, residing near Petersburg, Va. Isaac and Edmondson were to
have been sold, on New Year's day; a few days hence. How sad her

disappointment must have been on finding them gone, may be more easily imagined than described."

Edmondson is about twenty-five, a brother of Isaac, and a smart, good-looking young man, was owned by Mrs. Colley also. "This is just the class of fugitives to make good subjects for John Bull," thought the Committee, feeling pretty well assured that they would make good reports after having enjoyed free air in Canada for a short time. Of course, the Committee enjoined upon them very earnestly "not to forget their brethren left behind groaning in fetters; but to prove by their industry, uprightness, economy, sobriety and thrift, by the remembrance of their former days of oppression and their obligations to their God, that they were worthy of the country to which they were going, and so to help break the bands of the oppressors, and undo the heavy burdens of the oppressed." Similar advice was impressed upon the minds of all travelers passing over this branch of the Underground Rail Road. From hundreds thus admonished, letters came affording the most gratifying evidence that the counsel of the Committee was not in vain. The appended letter from the youngest brother, written with his own hand, will indicate his feelings and views in Canada:

HAMILTON, CANADA WEST Mar. 1, 1858.

MR. STILL, DEAR SIR:—I have taken the oppertunity to enform you yur letter came to hand 27th I ware glad to hear from you and yer famly i hope this letter May fine you and the famly Well i am Well my self My Brother join me in Love to you and all the frend. I ware sorry to hear of the death of Mrs freaman. We all must die sune or Late this a date we all must pay we must Perpar for the time she ware a nise lady dear sir the all is well and san thar love to you Emerline have Ben sick But is better at this time. I saw the hills the war well and san thar Love to you. I war sory to hear that My brother war sol i am glad that i did come away when i did god works all the things for the Best he is young he may get a long in the wole May god Bless hem ef you have any News from Petersburg Va Plas Rite me a word when you anser this Letter and ef any person came form home Letter Me know. Please sen me

one of your Paper that had the under grands R wrod give My Love
to Mr Careter and his family I am Seving with a barber at this time
he have promust to give me the trad ef i can lane it he is much of a
gentman. Mr Still sir i have writing a letter to Mr Brown of
Petersburg Va Pleas reed it and ef you think it right Plas sen it by
the Mail or by hand you wall see how i have writen it the will
know how sent it by the way this writing ef the ancer it you can
sen it to Me i have tol them direc to yor care for Ed. t. Smith
Philadelphia i hope it may be right i promorst to rite to hear
Please rite to me sune and let me know ef you do sen it on write
wit you did with that ma a bught the cappet Bage do not fergit to
rite tal John he mite rite to Me. I am doing as well is i can at this
time but i get no wagges But my Bord but is satfid at that thes hard
time and glad that i am Hear and in good helth. Northing More at
this time yor truly EDMUND TURNER.

———

The same writer sent to the Corresponding Secretary the following
"Warning to Slave-holders." At the time these documents were received, Slaveholders were never more defiant. The right to trample
on the weak in oppression was indisputable. "Cinnamon and odors,
and ointments, and frankincense, and wine, and oil, and fine flour
and wheat, and beasts, and sheep, and horses, and chariots, and
slaves, and souls of men," slave-holders believed doubtless were
theirs by Divine Right. Little dreaming that in less than three short
years—"Therefore shall her plagues come in one day, death, and
mourning, and famine." In view of the marvelous changes which
have been wrought by the hand of the Almighty, this warning to
slave-holders from one who felt the sting of Slavery, as evincing a
particular phase of simple faith and Christian charity is entitled to
a place in these records.

A WARNING TO SLAVE-HOLDERS.

Well may the Southern slaveholder say, that holding their Fellow
men in Bondage is no sin, because it is their delight as the Egyp-

tians, so do they; but nevertheless God in his own good time will bring them out by a mighty hand, as it is recorded in the sacred oracles of truth, that Ethiopia shall soon stretch out her hands to God, speaking in the positive (shall). And my prayer is to you, oh, slaveholder, in the name of that God who in the beginning said, Let there be light, and there was light. Let my People go that they may serve me; thereby good may come unto thee and to thy children's children. Slave-holder have you seriously thought upon the condition yourselves, family and slaves; have you read where Christ has enjoined upon all his creatures to read his word, thereby that they may have no excuse when coming before his judgment seat? But you say he shall not read his word, consequently his sin will be upon your head. I think every man has as much as he can do to answer for his own sins. And now my dear-slave-holder, who with you are bound and fast hastening to judgment? As one that loves your soul repent ye, therefore, and be converted, that your sins may be blotted out when the time of refreshing shall come from the presence of the Lord.

In the language of the poet:

> *Stop, poor sinner, stop and think,*
> *Before you further go;*
> *Think upon the brink of death*
> *Of everlasting woe.*
> *Say, have you an arm like God,*
> *That you his will oppose?*
> *Fear you not that iron rod*
> *With which he breaks his foes?*
> *Is the prayer of one that loves your souls.*
> *EDMUND TURNER.*

N.B. The signature bears the name of one who knows and felt the sting of Slavery; but now, thanks be to God, I am now where the poisonous breath taints not our air, but every one is sitting under his own vine and fig tree, where none dare to make him ashamed or afraid.

EDMUND TURNER, formerly of Petersburg, Va.

HAMILTON, June 22d, 1858, C.W.

To MR. WM. STILL, DEAR SIR:—A favorable opportunity
affords the pleasure of acknowledging the receipt of letters and
papers; certainly in this region they were highly appreciated, and I
hope the time may come that your kindness will be reciprocated
we are al well at present, but times continue dull. I also deeply
regret the excitement recently on the account of those slaves, you
will favor me by keeping me posted upon the subject. Those words
written to slaveholder is the thought of one who had sufferd, and
now I thought it a duty incumbent upon me to cry aloud and spare
not, &c., by sending these few lines where the slaveholder may
hear. You will still further oblige your humble servant also, to
correct any inaccuracy. My respects to you and your family and all
inquiring friends.

Your friend and well wisher, EDMUND TURNER.

The then impending judgments seen by an eye of faith as set
forth in this "Warning," soon fell with crushing weight upon the
oppressor, and Slavery died. But the old blind father of Jackson,
Isaac and Edmondson, still lives and may be seen daily on the streets
of Philadelphia; and though "halt, and lame, and blind, and poor,"
doubtless resulting from his early oppression, he can thank God
and rejoice that he has lived to see Slavery abolished.

ROBERT BROWN, ALIAS THOMAS JONES.

Crossing the River on Horseback in the Night.

In very desperate straits many new inventions were sought after by deep-thinking and resolute slaves, determined to be free at any cost. But it must here be admitted, that, in looking carefully over the more perilous methods resorted to, Robert Brown, alias Thomas Jones, stands second to none, with regard to deeds of bold daring. This hero escaped from Martinsburg, Va., in 1856. He was a man of medium size, mulatto, about thirty-eight years of age, could read and write, and was naturally sharp-witted. He had formerly been owned by Col. John F. Franie, whom Robert charged with various offences of a serious domestic character.

Furthermore, he also alleged, that his "mistress was cruel to all the slaves," declaring that "they (the slaves), could not live with her," that "she had to hire servants," etc.

In order to effect his escape, Robert was obliged to swim the Potomac river on horseback, on Christmas night, while the cold, wind, storm, and darkness were indescribably dismal. This daring bondman, rather than submit to his oppressor any longer, perilled his life as above stated. Where he crossed the river was about a half a mile wide. Where could be found in history a more noble and daring struggle for Freedom?

The wife of his bosom and his four children, only five days before he fled, were sold to a trader in Richmond, Va., for no other offence than simply "because she had resisted" the lustful designs of her master, being "true to her own companion." After this poor slave mother and her children were cast into prison for sale, the husband and some of his friends tried hard to find a purchaser in the neighborhood; but the malicious and brutal master refused to sell her—wishing to gratify his malice to the utmost, and to punish his victims all that lay in his power, he sent them to the place above named.

In this trying hour, the severed and bleeding heart of the husband resolved to escape at all hazards, taking with him a daguerreotype likeness of his wife which he happened to have on hand, and a lock of hair from her head, and from each of the children, as mementoes of his unbounded (though sundered) affection for them.

After crossing the river, his wet clothing freezing to him, he rode all night, a distance of about forty miles. In the morning he left his faithful horse tied to a fence, quite broken down. He then commenced his dreary journey on foot—cold and hungry—in a strange place, where it was quite unsafe to make known his condition and wants. Thus for a day or two, without food or shelter, he traveled until his feet were literally worn out, and in this condition he arrived at Harrisburg, where he found friends. Passing over many of the interesting incidents on the road, suffice it to say, he arrived safely in this city, on New Year's night, 1857, about two hours before day break (the telegraph having announced his coming from Harrisburg), having been a week on the way. The night he arrived was very cold; besides, the Underground train, that morning, was about three hours behind time; in waiting for it, entirely out in the cold, a member of the Vigilance Committee thought he was frosted. But when he came to listen to the story of the Fugitive's sufferings, his mind changed.

Scarcely had Robert entered the house of one of the Committee, where he was kindly received, when he took from his pocket his wife's likeness, speaking very touchingly while gazing upon it and showing it. Subsequently, in speaking of his family, he showed the locks of hair referred to, which he had carefully rolled up in paper separately. Unrolling them, he said, "this is my wife's;" "this is from my oldest daughter, eleven years old;" "and this is from my next oldest;" "and this from the next," "and this from my infant, only eight weeks old." These mementoes he cherished with the utmost care as the last remains of his affectionate family. At the sight of these locks of hair so tenderly preserved, the member of the Committee could fully appreciate the resolution of the fugitive in plunging into the Potomac, on the back of a dumb beast, in order to flee from a place and people who had made such barbarous havoc in his household.

His wife, as represented by the likeness, was of fair complexion, prepossessing, and good looking—perhaps not over thirty-three years of age.

BARNABY GRIGBY, ALIAS JOHN BOYER, AND MARY ELIZABETH, HIS WIFE; FRANK WANZER, ALIAS ROBERT SCOTT; EMILY FOSTER, ALIAS ANN WOOD. (TWO OTHERS WHO STARTED WITH THEM WERE CAPTURED.)

All these persons journeyed together from Loudon Co., Va. on horseback and in a carriage for more than one hundred miles. Availing themselves of a holiday and their master's horses and carriage, they as deliberately started for Canada, as though they had never been taught that it was their duty, as servants, to "obey their masters." In this particular showing a most utter disregard of the interest of their "kind-hearted and indulgent owners." They left home on Monday, Christmas Eve, 1855, under the leadership of Frank Wanzer, and arrived in Columbia the following Wednesday at one o'clock. As willfully as they had thus made their way along, they had not found it smooth sailing by any means. The biting frost and snow rendered their travel anything but agreeable. Nor did they escape the gnawings of hunger, traveling day and night. And whilst these "articles" were in the very act of running away with themselves and their kind master's best horses and carriage—when about one hundred miles from home, in the neighborhood of Cheat river, Maryland, they were attacked by "six white men, and a boy," who, doubtless, supposing that their intentions were of a "wicked and unlawful character" felt it to be their duty in kindness to their masters, if not to the travelers to demand of them an account of themselves. In other words, the assailants positively commanded the fugitives to "show what right" they possessed, to be found in a condition apparently so unwarranted.

The *spokesman* amongst the fugitives, affecting no ordinary amount of dignity, told their assailants plainly, that "no gentleman would interfere with persons riding along civilly"—not allowing it to be supposed that they were slaves, of course. These "gentlemen," however, were not willing to accept this account of the travelers, as their very decided steps indicated. Having the law on their side, they were for compelling the fugitives to surrender without further parley.

At this juncture, the fugitives verily believing that the time had arrived for the practical use of their pistols and dirks, pulled them out of their concealment—the young women as well as the young men—and declared they would not be "taken!" One of the white men raised his gun, pointing the muzzle directly towards one of the young women, with the threat that he would "shoot," etc. "Shoot! shoot!! shoot!!!" she exclaimed, with a double barrelled pistol in one hand and a long dirk knife in the other, utterly unterrified and fully ready for a death struggle. The male *leader* of the fugitives by this time had "pulled back the hammers" of his "pistols," and was about to fire! Their adversaries seeing the weapons, and the unflinching determination on the part of the *runaways* to stand their ground, "spill blood, kill, or die," rather than be "taken," very prudently "sidled over to the other side of the road," leaving at least four of the victors to travel on their way.

At this moment the four in the carriage lost sight of the two on horseback. Soon after the separation they heard firing, but what the result was, they knew not. They were fearful, however, that their companions had been captured.

The following paragraph, which was shortly afterwards taken from a Southern paper, leaves no room to doubt, as to the fate of the two.

Six fugitive slaves from Virginia were arrested at the Maryland line, near Hood's Mill, on Christmas day, but, after a severe fight, four of them escaped and have not since been heard of. They came from Loudoun and Fauquier counties.

Though the four who were successful, saw no "severe fight," it is not unreasonable to suppose, that there was a fight, nevertheless; but not till after the number of the fugitives had been reduced to two, instead of six. As chivalrous as slave-holders and slave-catchers were, they knew the value of their precious lives and the fearful risk of attempting a capture, when the numbers were equal.

The party in the carriage, after the conflict, went on their way rejoicing.

The young men, one cold night, when they were compelled to take rest in the woods and snow, in vain strove to keep the feet of their female companions from freezing by lying on them; but the frost was merciless and bit them severely, as their feet very plainly showed. The following disjointed report was cut from the *Frederick (Md.) Examiner,* soon after the occurrence took place:

"Six slaves, four men and two women, fugitives from Virginia, having with them two spring wagons and four horses, came to Hood's Mill, on the Baltimore and Ohio Railroad, near the dividing line between Frederick and Carroll counties, on Christmas day. After feeding their animals, one of them told a Mr. Dixon whence they came; believing them to be fugitives, he spread the alarm, and some eight or ten persons gathered round to arrest them; but the negroes drawing revolvers and bowie-knives, kept their assailants at bay, until five of the party succeeded in escaping in one of the wagons, and as the last one jumped on a horse to flee, he was fired at, the load taking effect in the small of the back. The prisoner says he belongs to Charles W. Simpson, Esq., of Fauquier county, Va., and ran away with the others on the preceding evening."

This report from the *Examiner,* while it is not wholly correct, evidently relates to the fugitives above described. Why the reporter made such glaring mistakes, may be accounted for on the ground that the bold stand made by the fugitives was so bewildering and alarming, that the "assailants" were not in a proper condition to make correct statements. Nevertheless the *Examiner's* report was preserved with other records, and is here given for what it is worth.

These victors were individually noted on the Record thus: Barnaby was owned by William Rogers, a farmer, who was considered a "moderate slaveholder," although of late "addicted to intemperance." He was the owner of about one "dozen head of slaves," and had besides a wife and two children.

Barnaby's chances for making extra "change" for himself were never favorable; sometimes of "nights" he would manage to earn a "trifle." He was prompted to escape because he "wanted to live by the sweat of his own brow," believing that all men ought so to live. This was the only reason he gave for fleeing.

Mary Elizabeth had been owned by Townsend McVee (likewise a farmer), and in Mary's judgment, he was "severe," but she added, "his wife made him so." McVee owned about twenty-five slaves; "he hardly allowed them to talk—would not allow them to raise chickens," and "only allowed Mary three dresses a year;" the rest she had to get as she could. Sometimes McVee would sell slaves—last year he sold two. Mary said that she could not say anything good of her mistress. On the contrary, she declared that her mistress "knew no mercy nor showed any favor."

It was on account of this "domineering spirit," that Mary was induced to escape.

Frank was owned by Luther Sullivan, "the meanest man in Virginia," he said; he treated his people just as bad as he could in every respect. "Sullivan," added Frank, "would 'lowance the slaves and stint them to save food and get rich," and "would sell and whip," etc. To Frank's knowledge, he had sold some twenty-five head. "He sold my mother and her two children to Georgia some four years previous." But the motive which hurried Frank to make his flight was his laboring under the apprehension that his master had some "pretty heavy creditors who might come on him at any time." Frank, therefore, wanted to be from home in Canada when these gentry should make their visit. My poor mother has been often flogged by master, said Frank. As to his mistress, he said she was "tolerably good."

Ann Wood was owned by McVee also, and was own sister to Elizabeth. Ann very fully sustained her sister Elizabeth's statement respecting the character of her master.

The above-mentioned four, were all young and likely. Barnaby was twenty-six years of age, mulatto, medium size, and intelligent—his wife was about twenty-four years of age, quite dark, good-looking, and of pleasant appearance. Frank was twenty-five years of age, mulatto, and very smart; Ann was twenty-two, good-looking, and smart. After their pressing wants had been met by the Vigilance Committee, and after partial recuperation from their hard travel, etc., they were forwarded on to the Vigilance Committee in New

York. In Syracuse, Frank (the leader), who was engaged to Emily, concluded that the knot might as well be tied on the U.G.R.R., although penniless, as to delay the matter a single day longer. Doubtless, the bravery, struggles, and trials of Emily throughout the journey, had, in his estimation, added not a little to her charms. Thus after consulting with her on the matter, her approval was soon obtained, she being too prudent and wise to refuse the hand of one who had proved himself so true a friend to Freedom, as well as so devoted to her. The twain were accordingly made one at the U.G.R.R. Station, in Syracuse, by Superintendent—Rev. J.W. Loguen. After this joyful event, they proceeded to Toronto, and were there gladly received by the Ladies' Society for aiding colored refugees.

The following letter from Mrs. Agnes Willis, wife of the distinguished Rev. Dr. Willis, brought the gratifying intelligence that these brave young adventurers, fell into the hands of distinguished characters and warm friends of Freedom:

TORONTO, 28th January, Monday evening, 1856.

MR. STILL, DEAR SIR:—I have very great pleasure in making you aware that the following respectable persons have arrived here in safety without being annoyed in any way after you saw them. The women, two of them, viz: Mrs. Greegsby and Mrs. Graham, have been rather ailing, but we hope they will very soon be well. They have been attended to by the Ladies' Society, and are most grateful for any attention they have received. The solitary person, Mrs. Graves, has also been attended to; also her box will be looked after. She is pretty well, but rather dull; however, she will get friends and feel more at home by and bye. Mrs. Wanzer is quite well; and also young William Henry Sanderson. They are all of them in pretty good spirits, and I have no doubt they will succeed in whatever business they take up. In the mean time the men are chopping wood, and the ladies are getting plenty sewing. We are always glad to see our colored refugees safe here. I remain, dear sir, yours respectfully,

AGNES WILLIS,
Treasurer to the Ladies' Society to aid colored refugees.

For a time Frank enjoyed his newly won freedom and happy
bride with bright prospects all around; but the thought of having
left sisters and other relatives in bondage was a source of sadness in
the midst of his joy. He was not long, however, in making up his
mind that he would deliver them or "die in the attempt." Deliberately forming his plans to go South, he resolved to take upon himself the entire responsibility of all the risks to be encountered. Not
a word did he reveal to a living soul of what he was about to undertake. With "twenty-two dollars" in cash and "three pistols" in his
pockets, he started in the lightning train from Toronto for Virginia.
On reaching Columbia in this State, he deemed it not safe to go any
further by public conveyance, consequently he commenced his
long journey on foot, and as he neared the slave territory he traveled by night altogether. For two weeks, night and day, he avoided
trusting himself in any house, consequently was compelled to lodge in
the woods. Nevertheless, during that space of time he succeeded in delivering one of his sisters and her husband, and another friend in the
bargain. You can scarcely imagine the Committee's amazement on
his return, as they looked upon him and listened to his "noble deeds
of daring" and his triumph. A more brave and self-possessed man
they had never seen.

He knew what Slavery was and the dangers surrounding him on
his mission, but possessing true courage unlike most men, he pictured no alarming difficulties in a distance of nearly one thousand
miles by the mail route, through the enemy's country, where he might
have in truth said, "I could not pass without running the gauntlet of
mobs and assassins, prisons and penitentiaries, bailiffs and constables,
&c." If this hero had dwelt upon and magnified the obstacles in his
way he would most assuredly have kept off the enemy's country, and
his sister and friends would have remained in chains.

The following were the persons delivered by Frank Wanzer.
They were his trophies, and this noble act of Frank's should ever be

held as a memorial and honor. The Committee's brief record made on their arrival runs thus:

"August 18, 1856. Frank Wanzer, Robert Stewart, alias Gasberry Robison, Vincent Smith, alias John Jackson, Betsey Smith, wife of Vincent Smith, alias Fanny Jackson. They all came from Alder, Loudon county, Virginia."

Robert is about thirty years of age, medium size, dark chestnut color, intelligent and resolute. He was held by the widow Hutchinson, who was also the owner of about one hundred others. Robert regarded her as a "very hard mistress" until the death of her husband, which took place the Fall previous to his escape. That sad affliction, he thought, was the cause of a considerable change in her treatment of her slaves. But yet "nothing was said about freedom," on her part. This reticence Robert understood to mean, that she was still unconverted on this great cardinal principle at least. As he could see no prospect of freedom through her agency, when Frank approached him with a good report from Canada and his friends there, he could scarcely wait to listen to the glorious news; he was so willing and anxious to get out of slavery. His dear old mother, Sarah Davis, and four brothers and two sisters, William, Thomas, Frederick and Samuel, Violet and Ellen, were all owned by Mrs. Hutchinson. Dear as they were to him, he saw no way to take them with him, nor was he prepared to remain a day longer under the yoke; so he decided to accompany Frank, let the cost be what it might.

Vincent is about twenty-three years of age, very "likely-looking," dark color, and more than ordinarily intelligent for one having only the common chances of slaves.

He was owned by the estate of Nathan Skinner, who was "looked upon," by those who knew him, "as a good slave-holder." In slave property, however, he was only interested to the number of twelve head. Skinner "neither sold nor emancipated." A year and a half before Vincent escaped, his master was called to give an account of his stewardship, and there in the spirit land Vincent was willing to let him remain, without much more to add about him.

Vincent left his mother, Judah Smith, and brothers and sisters, Edwin, Angeline, Sina Ann, Adaline Susan, George, John and Lewis, all belonging to the estate of Skinner.

Vincent was fortunate enough to bring his wife along with him. She was about twenty-seven years of age, of a brown color, and smart, and was owned by the daughter of the widow Hutchinson. This mistress was said to be a "clever woman."

WILLIAM JORDON, ALIAS
WILLIAM PRICE.

Under Governor Badger, of North Carolina, William had experienced Slavery in its most hateful form. True, he had only been twelve months under the yoke of this high functionary. But William's experience in this short space of time, was of a nature very painful.

Previous to coming into the governor's hands, William was held as the property of Mrs. Mary Jordon, who owned large numbers of slaves. Whether the governor was moved by this consideration, or by the fascinating charms of Mrs. Jordon, or both, William was not able to decide. But the governor offered her his hand, and they became united in wedlock. By this circumstance, William was brought into his unhappy relations with the Chief Magistrate of the State of North Carolina. This was the third time the governor had been married. Thus it may be seen, that the governor was a firm believer in wives as well as slaves. Commonly he was regarded as a man of wealth. William being an intelligent piece of property, his knowledge of the governor's rules and customs was quite complete, as he readily answered such questions as were propounded to him. In this way a great amount of interesting information was learned from William respecting the governor, slaves, on the plantation, in the swamps, etc. The governor owned large plantations, and was interested in raising cotton, corn, and peas, and was also a practical planter. He was willing to trust neither overseers nor slaves any further than he could help.

The governor and his wife were both equally severe towards them; would stint them shamefully in clothing and food, though they did not get flogged quite as often as some others on neighboring plantations. Frequently, the governor would be out on the plantation from early in the morning till noon, inspecting the operations of the overseers and slaves.

In order to serve the governor, William had been separated from his wife by sale, which was the cause of his escape. He parted not with his companion willingly. At the time, however, he was promised that he should have some favors shown him;—could make over-work, and earn a little money, and once or twice in the year, have the opportunity of making visits to her. Two hundred miles was the distance between them.

He had not been long on the governor's plantation before his honor gave him distinctly to understand that the idea of his going two hundred miles to see his wife was all nonsense, and entirely out of the question. "If I said so, I did not mean it," said his honor, when the slave, on a certain occasion, alluded to the conditions on which he consented to leave home, etc.

Against this cruel decision of the governor, William's heart revolted, for he was warmly attached to his wife, and so he made up his mind, if he could not see her "once or twice a year even," as he had been promised, he had rather "die," or live in a "cave in the wood," than to remain all his life under the governor's yoke. Obeying the dictates of his feelings, he went to the woods. For ten months before he was successful in finding the Underground Road, this brave-hearted young fugitive abode in the swamps—three months in a cave—surrounded with bears, wild cats, rattle-snakes and the like.

While in the swamps and cave, he was not troubled, however, about ferocious animals and venomous reptiles. He feared only man!

From his own story there was no escaping the conclusion, that if the choice had been left to him, he would have preferred at any time to have encountered at the mouth of his cave a ferocious bear than his master, the governor of North Carolina. How he managed to subsist, and ultimately effected his escape, was listened to with the deepest interest, though the recital of these incidents must here be very brief.

After night he would come out of his cave, and, in some instances, would succeed in making his way to a plantation, and if he could get nothing else, he would help himself to a "pig," or anything else he could conveniently convert into food. Also, as opportunity would offer, a friend of his would favor him with some meal, etc. With this mode of living he labored to content himself until he could do better. During these ten months he suffered indescribable hardships, but he felt that his condition in the cave was far preferable to that on the plantation, under the control of his Excellency, the Governor. All this time, however, William had a true friend, with whom he could communicate; one who was wide awake, and was on the alert to find a reliable captain from the North, who would consent to take this "property," or "freight," for a consideration. He heard at last of a certain Captain, who was then doing quite a successful business in an Underground way. This good news was conveyed to William, and afforded him a ray of hope in the wilderness. As Providence would have it, his hope did not meet with disappointment; nor did his ten months' trial, warring against the barbarism of Slavery, seem too great to endure for Freedom. He was about to leave his cave and his animal and reptile neighbors,— his heart swelling with gladness,—but the thought of soon being beyond the reach of his mistress and master thrilled him with inexpressible delight. He was brought away by Captain F., and turned over to the Committee, who were made to rejoice with him over the signal victory he had gained in his martyr-like endeavors to throw off the yoke, and of course they took much pleasure in aiding him. William was of a dark color, stout made physically, and well knew the value of Freedom, and how to hate and combat Slavery. It will be seen by the appended letter of Thomas Garrett, that William had the good luck to fall into the hands of this tried friend, by whom he was aided to Philadelphia:

WILMINGTON, 12th mo., 19th, 1855.

DEAR FRIEND, WILLIAM STILL:—The bearer of this is one of the twenty-one that I thought had all gone North; he left home on

Christmas day, one year since, wandered about the forests of North Carolina for about ten months, and then came here with those forwarded to New Bedford, where he is anxious to go. I have furnished him with a pretty good pair of boots, and gave him money to pay his passage to Philadelphia. He has been at work in the country near here for some three weeks, till taken sick; he is, by no means, well, but thinks he had better try to get farther North, which I hope his friends in Philadelphia will aid him to do. I handed this morning Captain Lambson's* wife twenty dollars to help fee a lawyer to defend him. She leaves this morning, with her child, for Norfolk, to be at the trial before the Commissioner on the 24th instant. Passmore Williamson agreed to raise fifty dollars for him. As none came to hand, and a good chance to send it by his wife, I thought best to advance that much.

Thy friend, THOS. GARRETT.

---

* Captain Lambson had been suspected of having aided in the escape of slaves from the neighborhood of Norfolk, and was in prison awaiting his trial.

JOSEPH GRANT AND JOHN SPEAKS.

Two Passengers on the Underground Rail Road, Via Liverpool.

It is to be regretted that, owing to circumstances, the account of these persons has not been fully preserved. Could justice be done them, probably their narratives would not be surpassed in interest by any other in the history of fugitives. In 1857, when these remarkable travelers came under the notice of the Vigilance Committee, as Slavery seemed likely to last for generations, and there was but little expectation that these records would ever have the historical value which they now possess, care was not always taken to prepare and preserve them. Besides, the cases coming under the notice of the Committee, were so numerous and so interesting, that it seemed almost impossible to do them anything like justice. In many instances the rapt attention paid by friends, when listening to the sad recitals of such passengers, would unavoidably consume so much time that but little opportunity was afforded to make any record of them. Particularly was this the case with regard to the above-mentioned individuals. The story of each was so long and sad, that a member of the Committee in attempting to write it out, found that the two narratives would take volumes. That all traces of these heroes might not be lost, a mere fragment is all that was preserved.

The original names of these adventurers were Joseph Grant and John Speaks. Between two and three years before escaping, they were sold from Maryland to John B. Campbell, a negro trader living in Baltimore, and thence to Campbell's brother, another trader in New Orleans, and subsequently to Daniel McBeans and Mr. Henry, of Harrison county, Mississippi.

Though both had to pass through nearly the same trial, and belonged to the same masters, this recital must be confined chiefly to the incidents in the career of Joseph. He was about twenty-seven years of age, well made, quite black, intelligent and self-possessed in his manner.

He was owned in Maryland by Mrs. Mary Gibson, who resided at St. Michael's on the Eastern Shore. She was a *nice woman* he said, but her property was under mortgage and had to be sold, and he was in danger of sharing the same fate.

Joseph was a married man, and spoke tenderly of his wife. She "promised" him when he was sold that she would "never marry," and earnestly entreated him, if he "ever met with the luck, to come and see her." She was unaware perhaps at that time of the great distance that was to divide them; his feelings on being thus sundered need not be stated. However, he had scarcely been in Mississippi three weeks, ere his desire to return to his wife, and the place of his nativity constrained him to attempt to return; accordingly he set off, crossing a lake eighty miles wide in a small boat, he reached Kent Island. There he was captured by the watchman on the Island, who with *pistols, dirk and cutlass* in hand, threatened if he resisted that death would be his instant doom. Of course he was returned to his master.

He remained there a few months, but could content himself no longer to endure the ills of his condition. So he again started for home, walked to Mobile, and thence he succeeded in stowing himself away in a steamboat and was thus conveyed to Montgomery, a distance of five hundred and fifty miles through solid slave territory. Again he was captured and returned to his owners; one of whom always went for immediate punishment, the other being mild thought persuasion the better plan in such cases. On the whole, Joseph thus far had been pretty fortunate, considering the magnitude of his offence.

A third time he summoned courage and steered his course homewards towards Maryland, but as in the preceding attempts, he was again unsuccessful.

In this instance Mr. Henry, the harsh owner, was exasperated, and the mild one's patience so exhausted that they concluded that nothing short of stern measures would cause Joe to reform. Said Mr.

Henry; *"I had rather lose my right arm than for him to get off without being punished, after having put us to so much trouble."*

Joseph will now speak for himself.

"He (master) sent the overseer to tie me. I told him I would not be tied. I ran and stayed away four days, which made Mr. Henry very anxious. Mr. Beans told the servants if they saw me, to tell me to come back and I should not be hurt. Thinking that Mr. Beans had always stood to his word, I was over persuaded and came back. He sent for me in his parlor, talked the matter over, sent me to the steamboat (perhaps the one he tried to escape on.) After getting cleverly on board the captain told me, I am sorry to tell you, you have to be tied. I was tied and Mr. Henry was sent for. He came; 'Well, I have got you at last, beg my pardon and promise you will never run away again and I will not be so hard on you.' I could not do it. He then gave me three hundred lashes well laid on. I was stripped entirely naked, and my flesh was as raw as a piece of beef. He made John (the companion who escaped with him) hold one of my feet which I broke loose while being whipped, and when done made him bathe me in salt and water.

"Then I resolved to 'go or die' in the attempt. Before starting, one week, I could not work. On getting better we went to Ship Island; the sailors, who were Englishmen, were very sorry to hear of the treatment we had received, and counselled us how we might get free."

The counsel was heeded, and in due time they found themselves in Liverpool. There their stay was brief. Utterly destitute of money, education, and in a strange land, they very naturally turned their eyes again in the direction of their native land. Accordingly their host, the keeper of a sailor's boarding-house, shipped them to Philadelphia.

But to go back, Joseph saw many things in New Orleans and Mississippi of a nature too horrible to relate, among which were the following:

"I have seen Mr. Beans whip one of his slaves to death, at the tree to which he was tied. Mr. Henry would make them lie down across a log, stripped naked, and with every stroke would lay the flesh open. Being used to it, some would lie on the log without being tied.

"In New Orleans, I have seen women stretched out just as naked as my hand, on boxes, and given one hundred and fifty lashes, four men holding them. I have helped hold them myself: when released they could hardly sit or walk. This whipping was at the "*Fancy House*."

The "chain-gangs" he also saw in constant operation. Four and five slaves chained together and at work on the streets, cleaning, &c., was a common sight. He could hardly tell Sunday from Monday in New Orleans, the slaves were kept so constantly going.

WILLIAM N. TAYLOR.

One Hundred Dollars Reward.

Ran away from Richmond City on Tuesday, the 2d of June, a negro man named WM. N. TAYLOR, belonging to Mrs. Margaret Tyler of Hanover county. Said negro was hired to Fitzhugh Mayo, Tobacconist; is quite black, of genteel and easy manners, about five feet ten or eleven inches high, has one front tooth broken, and is about 35 years old.

He is supposed either to have made his escape North, or attempted to do so. The above reward will be paid for his delivery to Messrs. Hill and Rawlings, in Richmond, or secured in jail, so that I get him again.

JAS. G. TYLER, Trustee for Margaret Tyler.
June 8th &c2t—*Richmond Enquirer, June 9, 57.*

William unquestionably possessed a fair share of common sense, and just enough distaste to Slavery to arouse him most resolutely to seek his freedom.

The advertisement of James G. Tyler was not altogether accurate with regard to his description of William; but notwithstanding, in handing William down to posterity, the description of Tyler has been adopted instead of the one engrossed in the records by the Committee. But as a simple matter of fair play, it seems fitting, that the description given by William, while on the Underground Rail Road, of his master, &c., should come in just here.

William acknowledged that he was the property of Walter H. Tyler, brother of EX-PRESIDENT TYLER, who was described as follows: "He (master) was about sixty-five years of age; was a barbarous man, very intemperate, horse racer, chicken-cock fighter and gambler. He had owned as high as forty head of slaves, but he had gambled them all away. He was a doctor, circulated high amongst southerners, though he never lived agreeably with his wife, would curse her and call her all kinds of names that he should not call a lady. From a boy of nine up to the time I was fifteen or sixteen, I don't reckon he whipped me less than a hundred times. He shot at me once with a double-barrelled gun.

"What made me leave was because I worked for him all my life-time and he never gave me but two dollars and fifteen cents in all his life. I was hired out this year for two hundred dollars, but when I would go to him to make complaints of hard treatment from the man I was hired to, he would say: "G—d d—n it, don't come to me, all I want is my money."

"Mr. Tyler was a thin raw-boned man, with a long nose, the picture of the president. His wife was a tolerably well-disposed woman in some instances—she was a tall, thin-visaged woman, and stood high in the community. Through her I fell into the hands of Tyler. At present she owns about fifty slaves. His own slaves, spoken of as having been gambled away, came by his father—he has been married the second time."

Twice William had been sold and bought in, on account of his master's creditors, and for many months had been expecting to be sold again, to meet pressing claims in the hands of the sheriff against Tyler. He, by the way, "now lives in Hanover county, about eighteen miles from Richmond, and for fear of the sheriff, makes himself very scarce in that city."

At fourteen years of age, William was sold for eight hundred dollars; he would have brought in 1857, probably twelve hundred and fifty dollars; he was a member of the Baptist Church in good and regular standing.

ARRIVAL FROM RICHMOND.

Jeremiah W. Smith and Wife Julia.

Richmond was a city noted for its activity and enterprise in slave trade. Several slave pens and prisons were constantly kept up to accommodate the trade. And slave auctions were as common in Richmond as dress goods auctions in Philadelphia; notwithstanding this fact, strange as it may seem, the Underground Rail Road brought away large numbers of passengers from Richmond, Petersburg and Norfolk, and not a few of them lived comparatively within a hair's breadth of the auction block. Many of those from these localities were amongst the most intelligent and respectable slaves in the South, and except at times when disheartened by some grave disaster which had befallen the road, as, for instance, when some friendly captain or conductor was discovered in aiding fugitives, many of the thinking bondmen were daily manoeuvering and watching for opportunities to escape or aid their friends so to do. This state of things of course made the naturally hot blood of Virginians fairly boil. They had preached long and loudly about the contented and happy condition of the slaves,—that the chief end of the black man was to worship and serve the white man, with joy and delight, with more willingness and obedience indeed than he would be expected to serve his Maker. So the slave-holders were utterly at a loss to account for the unnatural desire on the part of the slaves to escape to the North where they affirmed they would be far less happy in freedom than in the hands of those so "kind and indulgent towards them." Despite all this, daily the disposition increased, with the more intelligent slaves, to distrust the statements of their masters especially when they spoke against the North. For instance if the master was heard to curse Boston the slave was then satisfied that

Boston was just the place he would like to go to; or if the master told the slave that the blacks in Canada were freezing and starving to death by hundreds, his hope of trying to reach Canada was made tenfold stronger; he was willing to risk all the starving and freezing that the country could afford; his eagerness to find a conductor then would become almost painful.

The situations of Jeremiah and Julia Smith, however, were not considered very hard, indeed they had fared rather better than most slaves in Virginia, nevertheless it will be seen that they desired to better their condition, to keep off of the auction-block at least. Jeremiah could claim to have no mixture in his blood, as his color was of such a pure black; but with the way of the world, in respect to shrewdness and intelligence, he had evidently been actively conversant. He was about twenty-six years of age, and in stature only medium, with poor health.

The name of James Kinnard, whom he was obliged to call master and serve, was disgusting to him. Kinnard, he said, was a "close and severe man." At the same time he was not considered by the community "a hard man." From the age of fifteen years Jeremiah had been hired out, for which his owner had received from $50 to $130 per annum. In consequence of his master's custom of thus letting out Jeremiah, the master had avoided doctors' bills, &c. For the last two years prior to his escape, however, Jeremiah's health had been very treacherous, in consequence of which the master had been compelled to receive only $50 a year, sick or well. About one month before Jeremiah left, he was to have been taken on his master's farm, with the hope that he could be made more profitable there than he was in being hired out.

His owner had thought once of selling him, perhaps fearing that Jeremiah might unluckily die on his hands. So he put him in prison and advertised; but as he had the asthma pretty badly at that time, he was not saleable, the traders even declined to buy him.

While these troubles were presenting themselves to Jeremiah, Julia, his wife, was still more seriously involved, which added to Jeremiah's perplexities, of course.

Julia was of a dark brown color, of medium size, and thirty years of age. Fourteen years she had been the slave of A. Judson Crane, and under him she had performed the duties of nurse, chambermaid, etc., "faithfully and satisfactorily," as the certificate furnished her by this owner witnessed. She actually possessed a certificate, which he, Crane, gave her to enable her to find a new master, as she was then about to be sold. Her master had experienced a failure in business. This was the reason why she was to be sold.

Mrs. Crane, her mistress, had always promised Julia that she should be free at her death. But, unexpectedly, as Mrs. Crane was on her journey home from Cape May, where she had been for her health the summer before Julia escaped, she died suddenly in Philadelphia. Julia, however, had been sold twice before her mistress' death; once to the trader, Reed, and afterwards to John Freeland, and again was on the eve of being sold. Freeland, her last owner, thought she was unhappy because she was denied the privilege of going home of nights to her husband, instead of being on hand at the beck and call of her master and mistress day and night. So the very day Julia and her husband escaped, arrangements had been made to put her up at auction a third time. But both Julia and her husband had seen enough of Slavery to leave no room to hope that they could ever find peace or rest so long as they remained. So there and then, they resolved to strike for Canada, via the Underground Rail Road. By a little good management, berths were procured for them on one of the Richmond steamers (berths not known to the officers of the boat), and they were safely landed in the hands of the Vigilance Committee, and a most agreeable interview was had.

The Committee extended to them the usual hospitalities, in the way of board, accommodations, and free tickets Canadaward, and wished them a safe and speedy passage. The passengers departed, exceedingly light-hearted, Feb. 1, 1854.

BLOOD FLOWED FREELY.

Abram Galloway and Richard Eden, Two Passengers Secreted in a Vessel Loaded with Spirits of Turpentine. Shrouds Prepared to Prevent Being Smoked to Death.

The Philadelphia branch of the Underground Rail Road was not fortunate in having very frequent arrivals from North Carolina. Of course such of her slave population as managed to become initiated in the mysteries of traveling North by the Underground Rail Road were sensible enough to find out nearer and safer routes than through Pennsylvania. Nevertheless the Vigilance Committee of Philadelphia occasionally had the pleasure of receiving some heroes who were worthy to be classed among the bravest of the brave, no matter who they may be who have claims to this distinction.

In proof of this bold assertion the two individuals whose names stand at the beginning of this chapter are presented. Abram was only twenty-one years of age, mulatto, five feet six inches high, intelligent and the picture of good health. "What was your master's name?" inquired a member of the Committee. "Milton Hawkins," answered Abram. "What business did Milton Hawkins follow?" again queried said member. "He was chief engineer on the Wilmington and Manchester Rail Road" (not a branch of the Underground Rail Road), responded Richard. "Describe him," said the member. "He was a slim built, tall man with whiskers. He was a man of very good disposition. I always belonged to him; he owned three. He always said he would sell before he would use a whip. His wife was a very mean woman; she would whip contrary to his orders." "Who was your father?" was further inquired. "John Wesley Galloway," was the prompt response. "Describe your father?" "He was captain of a government vessel; he recognized me as his son, and protected me as far as he was allowed so to do; he lived at Smithfield, North Carolina. Abram's master, Milton Hawkins, lived at

Wilmington, N.C." "What prompted you to escape?" was next asked. "Because times were hard and I could not come up with my wages as I was required to do, so I thought I would try and do better." At this juncture Abram explained substantially in what sense times were hard, &c. In the first place he was not allowed to own himself; he, however, preferred hiring his time to serving in the usual way. This favor was granted Abram; but he was compelled to pay $15 per month for his time, besides finding himself in clothing, food, paying doctor bills, and a head tax of $15 a year.

Even under this master, who was a man of very good disposition, Abram was not contented. In the second place, he "always thought Slavery was wrong," although he had "never suffered any personal abuse." Toiling month after month the year round to support his master and not himself, was the one intolerable thought. Abram and Richard were intimate friends, and lived near each other. Being similarly situated, they could venture to communicate the secret feelings of their hearts to each other. Richard was four years older than Abram, with not quite so much Anglo-Saxon blood in his veins, but was equally as intelligent, and was by trade, a "fashionable barber," well-known to the ladies and gentlemen of Wilmington. Richard owed service to Mrs. Mary Loren, a widow. "She was very kind and tender to all her slaves." "If I was sick," said Richard, "she would treat me the same as a mother would." She was the owner of twenty, men, women and children, who were all hired out, except the children too young for hire. Besides having his food, clothing and doctor's expenses to meet, he had to pay the "very kind and tender-hearted widow" $12.50 per month, and head tax to the State, amounting to twenty-five cents per month. It so happened, that Richard at this time, was involved in a matrimonial difficulty. Contrary to the laws of North Carolina, he had lately married a free girl, which was an indictable offence, and for which the penalty was then in soak for him—said penalty to consist of thirty-nine lashes, and imprisonment at the discretion of the judge.

So Abram and Richard put their heads together, and resolved to try the Underground Rail Road. They concluded that liberty was worth dying for, and that it was their duty to strike for Freedom even if it should cost them their lives. The next thing needed, was information about the Underground Rail Road. Before a great while the captain of a schooner turned up, from Wilmington, Delaware. Learning that his voyage extended to Philadelphia, they sought to find out whether this captain was true to Freedom. To ascertain this fact required no little address. It had to be done in such a way, that even the captain would not really understand what they were up to, should he be found untrue. In this instance, however, he was the right man in the right place, and very well understood his business.

Abram and Richard made arrangements with him to bring them away; they learned when the vessel would start, and that she was loaded with tar, rosin, and spirits of turpentine, amongst which the captain was to secrete them. But here came the difficulty. In order that slaves might not be secreted in vessels, the slave-holders of North Carolina had procured the enactment of a law requiring all vessels coming North to be smoked.

To escape this dilemma, the inventive genius of Abram and Richard soon devised a safe-guard against the smoke. This safe-guard consisted in silk oil cloth shrouds, made large, with drawing strings, which, when pulled over their heads, might be drawn very tightly around their waists, whilst the process of smoking might be in operation. A bladder of water and towels were provided, the latter to be wet and held to their nostrils, should there be need. In this manner they had determined to struggle against death for liberty. The hour approached for being at the wharf. At the appointed time they were on hand ready to go on the boat; the captain secreted them, according to agreement. They were ready to run the risk of being smoked to death; but as good luck would have it, the law was not carried into effect in this instance, so that the "smell of smoke was not upon them." The effect of the turpentine, however, of the nature of which they were totally ignorant, was worse, if possible, than the smoke would have been. The blood was literally drawn from them at every pore in frightful quantities. But as heroes of the bravest type they resolved to continue steadfast as long as a pulse continued to beat, and thus they finally conquered.

The invigorating northern air and the kind treatment of the Vigilance Committee acted like a charm upon them, and they improved very rapidly from their exhaustive and heavy loss of blood. Desiring to retain some memorial of them, a member of the Committee begged one of their silk shrouds, and likewise procured an artist to take the photograph of one of them; which keepsakes have been valued very highly. In the regular order of arrangements the wants of Abram and Richard were duly met by the Committee, financially and otherwise, and they were forwarded to Canada. After their safe arrival in Canada, Richard addressed a member of the Committee thus:

KINGSTON, July 20, 1857.

MR. WILLIAM STILL—*Dear Friend:*—I take the opertunity of wrighting a few lines to let you no that we air all in good health hoping thos few lines may find you and your family engoying the same blessing. We arived in King all saft Canada West Abram Galway gos to work this morning at $1.75 per day and John pediford is at work for mr george mink and i will opne a shop for my self in a few days My wif will send a daugretipe to your cair whitch you will pleas to send on to me Richard Edons to the cair of George Mink Kingston C W Yours with Respect, RICHARD EDONS.

———

Abram, his comrade, allied himself faithfully to John Bull until Uncle Sam became involved in the contest with the rebels. In this hour of need Abram hastened back to North Carolina to help fight the battles of Freedom. How well he acted his part, we are not informed. We only know that, after the war was over, in the reconstruction of North Carolina, Abram was promoted to a seat in its Senate. He died in office only a few months since. The portrait is almost a "fac-simile."

ESCAPE OF A YOUNG SLAVE MOTHER.

Left Her Little Baby-Boy, Little Girl and Husband Behind.

She anxiously waits their coming in Syracuse, N.Y. Not until after the foregoing story headed, the "Escape of a Child," etc., had been put into the hands of the printer and was in type, was the story of the mother discovered, although it was among the records preserved. Under changed names, in many instances, it has been found to be no easy matter to cull from a great variety of letters, records and advertisements, just when wanted, all the particulars essential to complete many of these narratives. The case of the child, alluded to above, is a case in point. Thus, however, while it is impossible to introduce the mother's story in its proper place, yet, since it has been found, it is too important and interesting to be left out. It is here given as follows:

$300 REWARD.—RAN AWAY from the subscriber on Saturday, the 30th of August, 1856, my SERVANT WOMAN, named EMELINE CHAPMAN, about 25 years of age; quite dark, slender built, speaks short, and stammers some; with two children, one a female about two and a half years old; the other a male, seven or eight months old, bright color. I will give the above reward if they are delivered to me in Washington.

MRS. EMILY THOMPSON,

s23-TU, Th&st& Capitol Hill, Washington, D.C.

Emeline Chapman, so particularly described in the "Baltimore Sun" of the 23d of September, 1856, arrived by the regular Underground Rail Road train from Washington. In order to escape the responsibility attached to her original name, she adopted the name of

Susan Bell. Thus for freedom she was willing to forego her name, her husband, and even her little children. It was a serious sacrifice; but she had been threatened with the auction block, and she well understood what that meant. With regard to usage, having lived away from her owner, Emeline did not complain of any very hard times. True, she had been kept at work very constantly, and her owner had very faithfully received all her hire. Emeline had not even been allowed enough of her hire to find herself in clothing, or anything for the support of her two children—for these non-essentials, her kind mistress allowed her to seek elsewhere, as best she could. Emeline's husband was named John Henry; her little girl she called Margaret Ann, and her babe she had named after its father, all with the brand of Slavery upon them. The love of freedom, in the breast of this spirited young Slave-wife and mother, did not extinguish the love she bore to her husband and children, however otherwise her course, in leaving them, as she did, might appear. For it was just this kind of heroic and self-sacrificing struggle, that appealed to the hearts of men and compelled attention. The letters of Biglow and Stevens, relative to the little child, prove this fact, and additional testimony found in the appended letter from Rev. J.W. Loguen conclusively confirms the same. Indeed, who could close his eyes and ears to the plaintive cries of such a mother? Who could refrain from aiding on to freedom children honored in such a heroic parent?

SYRACUSE, Oct. 5, 1856.

DEAR FRIEND STILL:—I write to you for Mrs. Susan Bell, who was at your city some time in September last. She is from Washington city. She left her dear little children behind (two children). She is stopping in our city, and wants to hear from her children very much indeed. She wishes to know if you have heard from Mr. Biglow, of Washington city. She will remain here until she can hear from you. She feels very anxious about her children, I will assure you. I should have written before this, but I have been from home much of the time since she came to our city. She wants to know if Mr. Biglow has heard anything about her husband. If you have not written to Mr. Biglow, she wishes you would. She sends her love to you and your dear family. She says that you were all kind to her, and she does not forget it. You will direct your letter to me, dear brother, and I will see that she gets it.

Miss F.E. Watkins left our house yesterday for Ithaca, and other places in that part of the State. Frederick Douglass, Wm. J. Watkins and others were with us last week; Gerritt Smith with others. Miss Watkins is doing great good in our part of the State. We think much indeed of her. She is such a good and glorious speaker, that we are all charmed with her. We have had thirty-one fugitives in the last twenty-seven days; but you, no doubt, have had many more than that. I hope the good Lord may bless you and spare you long to do good to the hunted and outraged among our brethren.

Yours truly, J.W. LOGUEN,
Agent of the Underground Rail Road.

SAMUEL W. JOHNSON.

Arrival from the "Daily Dispatch" Office.

"Sam" was doing Slave labor at the office of the Richmond "Daily Dispatch," as a carrier of that thoroughly pro-slavery sheet. "Sam" had possessed himself somehow of a knowledge of reading and writing a little, and for the news of the day he had quite an itching ear. Also with regard to his freedom he was quite solicitous. Being of an ambitious turn of mind, he hired his time, for which he paid his master $175 per annum in regular quarterly payments. Besides paying this amount, he had to find himself in board, clothing, and pay doctor's expenses. He had had more than one owner in his life. The last one, however, he spoke of thus: "His name is James B. Foster, of Richmond, a very hard man. He owns three more Slaves besides myself." In escaping, "Sam" was obliged to leave his wife, who was owned by Christian Bourdon. His attachment to her, judging from his frequent warm expressions of affection, was very strong. But, as strong as it was, he felt that he could not consent to remain in slavery any longer. "Sam" had luckily come across a copy of Uncle Tom's Cabin, and in perusing it, all his notions with regard to "Masters and Servants," soon underwent an entire change, and he began to cast his eyes around him to see how he might get his freedom. One who was thoroughly awake as he was to the idea of being free, with a fair share of courage, could now and then meet with the opportunity to escape by the steamers or schooners coming North. Thus Samuel found the way open and on one of the steamers came to Philadelphia. On arriving, he was put at once in the charge of the Committee. While in their hands he seemed filled with astonishment at his own achievements, and such spontaneous expressions as naturally flowed from his heart thrilled and amazed his new-found friends, and abundant satisfaction was afforded, that Samuel Washington Johnson would do no discredit to his fugitive comrades in Canada. So the Committee gladly aided him on his journey.

After arriving in Canada, Samuel wrote frequently and intelligently. The subjoined letter to his wife shows how deeply he was attached to her, and, at the same time, what his views were of Slavery. The member of the Committee to whom it was sent with the request, that it should be forwarded to her, did not meet with the opportunity of doing so. A copy of it was preserved with other Underground Rail Road documents.

LETTER FROM SAMUEL W. JOHNSON TO HIS WIFE.

My Dear Wife I now embrace this golden opportunity of writing a few Lines to inform you that I am well at present engoying good health and hope that these few lines may find you well also My dearest wife I have Left you and now I am in a foreign land about fourteen hundred miles from you but though my wife my thoughts are upon you all the time My dearest Frances I hope you will remember me now gust as same as you did when I were there with you because my mind are with you night and day the Love that I bear for you in my breast is greater than I thought it was if I had thought I had so much Love for you I dont think I ever could Left being I have escape I and has fled into a land of freedom. I can but stop and look over my past Life and say what a fool I was for staying in bondage as Long My dear wife I dont want you to get married before you send me some letters because I never shall get married until I see you again My mind dont deceive and it appears to me as if I shall see you again at my time of writing this letter I am desitute of money I have not got in no business yet but when I do get into business I shall write you and also remember you Tell my Mother and Brother and all enquiring friends that I am now safe in free state I cant tell where I am at present but Direct your Letters to Mr. William Still in Philadelphia and I will get them Answer this as soon as you can if

you please for if you write the same day you receive it it will take
a fortnight to reach me No more to relate at present but still
remain your affectionate husband Mr. Still please defore this
piece out if you please

SAMUEL WASHINGTON JOHNSON.

Whether Samuel ever met with the opportunity of communicat-
ing with his wife, the writer cannot say. But of all the trials which
Slaves had to endure, the separations of husbands and wives were
the most difficult to bear up under. Although feeling keenly the loss
of his wife, Samuel's breast swelled with the thought of freedom, as
will be seen from the letter which he wrote immediately after landing in Canada:

ST. CATHARINE, UPPER CANADA WEST.

MR. WILLIAM STILL:—I am now in safety. I arrived at home
safe on the 11th inst at 12 o'clock M. So I hope that you will now
take it upon yourself to inform me something of that letter I left at
your house that night when I left there and write me word how
you are and how is your wife. I wish you may excuse this letter for
I am so full that I cannot express my mind at all. I am only got
$1.50 and I feel as if I had an independent fortune but I don't want
you to think that I am going to be idle because I am on free ground
and I shall always work though I am not got nothing to do at
present. Direct your letter to the post office as soon as possible.

SAMUEL W. JOHNSON.

TWO FEMALE PASSENGERS
FROM MARYLAND.

As the way of travel, *via* the Underground Rail Road, under the most favorable circumstances, even for the sterner sex, was hard enough to test the strongest nerves, and to try the faith of the bravest of the brave, every woman, who won her freedom, by this perilous undertaking, deserves commemoration. It is, therefore, a pleasure to thus transfer from the old Record book the names of Ann Johnson and Lavina Woolfley, who fled from Maryland in 1857. Their lives, however, had not been in any way very remarkable. Ann was tall, and of a dark chestnut color, with an intelligent countenance, and about twenty-four years of age. She had filled various situations as a Slave. Sometimes she was required to serve in the kitchen, at other times she was required to toil in the field, with the plow, hoe, and the like. Samuel Harrington, of Cambridge District, Maryland, was the name of the man for whose benefit Ann labored during her younger days. She had no hesitation in saying, that he was a very "ill-natured man;" he however, was a member of the "old time Methodist Church." In Slave property he had invested only to the extent of some five or six head. About three years previous to Ann's escape, one of her brothers fled and went to Canada. This circumstance so enraged the owner, that he declared he would "sell all" he owned. Accordingly Ann was soon put on the auction block, and was bought by a man who went by the name of William Moore. Moore was a married man, who, with his wife, was addicted to intemperance and carousing. Ann found that she had simply got "out of the fire into the frying-pan." She was really at a loss to tell when her lot was the harder, whether under the "rum drinker," or the old time Methodist. In this state of mind she decided to leave all and go to Canada, the refuge for the fleeing bondman. Lavina, Ann's companion, was the wife of James Woolfley. She and her husband set out together, with six others, and were of the party of eight who were betrayed into Dover jail, as has already been described in these pages. After fighting their way out of the jail, they separated (for prudential reasons). The husband of Lavina, immediately after the conflict at the jail, passed on to Canada, leaving his wife under the protection of friends. Since that time several months had elapsed, but of each other nothing had been known, before she received information on her arrival at Philadelphia. The Committee was glad to inform her, that her husband had safely passed on to Canada, and that she would be aided on also, where they could enjoy freedom in a free country.

CAPTAIN F. AND THE MAYOR OF NORFOLK.

Twenty-One Passengers Secreted in a Boat. November, 1855.

CAPTAIN F. was certainly no ordinary man. Although he had been living a sea-faring life for many years, and the marks of this calling were plainly enough visible in his manners and speech, he was, nevertheless, unlike the great mass of this class of men, not addicted to intemperance and profanity. On the contrary, he was a man of thought, and possessed, in a large measure, those humane traits of character which lead men to sympathize with suffering humanity wherever met with.

It must be admitted, however, that the first impressions gathered from a hasty survey of his rough and rugged appearance, his large head, large mouth, large eyes, and heavy eye-brows, with a natural gift at keeping concealed the inner-workings of his mind and feelings, were not calculated to inspire the belief, that he was fitted to be entrusted with the lives of unprotected females, and helpless children; that he could take pleasure in risking his own life to rescue them from the hell of Slavery; that he could deliberately enter the enemy's domain, and with the faith of a martyr, face the dread slave-holder, with his Bowie-knives and revolvers—Slave-hunters, and blood-hounds, lynchings, and penitentiaries, for humanity's sake. But his deeds proved him to be a true friend of the Slave; whilst his skill, bravery, and success stamped him as one of the most daring and heroic Captains ever connected with the Underground Rail Road cause.

At the time he was doing most for humanity in rescuing bondsmen from Slavery, Slave-laws were actually being the most rigidly executed. To show mercy, in any sense, to man or woman, who might be caught assisting a poor Slave to flee from the prison-house, was a matter not to be thought of in Virginia. This was perfectly well understood by Captain F.; indeed he did not hesitate to say, that his hazardous operations might any day result in the "sacrifice" of his life. But on this point he seemed to give himself no more concern than he would have done to know which way the wind would blow the next day. He had his own convictions about dying and the future, and he declared, that he had "no fear of death," however it might come. Still, he was not disposed to be reckless or needlessly to imperil his life, or the lives of those he undertook to aid. Nor was he averse to receiving compensation for his services. In Richmond, Norfolk, Petersburg, and other places where he traded, many slaves were fully awake to their condition. The great slave sales were the agencies that served to awaken a large number. Then the various mechanical trades were necessarily given to the Slaves, for the master had no taste for "greasy, northern mechanics." Then, again, the stores had to be supplied with porters, draymen, etc., from the slave population. In the hearts of many of the more intelligent amongst the slaves, the men, as mechanics, etc., the women, as dress-makers, chamber-maids, etc., notwithstanding all the opposition and hard laws, the spirit of Freedom was steadily burning. Many of the slaves were half brothers, and sisters, cousins, nephews, and nieces to their owners, and of course "blood would tell."

It was only necessary for the fact to be made known to a single reliable and intelligent slave, that a man with a boat running North had the love of Freedom for all mankind in his bosom to make that man an object of the greatest interest. If an angel had appeared amongst them doubtless his presence would not have inspired greater anxiety and hope than did the presence of Captain F. The class most anxious to obtain freedom could generally manage to acquire some means which they would willingly offer to captains or conductors in the South for such assistance as was indispensable to their escape. Many of the slaves learned if they could manage to cross Mason and Dixon's line, even though they might be utterly destitute and penniless, that they would then receive aid and protection from the Vigilance Committee. Here it may be well to state that, whilst the Committee gladly received and aided all who might come or be brought to them, they never employed agents or captains to go into the South with a view of enticing or running off slaves. So when captains operated, they did so with the full understanding that they alone were responsible for any failures attending their movements.

The way is now clear to present Captain F. with his schooner lying at the wharf in Norfolk, loading with wheat, and at the same time with twenty-one fugitives secreted therein. While the boat was thus lying at her mooring, the rumor was flying all over town that a number of slaves had escaped, which created a general excitement a degree less, perhaps, than if the citizens had been visited by an earthquake. The mayor of the city with a posse of officers with axes and long spears repaired to Captain F.'s boat. The fearless commander received his Honor very coolly, and as gracefully as the circumstances would admit. The mayor gave him to understand who he was, and by what authority he appeared on the boat, and what he meant to do. "Very well," replied Captain F., "here I am and this is my boat, go ahead and search." His Honor with his deputies looked quickly around, and then an order went forth from the mayor to "spear the wheat thoroughly." The deputies obeyed the command with alacrity. But the spears brought neither blood nor groans, and the sagacious mayor obviously concluded that he was "barking up the wrong tree." But the mayor was not there for nothing. "Take the axes and go to work," was the next order; and the axe was used with terrible effect by one of the deputies. The deck and other parts of the boat were chopped and split; no greater judgment being exercised when using the axe than when spearing the wheat; Captain F. all the while wearing an air of utter indifference or rather of entire composure. Indeed every step they took proved conclusively that they were wholly ignorant with regard to boat searching. At this point, with remarkable shrewdness, Captain F. saw wherein he could still further confuse them by a bold strategical move. As though about out of patience with the mayor's blunders, the captain instantly reminded his Honor that he had "stood still long enough" while his boat was being "damaged, chopped up," &c. "Now if you want to search," continued he, "give me the axe, and then point out

the spot you want opened and I will open it for you very quick."
While uttering these words he presented, as he was capable of
doing, an indignant and defiant countenance, and intimated that it
mattered not where or when a man died provided he was in the
right, and as though he wished to give particularly strong emphasis
to what he was saying, he raised the axe, and brought it down edge
foremost on the deck with startling effect, at the same time causing
the splinters to fly from the boards. The mayor and his posse
seemed, if not dreadfully frightened, completely confounded, and
by the time Captain F. had again brought down his axe with increased power, demanding where they would have him open, they
looked as though it was time for them to retire, and in a few minutes
after they actually gave up the search and left the boat without finding a soul. Daniel in the lions' den was not safer than were the
twenty-one passengers secreted on Captain F.'s boat. The law had
been carried out with a vengeance, but did not avail with this skilled
captain. The "five dollars" were paid for being searched, the amount
which was lawfully required of every captain sailing from Virginia.
And the captain steered direct for the City of Brotherly Love. The
wind of heaven favoring the good cause, he arrived safely in due
time, and delivered his precious freight in the vicinity of Philadelphia within the reach of the Vigilance Committee. The names of
the passengers were as follows:

ALAN TATUM, DANIEL CARR, MICHAEL VAUGHN,
THOMAS NIXON, FREDERICK NIXON, PETER PETTY, NA-
THANIEL GARDENER, JOHN BROWN, THOMAS FREE-
MAN, JAMES FOSTER, GODFREY SCOTT, WILLIS WILSON,
NANCY LITTLE, JOHN SMITH, FRANCIS HAINES, DAVID
JOHNSON, PHILLIS GAULT, ALICE JONES, NED WILSON,
and SARAH C. WILSON, and one other, who subsequently passed
on, having been detained on account of sickness. These passengers
were most "likely-looking articles;" a number of them, doubtless,
would have commanded the very highest prices in the Richmond
market. Among them were some good mechanics—one excellent
dress-maker, some "prime" waiters and chambermaids;—men and

women with brains, some of them evincing remarkable intelligence and decided bravery, just the kind of passengers that gave the greatest satisfaction to the Vigilance Committee. The interview with these passengers was extremely interesting. Each one gave his or her experience of Slavery, the escape, etc., in his or her own way, deeply impressing those who had the privilege of seeing and hearing them, with the fact of the growing spirit of Liberty, and the wonderful perception and intelligence possessed by some of the sons of toil in the South. While all the names of these passengers were duly entered on the Underground Rail Road records, the number was too large, and the time they spent with the attempts to escape were made by Daniel, after being sold to North Carolina; for this offence, he was on one occasion stripped naked, and flogged severely. This did not cure him. Prior to his joining Captain F.'s party, he had fled to the swamps, and dwelt there for three months, surrounded with wild animals and reptiles, and it was this state of solitude that he left directly before finding Captain F. Daniel had a wife in Portsmouth, to whom he succeeded in paying a private visit, when, to his unspeakable joy, he made the acquaintance of the noble Captain F., whose big heart was delighted to give him a passage North. Daniel, after being sold, had been allowed, within the two years, only one opportunity of visiting his wife; being thus debarred he resolved to escape. His wife, whose name was Hannah, had three children—slaves—their names were Sam, Dan, and "baby." The name of the latter was unknown to him.

MICHAEL VAUGHN. Michael was about thirty-one years of age, with superior physical proportions, and no lack of common sense. His color was without paleness—dark and unfading, and his manly appearance was quite striking. Michael belonged to a lady, whom he described as a "very disagreeable woman." "For all my life I have belonged to her, but for the last eight years I have hired my time. I paid my mistress $120 a year; a part of the time I had to find my board and all my clothing." This was the direct, and unequivocal testimony that Michael gave of his slave life, which was the foundation for alleging that his mistress was a "very disagreeable woman."

Michael left a wife and one child in Slavery; but they were not owned by his mistress. Before escaping, he felt afraid to lead his companion into the secret of his contemplated movements, as he felt, that there was no possible way for him to do anything for her deliverance; on the other hand, any revelation of the matter might prove too exciting for the poor soul;—her name was Esther. That he did not lose his affection for her whom he was obliged to leave so unceremoniously, is shown by the appended letter:

NEW BEDFORD, August 22d, 1855.

DEAR SIR:—I send you this to inform you that I expect my wife to come that way. If she should, you will direct her to me. When I came through your city last Fall, you took my name in your office, which was then given you, Michael Vaughn; since then my name is William Brown, No. 130 Kempton street. Please give my wife and child's name to Dr. Lundy, and tell him to attend to it for me. Her name is Esther, and the child's name Louisa.

Truly yours, WILLIAM BROWN.

Michael worked in a foundry. In church fellowship he was connected with the Methodists—his mistress with the Baptists.

THOMAS NIXON was about nineteen years of age, of a dark hue, and quite intelligent. He had not much excuse to make for leaving, except, that he was "tired of staying" with his "owner," as he "feared he might be sold some day," so he "thought" that he might as well save him the trouble. Thomas belonged to a Mr. Bockover, a wholesale grocer, No. 12 Brewer street. Thomas left behind him his mother and three brothers. His father was sold away when he was an infant, consequently he never saw him. Thomas was a member of the Methodist Church; his master was of the same persuasion.

FREDERICK NIXON was about thirty-three years of age, and belonged truly to the wide-awake class of slaves, as his marked physical and mental appearance indicated. He had a more urgent excuse for escaping than Thomas; he declared that he fled because, his owner wanted "to work him hard without allowing him any

chance, and had treated him rough." Frederick was also one of Mr.
Bockover's chattels; he left his wife, Elizabeth, with four children in
bondage. They were living in Eatontown, North Carolina. It had
been almost one year since he had seen them. Had he remained in
Norfolk he had not the slightest prospect of being reunited to his
wife and children, as he had been already separated from them for
about three years. This painful state of affairs only increased his
desire to leave those who were brutal enough to make such havoc in
his domestic relations.

PETER PETTY was about twenty-four years of age, and wore a
happy countenance; he was a person of agreeable manners, and
withal pretty smart. He acknowledged, that he had been owned by
Joseph Boukley, Hair Inspector. Peter did not give Mr. Boukley a
very good character, however; he said, that Mr. B. was "rowdyish in
his habits, was deceitful and sly, and would sell his slaves any time.
Hard bondage—something like the children of Israel," was his simple excuse for fleeing. He hired his time of his master, for which he
was compelled to pay $156 a year. When he lost time by sickness or
rainy weather, he was required to make up the deficiency, also find
his clothing. He left a wife—Lavinia—and one child, Eliza, both
slaves. Peter communicated to his wife his secret intention to leave,
and she acquiesced in his going. He left his parents also. All his sisters and brothers had been sold. Peter would have been sold too, but
his owner was under the impression, that he was "too good a Christian" to violate the laws by running away. Peter's master was quite a
devoted Methodist, and was attached to the same Church with
Peter. While on the subject of religion, Peter was asked about the
kind and character of preaching that he had been accustomed to
hear; whereupon he gave the following graphic specimen: "Servants
obey your masters; good servants make good masters; when your
mistress speaks to you don't pout out your mouths; when you want
to go to church ask your mistress and master," etc., etc. Peter declared, that he had never heard but one preacher speak against slavery, and that "one was obliged to leave suddenly for the North." He
said, that a Quaker lady spoke in meeting against Slavery one day,
which resulted in an outbreak, and final breaking up of the meeting.

PHILLIS GAULT. Phillis was a widow, about thirty years of age; the blood of two races flowed in about equal proportions through her veins. Such was her personal appearance, refinement, manners, and intelligence, that had the facts of her slave life been unknown, she would have readily passed for one who had possessed superior advantages. But the facts in her history proved, that she had been made to feel very keenly the horrifying effects of Slavery; not in the field, for she had never worked there; nor as a common drudge, for she had always been required to fill higher spheres; she was a dress-maker—but not without fear of the auction block. This dreaded destiny was the motive which constrained her to escape with the twenty others; secreted in the hold of a vessel expressly arranged for bringing away slaves. Death had robbed her of her husband at the time that the fever raged so fearfully in Norfolk. This sad event deprived her of the hope she had of being purchased by her husband, as he had intended. She was haunted by the constant thought of again being sold, as she had once been, and as she had witnessed the sale of her sister's four children after the death of their mother.

Phillis was, to use her own striking expression in a state of "great horror;" she felt, that nothing would relieve her but freedom. After having fully pondered the prospect of her freedom and the only mode offered by which she could escape, she consented to endure bravely whatever of suffering and trial might fall to her lot in the undertaking—and as was the case with thousands of others, she succeeded. She remained several days in the family of a member of the Committee in Philadelphia, favorably impressing all who saw her. As she had formed a very high opinion of Boston, from having heard it so thoroughly reviled in Norfolk, she desired to go there. The Committee made no objections, gave her a free ticket, etc. From that time to the present, she has ever sustained a good Christian character, and as an industrious, upright, and intelligent woman, she has been and is highly respected by all who know her. The following letter is characteristic of her:

BOSTON, March 22, 1858.

MY DEAR SIR—I received your photograph by Mr Cooper and it afforded me much pleasure to do so i hope that these few lines may find you and your family well as it leaves me and little Dicky at present i have no interesting news to tell you more than there is a great revival of religion through the land i all most forgoten to thank you for your kindness and our little Dick he is very wild and goes to school and it is my desire and prayer for him to grow up a useful man i wish you would try to gain some information from Norfolk and write me word how the times are there for i am afraid to write i wish yoo would see the Doctor for me and ask him if he could carefully find out any way that we could steal little Johny for i think to raise nine or ten hundred dollars for such a child is outraigust just at this time i feel as if i would rather steal him than to buy him give my kinde regards to the Dr and his family tell Miss Margret and Mrs Landy that i would like to see them out here this summer again to have a nice time in Cambridge Miss Walker that spent the evening with me in Cambridge sens much love to yoo and Mrs. Landy give my kindes regards to Mrs Still and children and receive a portion for yoo self i have no more to say at present but remain yoor respectfully.

FLARECE P. GAULT.

When you write direct yoo letters Mrs. Flarece P. Gault, No 62 Pinkney St.

ARRIVALS FROM DIFFERENT PLACES.

Matilda Mahoney—Dr. J.W. Pennington's Brother and Sons Captured and Carried Back.

While many sympathized with the slave in his chains, and freely wept over his destiny, or gave money to help buy his freedom, but few could be found who were willing to take the risk of going into the South, and standing face to face with Slavery, in order to conduct a panting slave to freedom. The undertaking was too fearful to think of in most cases. But there were instances when men and women too, moved by the love of freedom, would take their lives in their hands, beard the lion in his den, and nobly rescue the oppressed. Such an instance is found in the case of Matilda Mahoney, in Baltimore.

The story of Matilda must be very brief, although it is full of thrilling interest. She was twenty-one years of age in 1854, when she escaped and came to Philadelphia, a handsome young woman, of a light complexion, quite refined in her manners, and in short, possessing great personal attractions. But her situation as a slave was critical, as will be seen.

Her claimant was Wm. Rigard, of Frederick, Md., who hired her to a Mr. Reese, in Baltimore; in this situation her duties were general housework and nursing. With these labors, she was not, however, so much dissatisfied as she was with other circumstances of a more alarming nature: her old master was tottering on the verge of the grave, and his son, a trader in New Orleans. These facts kept Matilda in extreme anxiety. For two years prior to her escape, the young trader had been trying to influence his father to let him have her for the Southern market; but the old man had not consented. Of course the trader knew quite well, that an "article" of her appearance would command readily a very high price in the New

Orleans market. But Matilda's attractions had won the heart of a young man in the North, one who had known her in Baltimore in earlier days, and this lover was willing to make desperate efforts to rescue her from her perilous situation. Whether or not he had nerve enough to venture down to Baltimore to accompany his intended away on the Underground Rail Road, his presence would not have aided in the case. He had, however, a friend who consented to go to Baltimore on this desperate mission. The friend was James Jefferson, of Providence, R.I. With the strategy of a skilled soldier, Mr. Jefferson hurried to the Monumental City, and almost under the eyes of the slave-holders, and slave-catchers, despite of pro slavery breastworks, seized his prize and speeded her away on the Underground Railway, before her owner was made acquainted with the fact of her intended escape. On Matilda's arrival at the station in Philadelphia, several other passengers from different points, happened to come to hand just at that time, and gave great solicitude and anxiety to the Committee. Among these were a man and his wife and their four children, (noticed elsewhere), from Maryland. Likewise an interesting and intelligent young girl who had been almost miraculously rescued from the prison-house at Norfolk, and in addition to these, the brother of J.W. Pennington, D.D., with his two sons.

While it was a great gratification to have travelers coming along so fast, and especially to observe in every countenance, determination, rare manly and womanly bearing, with remarkable intelligence, it must be admitted, that the acting committee felt at the same time, a very lively dread of the slave-hunters, and were on their guard. Arrangements were made to send the fugitives on by different trains, and in various directions. Matilda and all the others with the exception of the father and two sons (relatives of Dr. Pennington) successfully escaped and reached their longed-for haven in a free land. The Penningtons, however, although pains had been taken to apprize the Doctor of the good news of the coming of his kin, whom he had not seen for many, many years, were captured after being in New York some twenty-four hours. In answer to an advisory letter from the secretary of the Committee the following from the Doctor is explicit, relative to his wishes and feelings with regard to their being sent on to New York.

29 6th AVENUE, NEW YORK, May 24th, 1854.

MY DEAR MR. STILL:—Your kind letter of the 22d inst has come to hand and I have to thank you for your offices of benevolence to my bone and my flesh, I have had the pleasure of doing a little for your brother Peter, but I do not think it an offset. My burden has been great about these brethren. I hope they have started on to me. Many thanks, my good friend. Yours Truly.

J.W.C. PENNINGTON.

This letter only served to intensify the deep interest which had already been awakened for the safety of all concerned. At the same time also it made the duty of the Committee clear with regard to forwarding them to N.Y. Immediately, therefore, the Doctor's brother and sons were furnished with free tickets and were as carefully cautioned as possible with regard to slave-hunters, if encountered on the road. In company with several other Underground Rail Road passengers, under the care of an intelligent guide, all were sent off in due order, looking quite as well as the most respectable of their race from any part of the country. The Committee in New York, with the Doctor, were on the look out of course; thus without difficulty all arrived safely in the Empire City.

It would seem that the coming of his brother and sons so overpowered the Doctor that he forgot how imminent their danger was. The meeting and interview was doubtless very joyous. Few perhaps could realize, even in imagination, the feelings that filled their hearts, as the Doctor and his brother reverted to their boyhood, when they were both slaves together in Maryland; the separation—the escape of the former many years previous—the contrast, one elevated to the dignity of a Doctor of Divinity, a scholar and noted clergyman, and as such well known in the United States, and Great Britain, whilst, at the same time, his brother and kin were held in chains, compelled to do unrequited labor, to come and go at the bidding of another. Were not these reflections enough to incapacitate the Doctor for the time being, for cool thought as to how he should best guard against the enemy? Indeed, in view of Slavery and its horrid features, the wonder is, not that more was not done, but that any thing was done, that the victims were not driven almost out of their senses. But time rolled on until nearly twenty-four hours had passed, and while reposing their fatigued and weary limbs in bed, just before day-break, hyena-like the slave-hunters pounced upon all three of them, and soon had them hand-cuffed and hurried off to a United States' Commissioner's office. Armed with the Fugitive Law, and a strong guard of officers to carry it out, resistance would have been simply useless. Ere the morning sun arose the sad news was borne by the telegraph wires to all parts of the country of this awful calamity on the Underground Rail Road.

Scarcely less painful to the Committee was the news of this accident, than the news of a disaster, resulting in the loss of several lives, on the Camden and Amboy Road, would have been to its managers. This was the first accident that had ever taken place on the road after passengers had reached the Philadelphia Committee, although, in various instances, slave-hunters had been within a hair's breadth of their prey.

All that was reported respecting the arrest and return of the Doctor's kin, so disgraceful to Christianity and civilization, is taken from the Liberator, as follows:

THREE FUGITIVE SLAVES ARRESTED IN NEW YORK, AND GIVEN UP TO THEIR OWNERS.

NEW YORK, May 25th.

About three o'clock this morning, three colored men, father and two sons, known as Jake, Bob, and Stephen Pennington, were arrested at the instance of David Smith and Jacob Grove, of Washington Co., Md., who claimed them as their slaves. They were taken before Commissioner Morton, of the United States Court, and it was understood that they would be examined at 11 o'clock; instead of that, however, the case was heard at once, no persons being present, when the claimnants testified that they were the owners of said slaves and that they escaped from their service at Baltimore, on Sunday last.

From what we can gather of the proceedings, the fugitives acknowledged themselves to be slaves of Smith and Grove. The commissioner considering the testimony sufficient, ordered their surrender, and they were accordingly given up to their claimants, who hurried them off at once, and they are now on their way to Baltimore. A telegraph despatch has been sent to Philadelphia, as it is understood an attempt will be made to rescue the parties, when the cars arrive. There was no excitement around the commissioner's office, owing to a misunderstanding as to the time of examination. The men were traced to this city by the claimants, who made application to the United States Court, when officers Horton and De Angeles were deputed by the marshal to effect their arrest, and those officers, with deputy Marshal Thompson scoured the city, and finally found them secreted in a house in Broome St. They were brought before Commissioner Morton this morning. No counsel appeared for the fugitives. The case being made out, the usual affidavits of fear of rescue were made, and the warrants thereupon issued, and the three fugitives were delivered over to the U.S. Marshal, and hurried off to Maryland. They were a father and his two sons, father about forty-five and sons eighteen or nineteen. The evidence shows them to have recently escaped. The father is the brother of the Rev. Dr. Pennington, a highly respected colored preacher of this city.

NEW YORK, May 28.

Last evening the church at the corner of Prince and Marion streets was filled with an intelligent audience of white and colored people, to hear Dr. Pennington relate the circumstance connected with the arrest of his brother and nephews. He showed, that he attempted to afford his brother the assistance of counsel, but was unable to do so, the officers at the Marshal's office having deceived him in relation to the time the trial was to take place before the Commissioners. Hon. E.F. Culver next addressed the audience, showing, that a great injustice had been done to the brother of Dr. Pennington, and though he, up to that time, had advocated peace, he now had the spirit to tear down the building over the Marshal's head. Intense interest was manifested during the proceedings, and much sympathy in behalf of Dr. Pennington.

THE FUGITIVE SLAVES IN BALTIMORE.

The U.S. Marshal, A.T. Hillyer, Esq., received a dispatch this morning from officers Horton and Dellugelis, at Baltimore, stating, that they had arrived there with the three slaves, arrested here yesterday (the Penningtons), the owners accompanying them. The officers will return to New York, this evening.—*N.Y. Express,* 27th.

NEW YORK, May 30.

The Rev. Dr. Pennington has received a letter from Mr. Grove, the claimant of his brother, who was recently taken back from this city, offering to sell him to Dr. Pennington, should he wish to buy him, and stating, that he would await a reply, before "selling him to the slave-drivers." Mr. Groce, who accompanied his "sweet heart," Matilda, in the same train which conveyed the Penningtons to New York, had reason to apprehend danger to all the Underground Rail Road passengers, as will appear from his subjoined letter:

ELMIRA, May 28th.

DEAR LUKE:—I arrived home safe with my precious charge, and found all well. I have just learned, that the Penningtons are taken. Had he done as I wished him he would never have been taken. Last night our tall friend from Baltimore came, and caused great excitement here by his information. The lady is perfectly safe now in Canada. I will write you and Mr. Still as soon as I get over the excitement. This letter was first intended for Mr. Gains, but I now send it to you. Please let me hear their movements. Yours truly,

C.L. GROCE.

But sadly as this blow was felt by the Vigilance Committee, it did not cause them to relax their efforts in the least. Indeed it only served to stir them up to renewed diligence and watchfulness, although for a length of time afterwards the Committee felt disposed, when sending, to avoid New York as much as possible, and in lieu thereof, to send *via* Elmira, where there was a depot under the agency of John W. Jones. Mr. Jones was a true and prompt friend of the fugitive, and wide-awake with regard to Slavery and slave-holders, and slave hunters, for he had known from sad experience in Virginia every trait of character belonging to these classes.

In the midst of the Doctor's grief, friends of the slave soon raised money to purchase his brother, about $1,000; but the unfortunate sons were doomed to the auction block and the far South, where, the writer has never exactly learned.

"FLEEING GIRL OF FIFTEEN," IN MALE ATTIRE.

Professors H. and T. Offer Their Services—Captains B. Also Are Enlisted—Slave-Trader Grasping Tightly His Prey, but She Is Rescued—Long Conflict, but Great Triumph—Arrival on Thanksgiving Day, Nov. 25, 1855.

It was the business of the Vigilance Committee, as it was clearly understood by the friends of the Slave, to assist all needy fugitives, who might in any way manage to reach Philadelphia, but, for various reasons, not to send agents South to incite slaves to run away, or to assist them in so doing. Sometimes, however, this rule could not altogether be conformed to. Cases, in some instances, would appeal so loudly and forcibly to humanity, civilization, and Christianity, that it would really seem as if the very stones would cry out, unless something was done. As an illustration of this point, the story of the young girl, which is now to be related, will afford the most striking proof. At the same time it may be seen how much anxiety, care, hazard, delay and material aid, were required in order to effect the deliverance of some who were in close places, and difficult of access. It will be necessary to present a considerable amount of correspondence in this case, to bring to light the hidden mysteries of this narrative. The first letter, in explanation, is the following:

LETTER FROM J. BIGELOW, ESQ.

————

WASHINGTON, D.C., June 27, 1854.

MR. WM. STILL—*Dear Sir:*—I have to thank you for the prompt answer you had the kindness to give to my note of 22d inst. Having found a correspondence so quick and easy, and withal so very flattering, I address you again more fully.

The liberal appropriation for *transportation* has been made chiefly on account of a female child of ten or eleven years old, for whose purchase I have been authorized to offer $700 (refused), and for whose sister I have paid $1,600, and some $1,000 for their mother, &c.

This child sleeps in the same apartment with its master and mistress, which adds to the difficulty of removal. She is some ten or twelve miles from the city, so that really the chief hazard will be in bringing her safely to town, and in secreting her until a few days of *storm* shall have abated. All this, I think, is now provided for with entire safety. The child has two cousins in the immediate vicinity; a young man of some twenty-two years of age, and his sister, of perhaps seventeen—*both Slaves*, but bright and clear-headed as anybody. The young man I have seen often—the services of *both* seem indispensable to the main object suggested; but having once rendered the service, they cannot, and ought not return to Slavery. They look for *freedom* as the reward of what they shall now do.

Out of the $300, cheerfully offered for the whole enterprise, I must pay some reasonable sum for transportation to the city and sustenance while here. It cannot be much; for the balance, I shall give a draft, which will be *promptly paid* on their arrival in New York.

If I have been understood to offer the whole $300, *it shall be paid*, though I have meant as above stated. Among the various ways that have been suggested, has been that of taking *all of them* into the cars here; that, I think, will be found impracticable. I find so much vigilance at the depot, that I would not deem it safe, though, in any kind of carriage they might leave in safety at any time.

All the rest I leave to the experience and sagacity of the gentleman who maps out the enterprise.

Now I will thank you to reply to this and let me know that it reaches you in safety, and is not put in a careless place, whereby I may be endangered; and state also, whether all my propositions are understood and acceptable, and whether, (pretty quickly after I shall inform you that *all things are ready*), the gentleman will make his appearance?

I live alone. My office and bed-room, &c., are at the corner of E. and 7th streets, opposite the east end of the General Post Office, where any one may call upon me.

It would, of course, be imprudent, that this letter, or any other *written* particulars, be in his pockets for fear of accident. Yours very respectfully, J. BIGELOW.

While this letter clearly brought to light the situation of things, its author, however, had scarcely begun to conceive of the numberless difficulties which stood in the way of success before the work could be accomplished. The information which Mr. Bigelow's letter contained of the painful situation of this young girl was submitted to different parties who could be trusted, with a view of finding a person who might possess sufficient courage to undertake to bring her away. Amongst those consulted were two or three captains who had on former occasions done good service in the cause. One of these captains was known in Underground Rail-Road circles as the "powder boy."* He was willing to undertake the work, and immediately concluded to make a visit to Washington, to see how the "land lay." Accordingly in company with another Underground Rail Road captain, he reported himself one day to Mr. Bigelow with as much assurance as if he were on an errand for an office under the government. The impression made on Mr. Bigelow's mind may be seen from the following letter; it may also be seen that he was fully alive to the necessity of precautionary measures.

SECOND LETTER FROM LAWYER BIGELOW.

WASHINGTON, D.C., September 9th, 1855.

MR. WM. STILL, DEAR SIR:—I strongly hope the little matter of business so long pending and about which I have written you so many times, will take a move now. I have the promise that the merchandize shall be delivered in this city to-night. Like so many

---

* He had been engaged at different times in carrying powder in his boat from a powder magazine, and from this circumstance, was familiarly called the "Powder Boy."

other promises, this also may prove a failure, though I have reason to believe that it will not. I shall, however, know before I mail this note. In case the goods arrive here I shall hope to see your long-talked of "Professional gentleman" in Washington, as soon as possible. He will find me by the enclosed card, which shall be a satisfactory introduction for him. You have never given me his name, nor am I anxious to know it. But on a pleasant visit made last fall to friend Wm. Wright, in Adams Co., I suppose I accidentally learned it to be a certain Dr. H———. Well, let him come.

I had an interesting call a week ago from two gentlemen, masters of vessels, and brothers, one of whom, I understand, you know as the "powder boy." I had a little light freight for them; but not finding enough other freight to ballast their craft, they went down the river looking for wheat, and promising to return soon.

I hope to see them often. I hope this may find you returned from your northern trip,* as your time proposed was out two or three days ago.

I hope if the whole particulars of Jane Johnson's case† are printed, you will send me the copy as proposed.

I forwarded some of her things to Boston a few days ago, and had I known its importance in court, I could have sent you one or two witnesses who would prove that her freedom was intended by her before she left Washington, and that a man was *engaged* here to go on to Philadelphia the same day with her to give notice there of her case, though I think he failed to do so. It was beyond all question her purpose, *before leaving Washington and provable too,* that if Wheeler should make her a free woman by taking her to a free state *"to use it rather."*

Tuesday, 11th September. The attempt was made on Sunday to forward the merchandize, but failed through no fault of any of the parties that I now know of. It will be repeated soon, and you shall know the result.

---

* Mr. Bigelow's correspondent had been on a visit to the fugitives to Canada.
† Jane Johnson of the Passmore Williamson Slave Case.

"Whorra for Judge Kane." I feel so indignant at the man, that it is not easy to write the foregoing sentence, and yet who is helping our cause like Kane and Douglas, not forgetting Stringfellow. I hope soon to know that this reaches you in safety.

It often happens that light freight would be offered to Captain B., but the owners cannot by possibility *advance* the amount of freight. I wish it were possible in some such extreme cases, that after advancing *all they have,* some public fund should be found to pay the balance or at least lend it.

[I wish here to caution you against the supposition that I would do any act, or say a word towards helping servants to escape. Although I hate slavery so much, I keep my hands clear of any such wicked or illegal act.]

Yours, very truly, J.B.

Will you recollect, hereafter, that in any of my future letters, in which I may use [ ] whatever words may be within the brackets are intended to have no signification whatever to you, only to blind the eyes of the uninitiated. You will find an example at the close of my letter.

Up to this time the chances seemed favorable of procuring the ready services of either of the above mentioned captains who visited Lawyer Bigelow for the removal of the merchandize to Philadelphia, providing the shipping master could have it in readiness to suit their convenience. But as these captains had a number of engagements at Richmond, Petersburg, &c., it was not deemed altogether safe to rely upon either of them, consequently in order to be prepared in case of an emergency, the matter was laid before two professional gentlemen who were each occupying chairs in one of the medical colleges of Philadelphia. They were known to be true friends of the slave, and had possessed withal some experience in Underground Rail Road matters. Either of these professors was willing to undertake the operation, provided arrangements could be completed in time to be carried out during the vacation. In this hopeful, although painfully indefinite position the matter remained for more than a year; but the correspondence and anxiety increased, and with them disappointments and difficulties multiplied. The hope of Freedom, however, buoyed up the heart of the young slave girl during the long months of anxious waiting and daily expectation for the hour of deliverance to come. Equally true and faithful also did Mr. Bigelow prove to the last; but at times he had some painfully dark seasons to encounter, as may be seen from the subjoined letter:

WASHINGTON, D.C., October 6th, 1855.

MR. STILL, DEAR SIR:—I regret exceedingly to learn by your favor of 4th instant, that all things are not ready. Although I cannot speak of any immediate and positive danger. [*Yet it is well known that the city is full of incendiaries.*]

Perhaps you are aware that any colored citizen is liable at any hour of day or night without any show of authority to have his house ransacked by constables, and if others do it and commit the most outrageous depredations none but white witnesses can convict them. Such outrages are always common here, and no kind of property exposed to colored protection only, can be considered safe. [I don't say that *much liberty* should not be given to constables on account of numerous runaways, but it don't always work for good.] Before advertising they go round and offer rewards to sharp colored men of perhaps *one or two hundred dollars,* to betray runaways, and having discovered their hiding-place, seize them and then cheat their informers out of the money.

[*Although a law-abiding man,*] I am anxious in this case of *innocence* to raise no conflict or suspicion. [*Be sure that the manumission is full and legal.*] And as I am *powerless* without your aid, *I pray you* don't lose a moment in giving me relief. The idea of waiting yet for weeks seems dreadful; do reduce it to days if possible, and give me notice of the *earliest possible time.*

The property is not yet advertised, but will be, [and if we delay too long, may be sold and lost.]

It was a great misunderstanding, though not your fault, that so much delay would be necessary. [I repeat again that I must have

the thing done legally, therefore, please get a good lawyer to draw
up the deed of manumission.]

Yours Truly, J. BIGELOW.

Great was the anxiety felt in Washington. It is certainly not too
much to say, that an equal amount of anxiety existed in Philadelphia respecting the safety of the merchandise. At this juncture Mr.
Bigelow had come to the conclusion that it was no longer safe to
write over his own name, but that he would do well to henceforth
adopt the name of the renowned Quaker, Wm. Penn, (he was worthy of it) as in the case of the following letter.

WASHINGTON, D.C., November 10th, 1855.

DEAR SIR:—Doctor T. presented my card last night about half
past eight which I instantly recognized. I, however, soon became
suspicious, and afterwards confounded, to find the doctor using
your name and the well known names of Mr. McK. and Mr. W. and
yet, neither he nor I, could conjecture the object of his visit.

The doctor is agreeable and sensible, and doubtless a true-
hearted man. He seemed to see the whole matter as I did, and was
embarrassed. He had nothing to propose, no information to give of
the "P. Boy," or of any substitute, and seemed to want no particular
information from me concerning my anxieties and perils, though I
stated them to him, but found him as powerless as myself to give
me relief. I had an agreeable interview with the doctor till after
ten, when he left, intending to take the cars at six, as I suppose he
did do, this morning.

This morning after eight, I got your letter of the 9th, but it gives
me but little enlightenment or satisfaction. You simply say that the
doctor is a *true man,* which I cannot doubt, that you thought it best
we should have an interview, and that you supposed I would meet
the expenses. You informed me also that the "P. Boy" left for
Richmond, on Friday, the 2d, to be gone *the length of time named in
your last,* I must infer that to be *ten days* though in your last *you
assured me* that the "P. Boy" would certainly start for *this place* (not
Richmond) in two or three days, though the difficulty about freight

might cause delay, and the whole enterprise might not be accomplished under ten days, &c., &c. That time having elapsed and I having agreed to an extra fifty dollars to ensure promptness. I have scarcely left my office since, except for my hasty meals, awaiting his arrival. You now inform me he has gone to Richmond, to be gone ten days, which will expire tomorrow, but you do not say he will return here or to Phila, or where, at the expiration of that time, and Dr. T. could tell me nothing whatever about him. Had he been able to tell me that this *best plan*, which I have so long rested upon, would fail, or was abandoned, I could then understand it, but he says no such thing, and you say, as you have twice before said, "ten days more."

Now, my dear sir, after this recapitulation, can you not see that I have reason for great embarrassment? I have given assurances, both here and in New York, founded on your assurances to me, and caused my friends in the latter place great anxiety, so much that I have had no way to explain my own letters but by sending your last two to Mr. Tappan.

I cannot doubt, I do not, but that you wish to help me, and the cause too, for which both of us have made many and large sacrifices with no hope of reward in this world. If in this case I have been very urgent since September Dr. T. can give you some of my reasons, they have not been selfish.

The whole matter is in a nutshell. Can I, in your opinion, depend on the "P. Boy," and when?

If he promises to come here next trip, will he come, or go to Richmond? This I think is the best way. Can I depend on it?

Dr. T. promised to write me some explanation and give some advice, and at first I thought to await his letter, but on second thought concluded to tell you how I feel, as I have done.

Will you answer my questions with some explicitness, and without delay?

I forgot to inquire of Dr. T. who is the head of your Vigilance Committee, whom I may address concerning other and further operations?

Yours very truly, WM. PENN.

P.S. I ought to say, that I have no doubt but there were good reasons for the P. Boy's going to Richmond instead of W.; *but what can they be?*

Whilst there are a score of other interesting letters, bearing on this case, the above must suffice, to give at least, an idea of the perplexities and dangers attending its early history. Having accomplished this end, a more encouraging and pleasant phase of the transaction may now be introduced. Here the difficulties, at least very many of them, vanish, yet in one respect, the danger became most imminent. The following letter shows that the girl had been successfully rescued from her master, and that a reward of five hundred dollars had been offered for her.

WASHINGTON, D.C., October 12, 1855.

MR. WM. STILL:—AS YOU PICK UP ALL THE NEWS THAT IS STIRRING, I CONTRIBUTE A FEW SCRAPS TO YOUR STOCK, GOING TO SHOW THAT THE POOR SLAVE-HOLDERS HAVE THEIR TROUBLES AS WELL AS OTHER PEOPLE.

FOUR HEAVY LOSSES ON ONE SMALL SCRAP CUT FROM A SINGLE NUMBER OF THE "SUN!" HOW VEXATIOUS! HOW PROVOKING! ON THE OTHER HAND, THINK OF THE POOR, TIMID, BREATHLESS, FLYING CHILD OF FIFTEEN! FIVE HUNDRED DOLLARS REWARD! OH, FOR SUCCOR! TO WHOM IN ALL THIS WIDE LAND OF FREEDOM SHALL SHE FLEE AND FIND SAFETY? ALAS!—ALAS!—THE LAW POINTS TO NO ONE! IS SHE STILL RUNNING WITH BLEEDING FEET?* OR HIDES SHE IN SOME COLD CAVE, TO REST AND

---

* At the time this letter was written, she was then under Mr. B.'s protection in Washington, and had to be so kept for six weeks. His question, therefore, "is she still running with bleeding feet," etc., was simply a precautionary step to blind any who might perchance investigate the matter.

STARVE? "$500 REWARD." YOURS, FOR THE WEAK AND
THE POOR. PERISH THE REWARD. J.B.

Having thus succeeded in getting possession of, and secreting
this fleeing child of fifteen, as best they could, in Washington, all
concerned were compelled to "possess their souls in patience,"
until the storm had passed. Meanwhile, the "child of fifteen" was
christened "Joe Wright," and dressed in male attire to prepare for
traveling as a lad. As no opportunity had hitherto presented itself,
whereby to prepare the "package" for shipment, from Washington,
neither the "powder boy" nor Dr. T.* was prepared to attend to the
removal, at this critical moment. The emergency of the case, however, cried loudly for aid. The other professional gentleman (Dr. H.),
was now appealed to, but his engagements in the college forbade his
absence before about Thanksgiving day, which was then six weeks
off. This fact was communicated to Washington, and it being the
only resource left, the time named was necessarily acquiesced in. In
the interim, "Joe" was to perfect herself in the art of wearing pantaloons, and all other male rig. Soon the days and weeks slid by, although at first the time for waiting seemed long, when, according to
promise, Dr. H. was in Washington, with his horse and buggy prepared for duty. The impressions made by Dr. H., on William Penn's
mind, at his first interview, will doubtless be interesting to all concerned, as may be seen in the following letter:

WASHINGTON, D.C., November 26, 1855.

MY DEAR SIR:—A recent letter from my friend, probably has led
you to expect this from me. He was delighted to receive yours of
the 23d, stating that the boy was *all right*. He found the "Prof.
gentleman" a *perfect gentleman;* cool, quiet, thoughtful, and *perfectly
competent to execute his undertaking*. At the first three minutes of their
interview, he felt assured that all would be right. He, and all

---

* Dr. T. was one of the professional gentlemen alluded to above, who had expressed a willingness to act as an agent in the matter.

concerned, give you and that gentleman sincere thanks for what you have done. May the blessings of Him, who cares for the poor, be on your heads.

The especial object of this, is to inform you that there is a half dozen or so of packages here, *pressing for transportation;* twice or thrice that number are also pressing, but less so than the others. Their aggregate means will average, say, $10 each; besides these, we know of a few, say three or four, *able and smart,* but utterly destitute, and kept so purposely by their oppressors. For all these, we feel deeply interested; $10 each would not be enough for the "powder boy." Is there any fund from which a pittance could be spared to help these poor creatures? I don't doubt but that they would honestly repay a small loan as soon as they could earn it. I know full well, that if you begin with such cases, there is no boundary at which you can stop. For years, one half at least, of my friend's time here has been gratuitously given to cases of distress among this class. He never expects or desires to do less; he literally has the *poor always with him.* He knows that it is so with you also, therefore, he only states the case, being especially anxious for at least those to whom I have referred.

I think a small lot of hard coal might always be sold here *from the vessel* at a profit. Would not a like lot of Cumberland coal always sell in Philadelphia?

My friend would be very glad to see the powder boy here again, and if he brings coal, there are those here, who would try to help him sell.

Reply to your regular correspondent as usual. WM. PENN.

By the presence of the Dr., confidence having been reassured that all would be right, as well as by the "inner light," William Penn experienced a great sense of relief. Everything having been duly arranged, the doctor's horse and carriage stood waiting before the White House (William Penn preferred this place as a starting point, rather than before his own office door). It being understood that "Joe" was to act as coachman in passing out of Washington, at this moment he was called for, and in the most polite and natural manner, with the fleetness of a young deer, he jumped into the carriage, took the reins and whip, whilst the doctor and William Penn were cordially shaking hands and bidding adieu. This done, the order was given to Joe, "drive on." Joe bravely obeyed. The faithful horse trotted off willingly, and the doctor sat in his carriage as composed as though he had succeeded in procuring an honorable and lucrative office from the White House, and was returning home to tell his wife the good news. The doctor had some knowledge of the roads, also some acquaintances in Maryland, through which State he had to travel; therefore, after leaving the suburbs of Washington, the doctor took the reins in his own hands, as he felt that he was more experienced as a driver than his young coachman. He was also mindful of the fact, that, before reaching Pennsylvania, his faithful beast would need feeding several times, and that they consequently would be obliged to pass one or two nights at least in Maryland, either at a tavern or farm-house.

In reflecting upon the matter, it occurred to the doctor, that in earlier days, he had been quite intimately acquainted with a farmer and his family (who were slave-holders), in Maryland, and that he would about reach their house at the end of the first day's journey. He concluded that he could do no better than to renew his acquaintance with his old friends on this occasion. After a very successful day's travel, night came on, and the doctor was safely at the farmer's door with his carriage and waiter boy; the doctor was readily recognized by the farmer and his family, who seemed glad to see him; indeed, they made quite a "fuss" over him. As a matter of strategy, the doctor made quite a "fuss" over them in return; nevertheless, he did not fail to assume airs of importance, which were calculated to lead them to think that he had grown older and wiser than when they knew him in his younger days. In casually referring to the manner of his traveling, he alluded to the fact, that he was not very well, and as it had been a considerable length of time since he had been through that part of the country, he thought that the drive would do him good, and especially the sight of old familiar places and people. The farmer and his family felt themselves exceedingly honored by the visit from the distinguished doctor, and manifested a marked willingness to spare no pains to render his night's lodging in every way comfortable.

The Dr. being an educated and intelligent gentleman, well posted on other questions besides medicine, could freely talk about farming in all its branches, and "niggers" too, in an emergency, so the evening passed off pleasantly with the Dr. in the parlor, and "Joe" in the kitchen. The Dr., however, had given "Joe" precept upon precept, "here a little, and there a little," as to how he should act in the presence of master white people, or slave colored people, and thus he was prepared to act his part with due exactness. Before the evening grew late, the Dr., fearing some accident, intimated, that he was feeling a "little languid," and therefore thought that he had better "retire." Furthermore he added, that he was "liable to vertigo," when not quite well, and for this reason he must have his boy "Joe" sleep in the room with him. "Simply give him a bed quilt and he will fare well enough in one corner of the room," said the Dr. The proposal was readily acceded to, and carried into effect by the accommodating host. The Dr. was soon in bed, sleeping soundly, and "Joe," in his new coat and pants, wrapped up in the bed quilt, in a corner of the room quite comfortably.

The next morning the Dr. arose at as early an hour as was prudent for a gentleman of his position, and feeling refreshed, partook of a good breakfast, and was ready, with his boy, "Joe," to prosecute their journey. Face, eyes, hope, and steps, were set as flint, Pennsylvania-ward. What time the following day or night they crossed Mason and Dixon's line is not recorded on the Underground Rail Road books, but at four o'clock on Thanksgiving Day, the Dr. safely landed the "fleeing girl of fifteen" at the residence of the writer in Philadelphia. On delivering up his charge, the Dr. simply remarked to the writer's wife, "I wish to leave this young lad with you a short while, and I will call and see further about him." Without further explanation, he stepped into his carriage and hurried away, evidently anxious to report himself to his wife, in order to relieve her mind of a great weight of anxiety on his account. The writer, who happened to be absent from home when the Dr. called, returned soon afterwards. "The Dr. has been here" (he was the family physician), "and left this 'young lad,' and said, that he would call again and see about him," said Mrs. S. The "young lad" was sitting quite composedly in the dining-room, with his cap on. The writer turned to him and inquired, "I suppose you are the person that the Dr. went to Washington after, are you not?" "No," said "Joe." "Where are you from then?" was the next question. "From York, sir." "From York? Why then did the Dr. bring you here?" was the next query, "the Dr. went expressly to Washington after a young girl, who was to be brought away dressed up as a boy, and I took you to be the person." Without replying "the lad" arose and walked out of the house. The querist, somewhat mystified, followed him, and then when the two were alone, "the lad" said, "I am the one the Dr. went after." After congratulating her, the writer asked why she had said, that she was not from Washington, but from York. She explained, that the Dr. had strictly charged her not to own to any person, except the writer, that she was from Washington, but from York. As there were persons present (wife, hired girl, and a fugitive woman), when the questions were put to her, she felt that it would be a violation of her pledge to answer in the affirmative. Before this examination, neither of the individuals present for a moment entertained the slightest doubt but that she was a "lad," so well had she acted her part in every particular. She was dressed in a new suit, which fitted her quite nicely, and with her unusual amount of common sense, she appeared to be in no respect lacking. To send off a prize so rare and remarkable, as she was, without affording some of the stock-holders and managers of the Road the pleasure of seeing her, was not to be thought of. In addition to the Vigilance Committee, quite a number of persons were invited to see her, and were greatly astonished. Indeed it was difficult to realize, that she was not a boy, even after becoming acquainted with the facts in the case.

The following is an exact account of this case, as taken from the Underground Rail Road records:

"THANKSGIVING DAY, Nov., 1855.
        Arrived, Ann Maria Weems, *alias* 'Joe Wright,' *alias* 'Ellen Capron,' from Washington, through the aid of Dr. H. She is about fif-

teen years of age, bright mulatto, well grown, smart and good-looking. For the last three years, or about that length of time, she has been owned by Charles M. Price, a negro trader, of Rockville, Maryland. Mr. P. was given to 'intemperance,' to a very great extent, and gross 'profanity.' He buys and sells many slaves in the course of the year. 'His wife is cross and peevish.' She used to take great pleasure in 'torturing' one 'little slave boy.' He was the son of his master (and was owned by him); this was the chief cause of the mistress' spite."

Ann Maria had always desired her freedom from childhood, and although not thirteen, when first advised to escape, she received the suggestion without hesitation, and ever after that time waited almost daily, for more than two years, the chance to flee. Her friends were, of course, to aid her, and make arrangements for her escape. Her owner, fearing that she might escape, for a long time compelled her to sleep in the chamber with "her master and mistress;" indeed she was so kept until about three weeks before she fled. She left her parents living in Washington. Three of her brothers had been sold South from their parents. Her mother had been purchased for $1,000, and one of her sisters for $1,600 for freedom. Before Ann Maria was thirteen years of age $700 was offered for her by a friend, who desired to procure her freedom, but the offer was promptly refused, as were succeeding ones repeatedly made. The only chance of procuring her freedom, depended upon getting her away on the Underground Rail Road. She was neatly attired in male habiliments, and in that manner came all the way from Washington. After passing two or three days with her new friends in Philadelphia, she was sent on (in male attire) to Lewis Tappan, of New York, who had likewise been deeply interested in her case from the beginning, and who held himself ready, as was understood, to cash a draft for three hundred dollars to compensate the man who might risk his own liberty in bringing her on from Washington. After having arrived safely in New York, she found a home and kind friends in the family of the Rev. A.N. Freeman, and received quite an ovation characteristic of an Underground Rail Road.

After having received many tokens of esteem and kindness from the friends of the slave in New York and Brooklyn, she was carefully forwarded on to Canada, to be educated at the "Buxton Settlement."

An interesting letter, however, from the mother of Ann Maria, conveying the intelligence of her late great struggle and anxiety in laboring to free her last child from Slavery is too important to be omitted, and hence is inserted in connection with this narrative.

LETTER FROM THE MOTHER.

WASHINGTON, D.C., September 19th, 1857.

WM. STILL, ESQ., Philadelphia, Pa. SIR:—I have just sent for my son Augustus, in Alabama. I have sent eleven hundred dollars which pays for his body and some thirty dollars to pay his fare to Washington. I borrowed one hundred and eighty dollars to make out the eleven hundred dollars. I was not very successful in Syracuse. I collected only twelve dollars, and in Rochester only two dollars. I did not know that the season was so unpropitious. The wealthy had all gone to the springs. They must have returned by this time. I hope you will exert yourself and help me get a part of the money I owe, at least. I am obliged to pay it by the 12th of next month. I was unwell when I returned through Philadelphia, or I should have called. I had been from home five weeks.

My son Augustus is the last of the family in Slavery. I feel rejoiced that he is soon to be free and with me, and of course feel the greatest solicitude about raising the one hundred and eighty dollars I have borrowed of a kind friend, or who has borrowed it for me at bank. I hope and pray you will help me as far as possible. Tell Mr. Douglass to remember me, and if he can, to interest his friends for me.

You will recollect that five hundred dollars of our money was taken to buy the sister of Henry H. Garnett's wife. Had I been able to command this I should not be necessitated to ask the favors and indulgences I do.

I am expecting daily the return of Augustus, and may Heaven grant him a safe deliverance and smile propitiously upon you and all kind friends who have aided in his return to me.

Be pleased to remember me to friends, and accept yourself the blessing and prayers of your dear friend,

EARRO WEEMS.

P.S. Direct your letter to E.L. Stevens, in Duff Green's Row,
Capitol Hill, Washington, D.C.
E.W.

That William Penn who worked so faithfully for two years for the deliverance of Ann Maria may not appear to have been devoting all his time and sympathy towards this single object it seems expedient that two or three additional letters, proposing certain grand Underground Rail Road plans, should have a place here. For this purpose, therefore, the following letters are subjoined.

LETTERS FROM WILLIAM PENN.

WASHINGTON, D.C., Oct. 3, 1854.

DEAR SIR:—I address you to-day chiefly at the suggestion of the Lady who will hand you my letter, and who is a resident of your city.

After stating to you, that the case about which I have previously written, remains just as it was when I wrote last—full of difficulty—I thought I would call your attention to another enterprise; it is this: to find a man with a large heart for doing good to the oppressed, who will come to Washington to live, and who will *walk out to Penn'a., or a part of the way there, once or twice a week.* He will find parties who will *pay him for doing so.* Parties of say, two, three, five or so, who will pay him *at least* $5 each, for the privilege of following him, but *will never speak to him;* but will keep just in sight of him and obey any sign he may give; say, he takes off his hat and scratches his head as a sign for them to go to some barn or wood to rest, &c. No living being shall be found to say he ever spoke to them. A white man would be best, and then even parties led out by him could not, if they would, testify to any *understanding* or anything else against a white man. I think he might make a good living at it. Can it not be done?

If one or two safe stopping-places could be found on the way—such as a barn or shed, they could walk quite safely all night and then sleep all day—about two, or *easily* three nights would convey them to a place of safety. The traveler might be a peddler or huckster, with an old horse and cart, and bring us in eggs and butter if he pleases. Let him once plan out his route, and he might then take ten or a dozen at a time, and they are often able and willing to pay $10 a piece.

I have a hard case now on hand; a brother and sister 23 to 25 years old, whose mother lives in your city. They are cruelly treated; they want to go, they *ought* to go; but they are utterly destitute. Can nothing be done for such cases? If you can think of anything let me know it. I suppose you know me?

WASHINGTON, D.C., April 3, 1856.

DEAR SIR:—I sent you the recent law of Virginia, under which all vessels are to be searched for fugitives within the waters of that State.

It was long ago suggested by a sagacious friend, that the "powder boy" might find a better port in the Chesapeake bay, or in the Patuxent river to communicate with this vicinity, than by entering the Potomac river, even were there no such law.

Suppose he opens a trade with some place south-west of Annapolis, 25 or 30 miles from here, or less. He might carry wood, oysters, &c., and all his customers from this vicinity might travel in *that direction* without any of the suspicions that might attend their journeyings *towards this city*. In this way, doubtless, a good business might be carried on without interruption or competition, and provided the plan was conducted without affecting the inhabitants along that shore, no suspicion would arise as to the manner or magnitude of his business operations. How does this strike you? What does the "powder boy" think of it?

I heretofore intimated a *pressing necessity* on the part of several females—they are variously situated—two have children, say a couple each; some have none—of the latter, one can raise $50, another, say 30 or 40 dollars—another who was gazetted last August (a copy sent you), can raise, through her friends, 20 or 30 dollars, &c., &c. None of these can walk so far or so fast as scores of *men* that are constantly leaving. I cannot shake off my anxiety for these poor creatures. Can you think of anything for any of these? Address your other correspondent in answer to this at your leisure. Yours,

WM. PENN.

P.S.—April 3d. Since writing the above, I have received yours of 31st. I am rejoiced to hear that business is so successful and prosperous—may it continue till *the article* shall cease to be merchandize.

I spoke in my last letter of the departure of a "few friends." I have since heard of their good health in Penn'a. Probably you may have seen them.

In reference to the expedition of which you think you can "hold out some little encouragement," I will barely remark, that I shall be glad, if it is undertaken, to have all the notice of the *time and manner* that is possible, so as to make ready.

A friend of mine says, anthracite coal will always pay here from Philadelphia, and thinks a small vessel might run often—that she never would be searched in the Potomac, unless she went outside.

You advise caution towards Mr. P. I am precisely of your opinion about him, that he is a "queer stick," and while I advised him carefully in reference to his own undertakings, I took no counsel of him concerning mine. Yours,

W.P.

WASHINGTON, D.C., April 23d, 1856.

DEAR SIR:—I have to thank you for your last two encouraging letters of 31st of March and 7th April. I have seen nothing in the papers to interest you, and having bad health and a press of other engagements, I have neglected to write you.

Enclosed is a list of persons referred to in my last letter, all most anxious to travel—all meritorious. In some of these I feel an especial interest for what they have done to help others in distress.

I suggest for yours and the "powder boy's" consideration the following plan: that he shall take in coal for Washington and come directly here—sell his coal and go to Georgetown for freight, and *wait* for it. If any fancy articles are sent on board, *I understand he has a place* to put them in, and *if he has* I suggest that he lies still, still waiting for freight till the first anxiety is over. Vessels that have *just left* are the ones that will be inquired after, and perhaps chased. If he lays still a day or two all suspicion will be prevented. If there shall be occasion to refer to any of them hereafter, it may be by their numbers in the list.

The family—5 to 11—will be missed and inquired after soon and urgently; 12 and 13 will also be soon missed, but *none of the others*.

If all this can be done, some little time or notice must be had to get them all ready. They tell me they can pay the sums marked to their names. The aggregate is small, but as I told you, they are poor. Let me hear from you when convenient.

Truly Yours, WM. PENN.

1. A woman, may be 40 years old $40.00
2. A woman, may be 40 years old, with 3 children, say 4, 6, and 8* 15.00
3. A sister of the above, younger............................... 10.00

---

* The children might be left behind.

4. A very genteel mulatto girl about 22. . . . . 25.00
5. A woman, say 45 . . . . .50.00*
6. A daughter, 18. . . . .
7. A son, 16 . . . .
8. A son, 14. . . . .
9. A daughter . . . .
10. A son, say 22 . . . .
11. A man, the Uncle, 40. . . . .
12. A very genteel mulatto girl, say 23 . . . . 25.00
13. A very genteel mulatto girl, say 24 . . . . 25.00

* For 5 through 11, "these are all one family, either of them leaving alone, they think, would cause the balance to be sold."

CHARLES GILBERT.

Fleeing from Davis a Negro Trader, Secreted Under a Hotel, up a Tree, Under a Floor, in a Thicket, on a Steamer.

In 1854 Charles was owned in the city of Richmond by Benjamin Davis, a notorious negro trader. Charles was quite a "likely-looking article," not too black or too white, but rather of a nice "ginger-bread color." Davis was of opinion that this "article" must bring him a tip-top price. For two or three months the trader advertised Charles for sale in the papers, but for some reason or other Charles did not command the high price demanded.

While Davis was thus daily trying to sell Charles, Charles was contemplating how he might escape. Being uncommonly shrewd he learned something about a captain of a schooner from Boston, and determined to approach him with regard to securing a passage. The captain manifested a disposition to accommodate him for the sum of ten dollars, provided Charles could manage to get to Old Point Comfort, there to embark. The Point was about one hundred and sixty miles distant from Richmond.

A man of ordinary nerve would have declined this condition un-hesitatingly. On the other hand it was not Charles' intention to let any offer slide; indeed he felt that he must make an effort, if he failed. He could not see how his lot could be made more miserable by attempting to flee. In full view of all the consequences he ventured to take the hazardous step, and to his great satisfaction he reached Old Point Comfort safely. In that locality he was well known, unfortunately too well known, for he had been raised partly there, and, at the same time, many of his relatives and acquaintances were still living there. These facts were evidently well known to the trader, who unquestionably had snares set in order to entrap Charles should he seek shelter among his relatives, a reasonable supposition. Charles had scarcely reached his old home before he was apprised of the fact that the hunters and watch dogs of Slavery were eagerly watching for him. Even his nearest relatives, through fear of consequences had to hide their faces as it were from him. None dare offer him a night's lodging, scarcely a cup of water, lest such an act might be discovered by the hunters, whose fiendish hearts would have found pleasure in meting out the most dire punishments to those guilty of thus violating the laws of Slavery. The prospect, if not utterly hopeless, was decidedly discouraging. The way to Boston was entirely closed. A "reward of $200" was advertised for his capture. For the first week after arriving at Old Point he entrusted himself to a young friend by the name of E.S. The fear of the pursuers drove him from his hiding-place at the expiration of the week. Thence he sought shelter neither with kinfolks, Christians, nor infidels, but in this hour of his calamity he made up his mind that he would try living under a large hotel for a while. Having watched his opportunity, he managed to reach Higee hotel, a very large house without a cellar, erected on pillars three or four feet above the ground. One place alone, near the cistern, presented some chance for a hiding-place, sufficient to satisfy him quite well under the circumstances. This dark and gloomy spot he at once willingly occupied rather than return to Slavery. In this refuge he remained four weeks. Of course he could not live without food; but to communicate with man or woman would inevitably subject him to danger. Charles' experience in the neighborhood of his old home left no ground for him to hope that he would be likely to find friendly aid anywhere under the shadow of Slavery. In consequence of these fears he received his food from the "slop tub," securing this diet in the darkness of night after all was still and quiet around the hotel. To use his own language, the meals thus obtained were often "sweet" to his taste.

One evening, however, he was not a little alarmed by the approach of an Irish boy who came under the hotel to hunt chickens. While prowling around in the darkness he appeared to be making his way unconsciously to the very spot where Charles was reposing. How to meet the danger was to Charles' mind at first very puzzling, there was no time now to plan. As quick as thought he feigned the bark of a savage dog accompanied with a furious growl and snarl which he was confident would frighten the boy half out of his senses, and cause him to depart quickly from his private apartment. The trick succeeded admirably, and the emergency was satisfactorily met, so far as the boy was concerned, but the boy's father hearing the attack of the dog, swore that he would kill him. Charles was a silent listener to the threat, and he saw that he could no longer remain in safety in his present quarter. So that night he took his departure for Bay Shore; here he decided to pass a day in the woods, but the privacy of this place was not altogether satisfactory to Charles' mind; but where to find a more secure retreat he could not,—dared not venture to ascertain that day. It occurred to him, however, that he would be much safer up a tree than hid in the bushes and undergrowth. He therefore climbed up a large acorn tree and there passed an entire day in deep meditation. No gleam of hope appeared, yet he would not suffer himself to think of returning to bondage. In this dilemma he remembered a poor washerwoman named Isabella, a slave who had charge of a wash-house. With her he resolved to seek succor. Leaving the woods he proceeded to the wash-house and was kindly received by Isabella, but what to do with him or how to afford him any protection she could see no way whatever. The schooling which Charles had been receiving a number of weeks in connection with the most fearful looking-for of the threatened wrath of the trader made it much easier for him than for her to see how he could be provided for. A room and comforts he was not accustomed to. Of course he could not expect such comforts now. Like many another escaping from the relentless tyrant, Charles could contrive methods which to his venturesome mind would afford hope, however desperate they might appear to others. He thought that he might be safe under the floor. To Isabella the idea was new, but her sympathies were strongly with Charles, and she readily consented to accommodate him under the floor of the wash-house. Isabella and a friend of Charles, by the name of John Thomas, were the only persons who were cognizant of this arrangement. The kindness of these friends, manifested by their willingness to do anything in their power to add to the comfort of Charles, was proof to him that his efforts and sufferings had not been altogether in vain. He remained under the floor two weeks, accessible to kind voices and friendly ministrations. At the end of this time his repose was again sorely disturbed by reports from without that suspicion had been awakened towards the wash-house. How this happened neither Charles nor his friends could conjecture. But the arrival of six officers whom he could hear talking very plainly in the house, whose errand was actually to search for him, convinced him that he had never for a single moment been in greater danger. The officers not only searched the house, but they offered his friend John Thomas $25 if he would only put them on Charles' track. John professed to know nothing; Isabella was equally ignorant. Discouraged with their efforts on this occasion, the officers gave up the hunt and left the house. Charles, however, had had enough of the floor accommodations. He left that night and returned to his old quarters under the hotel. Here he stayed one week, at the expiration of which time the need of fresh air was so imperative, that he resolved to go out at night to Allen's cottage and spend a day in the woods. He had knowledge of a place where the undergrowth and bushes were almost impenetrable. To rest and refresh himself in this thicket he felt would be a great comfort to him. Without serious difficulty he reached the thicket, and while pondering over the all-absorbing matter as to how he should ever manage to make his escape, an old man approached. Now while Charles had no reason to think that he was sought by the old intruder, his very near approach admonished him that it would neither be safe nor agreeable to allow him to come nearer. Charles remembering that his trick of playing the dog, when previously in danger under the hotel, had served a good end, thought that it would work well in the thicket. So he again tried his power at growling and barking hideously for a moment or two, which at once caused the man to turn his course. Charles could hear him distinctly retreating, and at the same time cursing the dog. The owner of the place had the reputation of keeping "bad dogs," so the old man poured out a dreadful threat against "Stephens' dogs," and was soon out of the reach of the one in the thicket.

Notwithstanding his success in frightening off the old man, CHARLES felt that the thicket was by no means a safe place for him. He concluded to make another change. This time he sought a marsh; two hours' stay there was sufficient to satisfy him, that that too was no place to tarry in, even for a single night. He, therefore, left immediately. A third time, he returned to the hotel, where he remained only two days. His appeals had at last reached the heart of his mother—she could no longer bear to see him struggling, and suffering, and not render him aid, whatever the consequences might be. If she at first feared to lend him a helping hand, she now resolutely worked with a view of saving money to succor him. Here the prospect began to brighten.

A passage was secured for him on a steamer bound for Philadelphia. One more day, and night must elapse, ere he could be received on board. The joyful anticipations which now filled his breast left no room for fear; indeed, he could scarcely contain himself; he was drunk with joy. In this state of mind he concluded that nothing would afford him more pleasure before leaving, than to spend his last hours at the wash house, "under the floor." To this place he went with no fear of hunters before his eyes. Charles had scarcely been three hours in this place, however, before three officers came in search of him. Two of them talked with Isabella, asked her about her "boarders," etc.; in the meanwhile, one of them uninvited, made his way up stairs. It so happened, that Charles was in this very portion of the house. His case now seemed more hopeless than ever. The officer up stairs was separated from him simply by a thin curtain. Women's garments hung all around. Instead of fainting or surrendering, in the twinkling of an eye, Charles' inventive intellect, led him to enrobe himself in female attire. Here, to use his own language, a "thousand thoughts" rushed into his mind in a minute. The next instant he was going down stairs in the presence of the officers, his old calico dress, bonnet and rig, attracting no further attention than simply to elicit the following simple questions: "Whose gal are you?" "Mr. Cockling's, sir." "What is your name?"

"Delie, sir." "Go on then!" said one of the officers, and on Charles went to avail himself of the passage on the steamer which his mother had procured for him for the sum of thirty dollars.

In due time, he succeeded in getting on the steamer, but he soon learned, that her course was not direct to Philadelphia, but that some stay would be made in Norfolk, Va. Although disappointed, yet this being a step in the right direction, he made up his mind to be patient. He was delayed in Norfolk four weeks. From the time Charles first escaped, his owner (Davis the negro trader), had kept a standing reward of $550 advertised for his recovery. This showed that Davis was willing to risk heavy expenses for Charles as well as gave evidence that he believed him still secreted either about Richmond, Petersburg, or Old Point Comfort. In this belief he was not far from being correct, for Charles spent most of his time in either of these three places, from the day of his escape until the day that he finally embarked. At last, the long looked-for hour arrived to start for Philadelphia.

He was to leave his mother, with no hope of ever seeing her again, but she had purchased herself and was called free. Her name was Margaret Johnson. Three brothers likewise were ever in his thoughts, (in chains), "Henry," "Bill," and "Sam," (half brothers). But after all the hope of freedom outweighed every other consideration, and he was prepared to give up all for liberty. To die rather than remain a slave was his resolve.

Charles arrived per steamer, from Norfolk, on the 11th day of November, 1854. The Richmond papers bear witness to the fact, that Benjamin Davis advertised Charles Gilbert, for months prior to this date, as has been stated in this narrative. As to the correctness of the story, all that the writer has to say is, that he took it down from the lips of Charles, hurriedly, directly after his arrival, with no thought of magnifying a single incident. On the contrary, much that was of interest in the story had to be omitted. Instead of being overdrawn, not half of the particulars were recorded. Had the idea then been entertained, that the narrative of this young slave-warrior was to be brought to light in the manner and time that it now is, a far more thrilling account of his adventures might have been written. Other colored men who knew both Davis and Charles, as well as one man ordinarily knows another, rejoiced at seeing Charles in Philadelphia, and they listened with perfect faith to his story. So marvellous were the incidents of his escape, that his sufferings in Slavery, previous to his heroic struggles to throw off the yoke, were among the facts omitted from the records. While this may be regretted it is, nevertheless, gratifying on the whole to have so good an account of him as was preserved. It is needless to say, that the Committee took especial pleasure in aiding him, and listening to so remarkable a story narrated so intelligently by one who had been a slave.

SALT-WATER FUGITIVE.

This was an exceptional case, as this passenger did not reach the Vigilance Committee of Philadelphia, yet to exclude him on this account, would be doing an injustice to history.

The facts in his case were incontestably established in the Philadelphia Register in April, 1854, from which the following thrilling account is taken:

The steamship, Keystone State, which arrived at this port on Saturday morning, had just entered Delaware Bay, when a man was discovered secreted outside of the vessel and under the guards. When brought from his hiding-place, he was found to be a Fugitive Slave, who had secreted himself there before the vessel left Savannah on Wednesday, and had remained in that place from the time of starting!

His position was such, that the water swept over and around him almost constantly. He had some bread in his pocket, which he had intended for subsistence until he could reach a land of liberty. It was saturated with sea-water and dissolved to a pulp.

When our readers remember the high winds of Friday, and the sudden change to cold during that night, and the fact that the fugitive had remained in that situation for three days and nights, we think it will be conceded that he fully earned his liberty, and that the "institution," which was so intolerable that he was willing to run the risk of almost certain death to escape from it had no very great attractions for him. But the poor man was doomed to disappointment. The captain ordered the vessel to put into Newcastle, where, the fugitive, hardly able to stand, was taken on shore and incarcerated, and where he now awaits the order of his owner in Savannah. The following additional particulars are from the same paper of the 21st.

The Keystone State case.—Our article yesterday morning brought us several letters of inquiry and offers of contributions to aid in the purchase from his master of the unfortunate inmate of Newcastle jail. In answer to the former, we would say, that the steamer Keystone State, left Savannah, at 9 A.M., last Wednesday. It was about the same hour next morning that the men engaged in heaving lead, heard a voice from under the guards imploring help. A rope was procured, and the man relieved from his dangerous and suffering situation. He was well cared for immediately; a suit of dry clothes was furnished him, and he was given his share of the contents of the boat pantry. On arriving at Newcastle, the captain had him placed in jail, for the purpose, as we are informed, of taking him back to Savannah.

To those who have offered contributions so liberally, we answer, that the prospect is, that only a small amount will be needed—enough to fee a lawyer to sue out a writ of habeas corpus. The salt water fugitive claims to be a free man, and a native of Philadelphia. He gives his name as Edward Davis, and says that he formerly lived at No. 5 Steel's court, that he was a pupil in Bird's school, on Sixth St. above Lombard, and that he has a sister living at Mr. Diamond's, a distiller, on South St. We are not informed why he was in Georgia, from which he took such an extraordinary means to effect his escape. If the above assertion be true, we apprehend little trouble in restoring the man to his former home. The claim of the captain to take him back to Savannah, will not be listened to for a moment by any court. The only claim the owners of the "Keystone State" or the captain can have on salt water Davis, is for half passenger fare; he came half the way as a fish. A gentleman who came from Wilmington yesterday, assures us that the case is in good hands at Newcastle.

FULL PARTICULARS OF THE ABDUCTION, ENSLAVING AND ESCAPE OF DAVIS. ATTEMPT TO SEDUCE HIM TO SLAVERY AGAIN.

The case of the colored man Davis, who made such a bold stroke to regain his liberty, by periling his life on board the steamer Keystone

State, has excited very general attention. He has given a detailed account of his abduction and sale as a slave in the State of Maryland and Georgia, and some of his adventures up to the time of reaching Delaware. His own story is substantially as follows:

He left Philadelphia on the 15th of September, 1851, and went to Harrisburg, intending to go to Hollidaysburg; took a canal boat for Havre de Grace, where he arrived next day. There he hired on board the schooner Thomas and Edward (oyster boat), of Baltimore. Went from Havre de Grace to St. Michael's, for oysters, thence to Baltimore, and thence to Havre de Grace again.

He then hired to a Mr. Sullivan, who kept a grocery store, to do jobs. While there, a constable, named Smith, took him before a magistrate named Graham, who fined him fifteen or twenty dollars for violating the law in relation to free negroes coming into the State. This fine he was not able to pay, and Smith took him to Bell Air prison. Sheriff Gaw wrote to Mr. Maitland in Philadelphia, to whom he referred, and received an answer that Mr. Maitland was dead and none of the family knew him. He remained in that prison nearly two months. He then had a trial in court before a Judge Grier (most unfortunate name), who sentenced him to be sold to pay his fine and expenses, amounting to fifty dollars.

After a few days and *without being offered at public sale*, he was taken out of jail at two o'clock in the morning and carried to Campbell's slave pen, in Baltimore, where he remained several months. While there, he was employed to cook for some fifty or sixty slaves, being told that he was working out his fine and jail fees. After being there about six months, he was taken out of prison, handcuffed by one Winters, who took him and two or three others to Washington and thence to Charleston, S.C. Here Winters left them, and they were taken by steamboat to Savannah. While on board the boat, he learned that himself and the other two had been sold to Mr. William Dean, of Macon, where he stayed two days, and was taken from that place to the East Valley Railroad.

Subsequently he was sent to work on the Possum Tail Railroad. Here he was worked so hard, that in one month he lost his health. The other two men taken on with him, failed before he did. He was then sent to Macon, and thence to the cotton plantation again.

During the time he worked on the railroad he had allowed him for food, one peck of corn meal, four pounds of bacon, and one quart of molasses per week. He cooked it himself at night, for the next day's use. He worked at packing cotton for four or five months, and in the middle of November, 1852, was sent back to the railroad, where he was again set to wheeling.

He worked at "task work" two months, being obliged to wheel *sixteen* square yards per day. At the end of two months he broke down again, and was sick. They tried one month to cure him, but did not succeed. In July, 1853, he was taken to an infirmary in Macon. Dr. Nottinghan and Dr. Harris, of that institution, both stated that his was the worst case of the kind they ever had. He remained at the infirmary two months and partially recovered. He told the story of his wrongs to these physicians, who tried to buy him. One of his legs was drawn up so that he could not walk well, and they offered four hundred dollars for him, which his master refused. The doctors wanted him to attend their patients, (mostly slaves). While in Georgia he was frequently asked where he came from, being found more intelligent than the common run of slaves.

On the 12th of March he ran away from Macon and went to Savannah. There he hid in a stable until Tuesday afternoon at six o'clock, when he secreted himself on board the Keystone State. At 9 o'clock the next morning the Keystone State left with Davis secreted, as we have before stated. With his imprisonment in Newcastle, after being pronounced free, our readers are already familiar. We subjoin the documents on which he was discharged from his imprisonment in Newcastle, and his subsequent re-committal on the oath of Capt. Hardie.

COPY OF FIRST ORDER OF COMMITMENT.

New Castle county, ss., State of Delaware.—To Wm. R. Lynam, Sheriff of said county.——Davis (Negro) is delivered to your custody for further examination and hearing for traveling without a pass, and supposed to be held a Slave to some person in the State of Georgia.

[Seal]. Witness the hand and seal of John Bradford, one of the Justices of the Peace for the county of Newcastle, the 17th day of March, 1854.

JOHN BRADFORD, J.P.

COPY OF DISCHARGE.

To Wm. R. Lynam, Sheriff of Newcastle county: You will discharge——Davis from your custody, satisfactory proof having been made before me that he is a free man. JOHN BRADFORD, J.P.

Witnesses—Joanna Diamond, John H. Brady, Martha C. Maguire.

COPY OF ORDER OF RE-COMMITMENT.

New Castle county, ss., the State of Delaware to Wm. R. Lynam, and to the Sheriff or keeper of the Common Jail of said county, Whereas——Davis hath this day been brought before me, the subscriber, one of the Justices of the Peace, in and for the said county, charged upon the oath of Robert Hardie with being a runaway slave, and also as a suspicious person, traveling without a pass, these are therefore to command you, the said Wm. R. Lynam, forthwith to convey and deliver into the custody of the said Sheriff, or keeper of the said jail, the body of the said Davis, and you the said Sheriff or receiver of the body of the said Davis into your custody in the said jail, and him there safely keep until he be thence delivered by due course of the law.

Given under my hand and seal at New Castle this 21st day of March, A.D., 1854.

JOHN BRADFORD, J.P.

On the fourth of April, the Marshal of Macon called at the jail in Newcastle, and demanded him as a fugitive slave, but the Sheriff refused to give him up until a fair hearing could be had according to the laws of the State of Delaware. The Marshal has returned to Georgia, and will probably bring the claimant on the next trip of the Keystone State. The authorities of Delaware manifest no disposition to deliver up a man whose freedom has been so clearly proved; but every effort will be made to reduce him again to slavery by the man who claims him, in which, it seems, he has the hearty co-operation of Capt. Hardie. A trial will be had before U.S. Commissioner Guthrie, and we have every reason to suppose it will be a fair one. The friends of right and justice should remember that such a trial will be attended with considerable expense, and that the imprisoned man has been too long deprived of his liberty to have money to pay for his own defence.

SAMUEL GREEN ALIAS WESLEY KINNARD,
AUGUST 28TH, 1854.

Ten Years in the Penitentiary for Having a Copy of Uncle Tom's Cabin.

The passenger answering to the above name, left Indian Creek, Chester Co., Md., where he had been held to service or labor, by Dr. James Muse. One week had elapsed from the time he set out until his arrival in Philadelphia. Although he had never enjoyed school privileges of any kind, yet he was not devoid of intelligence. He had profited by his daily experience as a slave, and withal, had managed to learn to read and write a little, despite law and usage to the contrary. Sam was about twenty-five years of age and by trade, a blacksmith. Before running away, his general character for sobriety, industry, and religion, had evidently been considered good, but in coveting his freedom and running away to obtain it, he had sunk far below the utmost limit of forgiveness or mercy in the estimation of the slave-holders of Indian Creek.

During his intercourse with the Vigilance Committee, while rejoicing over his triumphant flight, he gave, with no appearance of excitement, but calmly, and in a common-sense like manner, a brief description of his master, which was entered on the record book substantially as follows: "Dr. James Muse is thought by the servants to be the worst man in Maryland, inflicting whipping and all manner of cruelties upon the servants."

While Sam gave reasons for this sweeping charge, which left no room for doubt, on the part of the Committee, of his sincerity and good judgment, it was not deemed necessary to make a note of more of the doctor's character than seemed actually needed, in order to show why "Sam" had taken passage on the Underground Rail Road. For several years, "Sam" was hired out by the doctor at blacksmithing; in this situation, daily wearing the yoke of unrequited labor, through the kindness of Harriet Tubman (sometimes called "Moses"), the light of the Underground Rail Road and Canada suddenly illuminated his mind. It was new to him, but he was quite too intelligent and liberty-loving, not to heed the valuable information which this sister of humanity imparted. Thenceforth he was in love with Canada, and likewise a decided admirer of the U.R. Road. Harriet was herself, a shrewd and fearless agent, and well understood the entire route from that part of the country to Canada. The spring previous, she had paid a visit to the very neighborhood in which "Sam" lived, expressly to lead her own brothers out of "Egypt." She succeeded. To "Sam" this was cheering and glorious news, and he made up his mind, that before a great while, Indian Creek should have one less slave and that Canada should have one more citizen. Faithfully did he watch an opportunity to carry out his resolution. In due time a good Providence opened the way, and to "Sam's" satisfaction he reached Philadelphia, having encountered no peculiar difficulties. The Committee, perceiving that he was smart, active, and promising, encouraged his undertaking, and having given him friendly advice, aided him in the usual manner. Letters of introduction were given him, and he was duly forwarded on his way. He had left his father, mother, and one sister behind. Samuel and Catharine were the names of his parents. Thus far, his escape would seem not to affect his parents, nor was it apparent that there was any other cause why the owner should revenge himself upon them.

The father was an old local preacher in the Methodist Church— much esteemed as an inoffensive, industrious man; earning his bread by the sweat of his brow, and contriving to move along in the narrow road allotted colored people bond or free, without exciting a spirit of ill will in the pro-slavery power of his community. But the rancor awakened in the breast of slave-holders in consequence of the high-handed step the son had taken, brought the father under suspicion and hate. Under the circumstances, the eye of Slavery could do nothing more than watch for an occasion to pounce upon him. It was not long before the desired opportunity presented itself. Moved by parental affection, the old man concluded to pay a visit to his boy, to see how he was faring in a distant land, and among strangers. This resolution he quietly carried into effect. He found his son in Canada, doing well; industrious; a man of sobriety, and following his father's footsteps religiously. That the old man's heart was delighted with what his eyes saw and his ears heard in Canada, none can doubt. But in the simplicity of his imagination, he never dreamed that this visit was to be made the means of his destruction. During the best portion of his days he had faithfully worn the badge of Slavery, had afterwards purchased his freedom, and thus become a free man. He innocently conceived the idea that he was doing no harm in availing himself not only of his God-given rights, but of the rights that he had also purchased by the hard toil of his own hands. But the enemy was lurking in ambush for him—thirsting for his blood. To his utter consternation, not long after his return from his visit to his son "a party of gentlemen from the New Market district, went at night to Green's house and made search, whereupon was found a copy of Uncle Tom's Cabin, etc." This was enough—the hour had come, wherein to wreak vengeance upon poor Green. The course pursued and the result, may be seen in the following statement taken from the Cambridge (Md.), "Democrat," of April 29th, 1857, and communicated by the writer to the "Provincial Freeman."

SAM GREEN.

The case of the State against Sam Green (free negro) indicted for having in his possession, papers, pamphlets and pictorial representations, having a tendency to create discontent, etc., among the people of color in the State, was tried before the court on Friday last.

This case was of the utmost importance, and has created in the public mind a great deal of interest—it being the first case of the kind ever having occurred in our country.

It appeared, in evidence, that this Green has a son in Canada, to whom Green made a visit last summer. Since his return to this county, suspicion has fastened upon him, as giving aid and assisting slaves who have since absconded and reached Canada, and several weeks ago, a party of gentlemen from New Market district, went at night, to Green's house and made search, whereupon was found a volume of "Uncle Tom's Cabin," a map of Canada, several schedules of routes to the North, and a letter from his son in Canada, detailing the pleasant trip he had, the number of friends he met with on the way, with plenty to eat, drink, etc., and concludes with a request to his father, that he shall tell certain other slaves, naming them, to come on, which slaves, it is well known, did leave shortly afterwards, and have reached Canada. The case was argued with great ability, the counsel on both sides displaying a great deal of ingenuity, learning and eloquence. The first indictment was for the having in possession the letter, map and route schedules.

Notwithstanding the mass of evidence given, to show the prisoner's guilt, in unlawfully having in his possession these documents, and the nine-tenths of the community in which he lived, believed that he had a hand in the running away of slaves, it was the opinion of the court, that the law under which he was indicted, was not applicable to the case, and that he must, accordingly, render a verdict of not guilty.

He was immediately arraigned upon another indictment, for having in possession "Uncle Tom's Cabin," and tried; in this case the court has not yet rendered a verdict, but holds it under *curia* till after the Somerset county court. It is to be hoped, the court will find the evidence in this case sufficient to bring it within the scope of the law under which the prisoner is indicted (that of 1842, chap. 272), and that the prisoner may meet his due reward—be that what it may.

That there is something required to be done by our Legislators, for the protection of slave property, is evident from the variety of constructions put upon the statute in this case, and we trust, that at the next meeting of the Legislature there will be such amendments, as to make the law on this subject, perfectly clear and comprehensible to the understanding of every one.

In the language of the assistant counsel for the State, "Slavery must be protected or it must be abolished."

—

From the same sheet, of May 20th, the terrible doom of Samuel Green, is announced in the following words:

> In the case of the State against Sam Green, (free negro) who was tried at the April term of the Circuit Court of this county, for having in his possession abolition pamphlets, among which was "Uncle Tom's Cabin," has been found guilty by the court, and sentenced to the penitentiary for the term of ten years—until the 14th of May, 1867.

The son, a refugee in Canada, hearing the distressing news of his father's sad fate in the hands of the relentless "gentlemen," often wrote to know if there was any prospect of his deliverance. The subjoined letter is a fair sample of his correspondence:

SALFORD, 22, 1857.

Dear Sir I take my pen in hand to Request a faver of you if you can by any means without duin InJestus to your self or your Bisness to grant it as I Bleve you to be a man that would Sympathize in such a ones Condition as my self I Reseved a letter that Stats to me that my Fater has ben Betraed in the act of helping sum frend to Canada and the law has Convicted and Sentanced him to the Stats prison for 10 yeares his White Frands ofered 2 thousen Dollers to Redem him but they would not short three thousen. I am in Canada and it is a Dificult thing to get a letter to any of my Frands in Maryland so as to get prop per infermation abot it—if you can by any means get any in telligence from Baltimore City a bot this Event Plese do so and Rit word and all so all the inform mation that you think prop per as Regards the Evant and the best mathod to Redeme him and so Plese Rite soon as you can You will oblige your sir Frand and Drect your letter to Salford P. office C.W.

SAMUEL GREEN.

In this dark hour the friends of the Slave could do but little more than sympathize with this heart-stricken son and grey-headed father. The aged follower of the Rejected and Crucified had like

Him to bear the "reproach of many," and make his bed with the
wicked in the Penitentiary. Doubtless there were a few friends in his
neighborhood who sympathized with him, but they were powerless
to aid the old man. But thanks to a kind Providence, the great deliverance brought about during the Rebellion by which so many cap-
tives were freed, also unlocked Samuel Green's prison-doors and he
was allowed to go free. After his liberation from the Penitentiary, we
had from his own lips narrations of his years of suffering—of the
bitter cup, that he was compelled to drink, and of his being sustained by the Almighty Arm—but no notes were taken at the time,
consequently we have nothing more to add concerning him, save
quite a faithful likeness.

AN IRISH GIRL'S DEVOTION TO FREEDOM.

*In Love with a Slave—Gets Him off to Canada—Follows Him—
Marriage, &C.*

Having dwelt on the sad narratives of Samuel Green and his son
in the preceding chapter, it is quite a relief to be able to introduce a traveler whose story contains incidents less painful to
contemplate. From the record book the following brief account is
taken:

"April 27, 1855. John Hall arrived safely from Richmond, Va., per
schooner, (Captain B). One hundred dollars were paid for his passage." In Richmond he was owned by James Dunlap, a merchant. John
had been sold several times, in consequence of which, he had possessed very good opportunities of experiencing the effect of change
of owners. Then, too, the personal examination made before sale, and
the gratification afforded his master when he (John), brought a good
price—left no very pleasing impressions on his mind.

By one of his owners, named Burke, John alleged that he had
been "cruelly used." When quite young, both he and his sister, together with their mother, were sold by Burke. From that time he
had seen neither mother nor sister—they were sold separately. For
three or four years the desire to seek liberty had been fondly cherished, and nothing but the want of a favorable opportunity had de-
terred him from carrying out his designs. He considered himself
much "imposed upon" by his master, particularly as he was allowed
"no choice about living" as he "desired." This was indeed ill-
treatment as John viewed the matter. John may have wanted too
much. He was about thirty-five years of age, light complexion—
tall—rather handsome-looking, intelligent, and of good manners.
But notwithstanding these prepossessing features, John's owner valued him at only $1,000. If he had been a few shades darker and only

about half as intelligent as he was, he would have been worth at least $500 more. The idea of having had a white father, in many instances, depreciated the pecuniary value of male slaves, if not of the other sex. John emphatically was one of this injured class; he evidently had blood in his veins which decidedly warred against submitting to the yoke. In addition to the influence which such rebellious blood exerted over him, together with a considerable amount of intelligence, he was also under the influence and advice of a daughter of old Ireland. She was heart and soul with John in all his plans which looked Canada-ward. This it was that "sent him away."

It is very certain, that this Irish girl was not annoyed by the kinks in John's hair. Nor was she overly fastidious about the small percentage of colored blood visible in John's complexion. It was, however, a strange occurrence and very hard to understand. Not a stone was left unturned until John was safely on the Underground Rail Road. Doubtless she helped to earn the money which was paid for his passage. And when he was safe off, it is not too much to say, that John was not a whit more delighted than was his intended Irish lassie, Mary Weaver. John had no sooner reached Canada than Mary's heart was there too. Circumstances, however, required that she should remain in Richmond a number of months for the purpose of winding up some of her affairs. As soon as the way opened for her, she followed him. It was quite manifest, that she had not let a single opportunity slide, but seized the first chance and arrived partly by means of the Underground Rail Road and partly by the regular train. Many difficulties were surmounted before and after leaving Richmond, by which they earned their merited success. From Canada, where they anticipated entering upon the matrimonial career with mutual satisfaction, it seemed to afford them great pleasure to write back frequently, expressing their heartfelt gratitude for assistance, and their happiness in the prospect of being united under the favorable auspices of freedom! At least two or three of these letters, bearing on particular phases of their escape, etc., are too valuable not to be published in this connection:

FIRST LETTER.

HAMILTON, March 25th, 1856.

Mr. Still:—Sir and Friend—I take the liberty of addressing you with these few lines hoping that you will attend to what I shall request of you.

I have written to Virginia and have not received an answer yet. I want to know if you can get any one of your city to go to Richmond for me. If you can, I will pay the expense of the whole. The person that I want the messenger to see is a white girl. I expect you know who I allude to, it is the girl that sent me away. If you can get any one to go, you will please write right away and tell me the cost, &c. I will forward the money and a letter. Please use your endeavors. Yours Respectfuliy, JOHN HALL.

Direct yours to Mr. Hill.

SECOND LETTER.

HAMILTON, Sept. 15th, 1856.

To Mr. Still, Dear Sir:—I take this opportunity of addressing these few lines to you hoping to find you in good health I am happy to inform you that Miss Weaver arrived here on Tuesday last, and I can assure you it was indeed a happy day. As for your part that you done I will not attempt to tell you how thankful I am, but I hope that you can imagine what my feelings are to you. I cannot find words sufficient to express my gratitude to you, I think the wedding will take place on Tuesday next, I have seen some of the bread from your house, and she says it is the best bread she has had since she has been in America. Sometimes she has impudence enough to tell me she would rather be where you are in Philadelphia than to be here with me. I hope this will be no admiration to you for no honest hearted person ever saw you that would not desire to be where you are, No flattery, but candidly speaking, you are worthy all the praise of any person who has ever been with you, I am now like a deserted

Christian, but yet I have asked so much, and all has been done yet I must ask again, My love to Mrs. Still. Dear Mr. Still I now ask you please to exercise all your influence to get this young man Willis Johnson from Richmond for me It is the young man that Miss Weaver told you about, he is in Richmond I think he is at the corner of Fushien Street, & Grace in a house of one Mr. Rutherford, there is several Rutherford in the neighborhood, there is a church call'd the third Baptist Church, on the R.H. side going up Grace street, directly opposite the Baptist church at the corner, is Mrs. Meads Old School at one corner, and Mr. Rutherfords is at the other corner. He can be found out by seeing Fountain Tombs who belongs to Mr. Rutherford and if you should not see him, there is James Turner who lives at the Governors, Please to see Captain Bayliss and tell him to take these directions and go to John Hill, in Petersburgh, and he may find him. Tell Captain Bayliss that if he ever did me a friendly thing in his life which he did do one friendly act, if he will take this on himself, and if money should be lacking I will forward any money that he may require, I hope you will sympathize with the poor young fellow, and tell the captain to do all in his power to get him and the costs shall be paid. He lies now between death or victory, for I know the man he belongs to would just as soon kill him as not, if he catches him, I here enclose to you a letter for Mr. Wm. C. Mayo, and please to send it as directed. In this letter I have asked him to send a box to you for me, which you will please pay the fare of the express upon it, when you get it please to let me know, and I will send you the money to pay the expenses of the carriage clear through. Please to let Mr. Mayo know how to direct a box to you, and the best way to send it from Richmond to Philadelphia. You will greatly oblige me by so doing. In this letter I have enclosed a trifle for postage which you will please to keep on account of my letters I hope you wont think hard of me but I simply send it because I know you have done enough, and are now doing more, without imposing in the matter I have done it a great many more of our people who you have done so much fore. No more from your humble and oldest servant.

JOHN HALL, Norton's Hotel, Hamilton.

THIRD LETTER.

MONDAY, Sept. 29, 56.

Sir:—I take this opportunity of informing you that we are in excellent health, and hope you are the same, I wrote a letter to you about 2 weeks ago and have not yet had an answer to it I wish to inform you that the wedding took place on Tuesday last, and Mrs. Hall now sends her best love to you, I enclose a letter which I wish you to forward to Mr. Mayo, you will see in his letter what I have said to him and I wish you would furnish him with such directions as it requires for him to send them things to you. I have told him not to pay for them but to send them to you so when you get them write me word what the cost of them are, and I will send you the money for them. Mary desires you to give her love to Mrs. Still. If any letters come for me please to send to me at Nortons Hotel, Please to let me know if you had a letter from me about 12 days ago. You will please Direct the enclosed to Mr. W.C. Mayo, Richmond, Va. Let me know if you have heard anything of Willis Johnson Mr. & Mrs. Hill send their kind love to you, they are all well, no more at present from your affect.,

JOHN HALL Nortons Hotel.

FOURTH LETTER.

HAMILTON, December 23d, 1856.

DEAR SIR:—I am happy to inform you that we are both enjoying good health and hope you are the same. I have been expecting a letter from you for some time but I suppose your business has prevented you from writing. I suppose you have not heard from any of my friends at Richmond. I have been longing to hear some news from that part, you may think "Out of sight and out of mind," but I can assure you, no matter how far I may be, or in what distant land, I shall never forget you, if I can never reach you by letters you may be sure I shall always think of you. I have found a great many friends in my life, but I must say you are the best one I ever met with, except one, you must know who that is, 'tis one who if I did not consider a friend, I could not consider any other person a friend, and that is Mrs. Hall. Please to let me know if the navigation between New York & Richmond is closed. Please to let me know whether it would be convenient to you to go to New York if it is please let me know what is the expense. Tell Mrs Still that my wife would be very happy to receive a letter from her at some moment when she is at leisure, for I know from what little I have seen of domestic affairs it keeps her pretty well employed, And I know she has not much time to write but if it were but two lines, she would be happy to receive it from her, my reason for wanting you to go to New York, there is a young man named Richard Myers and I should like for you to see him. He goes on board the Orono to Richmond and is a particular friend of mine and by seeing him I could get my clothes from Richmond, I expect to be out of employ in a few days, as the hotel is about to close on the 1st January and I hope you will write to me soon I want you to send me word how you and all the family are and all the news you can, you must excuse my short letter, as it is now near one o'clock and I must attend to business, but I have not written half what I intended to, as time is short, hoping to hear from you soon I remain yours sincerely,

JOHN HALL.

Mr. and Mrs. Hill desire their best respects to you and Mrs. Still.

It cannot be denied that this is a most extraordinary occurrence. In some respects it is without a parallel. It was, however, no uncommon thing for white men (slave-holders) in the South to have colored wives and children whom, they did not hesitate to live with and acknowledge by their actions, with their means, and in their wills as the rightful heirs of their substance. Probably there is not a state in the Union where such relations have not existed. Seeing such usages, Mary might have reasoned that she had as good a right to marry the one she loved most as anybody else, particularly as she was in a "free country."

"SAM" NIXON ALIAS DR. THOMAS BAYNE.

The Escape of a Dentist on the U.G.R.R.—He Is Taken for an
Impostor—Elected a Member of City Council in New Bedford—
Studying Medicine, Etc.

But few could be found among the Underground Rail Road passengers who had a stronger repugnance to the unrequited labor system, or the recognized terms of "master and slave," than Dr. Thomas
Bayne. Nor were many to be found who were more fearless and
independent in uttering their sentiments. His place of bondage was
in the city of Norfolk, Va., where he was held to service by Dr. C.F.
Martin, a dentist of some celebrity. While with Dr. Martin, "Sam"
learned dentistry in all its branches, and was often required by his
master, the doctor, to fulfil professional engagements, both at home
and at a distance, when it did not suit his pleasure or convenience
to appear in person. In the mechanical department, especially,
"Sam" was called upon to execute the most difficult tasks. This was
not the testimony of "Sam" alone; various individuals who were
with him in Norfolk, but had moved to Philadelphia, and were living there at the time of his arrival, being invited to see this distinguished professional piece of property, gave evidence which fully
corroborated his. The master's professional practice, according to
"Sam's" calculation, was worth $3,000 per annum. Full $1,000 of this
amount in the opinion of "Sam" was the result of his own fettered
hands. Not only was "Sam" serviceable to the doctor in the mechanical and practical branches of his profession, but as a sort of
ready reckoner and an apt penman, he was obviously considered by
the doctor, a valuable "article." He would frequently have "Sam" at
his books instead of a book-keeper. Of course, "Sam" had never
received, from Dr. M., an hour's schooling in his life, but having
perceptive faculties naturally very large, combined with much self-
esteem, he could hardly help learning readily. Had his master's de-

sign to keep him in ignorance been ever so great, he would have found it a labor beyond his power. But there is no reason to suppose that Dr. Martin was opposed to Sam's learning to read and write. We are pleased to note that no charges of ill-treatment are found recorded against Dr. M. in the narrative of "Sam."

True, it appears that he had been sold several times in his younger days, and had consequently been made to feel keenly, the smarts of Slavery, but nothing of this kind was charged against Dr. M., so that he may be set down as a pretty fair man, for aught that is known to the contrary, with the exception of depriving "Sam" of the just reward of his labor, which, according to St. James, is pronounced a "fraud." The doctor did not keep "Sam" so closely confined to dentistry and book-keeping that he had no time to attend occasionally to outside duties. It appears that he was quite active and successful as an Underground Rail Road agent, and rendered important aid in various directions. Indeed, Sam had good reason to suspect that the slave-holders were watching him, and that if he remained, he would most likely find himself in "hot water up to his eyes." Wisdom dictated that he should "pull up stakes" and depart while the way was open. He knew the captains who were then in the habit of taking similar passengers, but he had some fears that they might not be able to pursue the business much longer. In contemplating the change which he was about to make, "Sam" felt it necessary to keep his movements strictly private. Not even was he at liberty to break his mind to his wife and child, fearing that it would do them no good, and might prove his utter failure. His wife's name was Edna and his daughter was called Elizabeth; both were slaves and owned by E.P. Tabb, Esq., a hardware merchant of Norfolk.

No mention is made on the books, of ill-treatment, in connection with his wife's servitude; it may therefore be inferred, that her situation was not remarkably hard. It must not be supposed that "Sam" was not truly attached to his wife. He gave abundant proof of true matrimonial devotion, notwithstanding the secrecy of his arrangements for flight. Being naturally hopeful, he concluded that he could better succeed in securing his wife after obtaining freedom himself, than in undertaking the task beforehand.

The captain had two or three other Underground Rail Road male passengers to bring with him, besides "Sam," for whom, arrangements had been previously made—no more could be brought that trip. At the appointed time, the passengers were at the disposal of the captain of the schooner which was to bring them out of Slavery into freedom. Fully aware of the dangerous consequences should he be detected, the captain, faithful to his promise, secreted them in the usual manner, and set sail northward. Instead of landing his passengers in Philadelphia, as was his intention, for some reason or other (the schooner may have been disabled), he landed them on the New Jersey coast, not a great distance from Cape Island. He directed them how to reach Philadelphia. Sam knew of friends in the city, and straightway used his ready pen to make known the distress of himself and partners in tribulation. In making their way in the direction of their destined haven, they reached Salem, New Jersey, where they were discovered to be strangers and fugitives, and were directed to Abigail Goodwin, a Quaker lady, an abolitionist, long noted for her devotion to the cause of freedom, and one of the most liberal and faithful friends of the Vigilance Committee of Philadelphia.

This friend's opportunities of witnessing fresh arrivals had been rare, and perhaps she had never before come in contact with a "chattel" so smart as "Sam." Consequently she was much embarrassed when she heard his story, especially when he talked of his experience as a "Dentist." She was inclined to suspect that he was a "shrewd impostor" that needed "watching" instead of aiding. But her humanity forbade a hasty decision on this point. She was soon persuaded to render him some assistance, notwithstanding her apprehensions. While tarrying a day or two in Salem, "Sam's" letter was received in Philadelphia. Friend Goodwin was written to in the meantime, by a member of the Committee, directly with a view of making inquires concerning the stray fugitives, and at the same time to inform her as to how they happened to be coming in the direction found by her. While the mind of the friend was much relieved by the letter she received, she was still in some doubt, as will be seen by the appended extract from a letter on the subject:

LETTER FROM A. GOODWIN.

SALEM, 3 mo., 25, '55.

DEAR FRIEND:—Thine of the 22d came to hand yesterday noon.

I do not believe that any of them are the ones thee wrote about, who wanted Dr. Lundy to come for them, and promised they would pay his expenses. They had no money, the minister said, but were pretty well off for clothes. I gave him all I had and more, but it seemed very little for four travelers—only a dollar for each— but they will meet with friends and helpers on the way. He said they expected to go away to-morrow. I am afraid, it's so cold, and one of them had a sore foot, they will not get away—it's dangerous staying here. There has been a slave-hunter here lately, I was told yesterday, in search of a woman; he tracked her to our Almshouse—she had lately been confined and was not able to go—he will come back for her and his infant—and will not wait long I expect. I want much to get her away first—and if one had a C.C. Torney here no doubt it would be done; but she will be well guarded. How much I wish the poor thing could be secreted in some safe place till she is able to travel Northward; but where that could be it's not easy to see. I presume the Carolina freed people have arrived ere now. I hope they will meet many friends, and be well provided for. Mary Davis will be then paid—her cousins have sent her twenty-four dollars, as it was not wanted for the purchase money—it was to be kept for them when they arrive. I am glad thee did keep the ten for the fugitives.

Samuel Nixon is now here, just come—a smart young man— they will be after him soon. I advise him to hurry on to Canada; he will leave here to-morrow, but don't say that he will go straight to the city. I would send this by him if he did. I am afraid he will loiter about and be taken—do make them go on fast—he has left. I could not hear much he said—some who did don't like him at all—think him an impostor—a great brag—said he was a dentist ten years. He was asked where he came from, but would not tell till he looked at the letter that lay on the table and that he had just brought back. I don't feel much confidence in him—don't believe he is the one thee alluded to. He was asked his name—he looked at the letter to find it out. Says nobody can make a better set of teeth than he can. He said they will go on to-morrow in the stage—he took down the number and street of the Anti-slavery office—you will be on your guard against imposition—he kept the letter thee sent from Norfolk. I had then no doubt of him, and had no objection to it. I now rather regret it. I would send it to thee if I had it, but perhaps it is of no importance.

He wanted the names taken down of nine more who expected to get off soon and might come here. He told us to send them to him, but did not seem to know where he was going to. He was well dressed in fine broad-cloth coat and overcoat, and has a very active tongue in his head.

But I have said enough—don't want to prejudice thee against him, but only be on thy guard, and do not let him deceive thee, as I fear he has some of us here.

With kind regards, A. GOODWIN.

In due time Samuel and his companions reached Philadelphia, where a cordial welcome awaited them. The confusion and difficulties into which they had fallen, by having to travel an indirect route, were fully explained, and to the hearty merriment of the Committee and strangers, the dilemma of their good Quaker friend Goodwin at Salem was alluded to. After a sojourn of a day or two in Philadelphia, Samuel and his companions left for New Bedford. Canada was named to them as the safest place for all Refugees; but it was in vain to attempt to convince "Sam" that Canada or any other place on this Continent, was quite equal to New Bedford. His heart was there, and there he was resolved to go—and there he did go too, bearing with him his resolute mind, determined, if possible, to work his way up to an honorable position at his old trade, Dentistry, and that too for his own benefit.

Aided by the Committee, the journey was made safely to the desired haven, where many old friends from Norfolk were found. Here our hero was known by the name of Dr. Thomas Bayne—he was no longer "Sam." In a short time the Dr. commenced his profession in an humble way, while, at the same time, he deeply interested himself in his own improvement, as well as the improvement of others, especially those who had escaped from Slavery as he himself had. Then, too, as colored men were voters and, therefore, eligible to office in New Bedford, the Doctor's naturally ambitious and intelligent, turn of mind led him to take an interest in politics, and before he was a citizen of New Bedford four years, he was duly elected a member of the City Council. He was also an outspoken advocate of the cause of temperance, and was likewise a ready speaker at Anti-slavery meetings held by his race. Some idea of his abilities, and the interest he took in the Underground Rail Road, education, etc., may be gathered from the appended letters:

NEW BEDFORD, June 23d, 1855.

W. Still:—Sir—I write you this to inform you that I has received my things and that you need not say any thing to Bagnul about them—I see by the Paper that the under ground Rail Road is in operation. Since 2 weeks a go when Saless Party was betrayed by that Capt whom we in mass. are so anxious to Learn his name— There was others started last Saturday night—They are all my old friends and we are waiting their arrival, we hope you will look out for them they may come by way of Salem, N.J. if they be not overtaken. They are from Norfolk—Times are very hard in Canada 2 of our old friends has left Canada and come to Bedford for a living. Every thing are so high and wages so low They cannot make a living (owing to the War) others are Expected shortly—let me hear from Sales and his Party. Get the Name of the Capt. that betrayed him let me know if Mrs. Goodwin of Salem are at the same place yet—John Austin are with us. C. Lightfoot is well and remembers you and family. My business increases more since I has got an office. Send me a Norfolk Paper or any other to read when convenient.

Let me hear from those People as soon as possible. They consist of woman and child 2 or 3 men belonging to Marsh Bottimore,

L. Slosser and Herman & Co—and Turner—all of Norfolk, Va. Truly yours, THOS. BAYNE.

Direct to Box No. 516, New Bedford, Mass. Don't direct my letters to my office. Direct them to my Box 516. My office is 66-½ William St. The same street the Post office is near the city market.

The Doctor, feeling his educational deficiency in the enlightened city of New Bedford, did just what every uncultivated man should, devoted himself assiduously to study, and even applied himself to abstruse and hard subjects, medicine, etc., as the following letters will show:

NEW BEDFORD, Jan., 1860.
No. 22, Cheapside, opposite City Hall.

My Dear Friend:—Yours of the 3d inst. reached me safely in the midst of my misfortune. I suppose you have learned that my office and other buildings burned down during the recent fire. My loss is $550, insured $350.

I would have written you before, but I have been to R.I. for some time and soon after I returned before I examined the books, the fire took place, and this accounts for my delay. In regard to the books I am under many obligations to you and all others for so great a piece of kindness, and shall ever feel indebted to you for the same. I shall esteem them very highly for two reasons, first, The way in which they come, that is through and by your Vigilance as a colored man helping a colored man to get such knowledge as will give the lie to our enemies. Secondly—their contents being just the thing I needed at this time. My indebtedness to you and all concerned for me in this direction is inexpressible. There are some books the Doctor says I must have, such as the Medical Dictionary, Physician's Dictionary, and a work on Anatomy. These I will have to get, but any work that may be of use to a student of anatomy or medicine will be thankfully received. You shall hear from me again soon. Truly Yours, THOS. BAYNE.

NEW BEDFORD, March 18th, 1861.

Mr. Wm. Still:—Dear Sir—Dr. Powell called to see me and
informed me that you had a medical lexicon (Dictionary) for me.
If you have such a book for me, it will be very thankfully received,
and any other book that pertains to the medical or dental
profession. I am quite limited in means as yet and in want of books
to prosecute my studies. The books I need most at present is such
as treat on midwifery, anatomy, &c. But any book or books in
either of the above mentioned cases will be of use to me. You can
send them by Express, or by any friend that may chance to come
this way, but by Express will be the safest way to send them. Times
are quite dull. This leaves me well and hope it may find you and
family the same. My regards to your wife and all others.

Yours, &c., THOMAS BAYNE,
22 Cheapside, opposite City Hall.

Thus the doctor continued to labor and improve his mind until
the war removed the hideous institution of Slavery from the nation;
but as soon as the way opened for his return to his old home, New
Bedford no longer had sufficient attractions to retain him. With all
her faults he conceived that "Old Virginia" offered decided induce-
ments for his return. Accordingly he went directly to Norfolk,
whence he escaped. Of course every thing was in the utmost confusion and disorder when he returned, save where the military held
sway. So as soon as the time drew near for reorganizing, elections,
&c., the doctor was found to be an aspirant for a seat in Congress,
and in "running" for it, was found to be a very difficult candidate to
beat. Indeed in the first reports of the election his name was amongst
the elected; but subsequent counts proved him to be among the
defeated by only a very slight majority.

At the time of the doctor's escape, in 1855, he was thirty-one
years of age, a man of medium size, and about as purely colored,
as could readily be found, with a full share of self-esteem and
pluck.

SLAVE-TRADER HALL IS FOILED.

Robert McCoy Alias William Donar.

In October, 1854, the Committee received per steamer, directly from Norfolk, Va., Robert McCoy and Elizabeth Saunders. Robert had constantly been in the clutches of the negro-trader Hall, for the last sixteen years, previous to his leaving, being owned by him. He had, therefore, possessed very favorable opportunities for varied observation and experience relative to the trader's conduct in his nefarious business, as well as for witnessing the effects of the auction-block upon all ages—rending asunder the dearest ties, despite the piteous wails of childhood or womanhood, parental or conjugal relations. But no attempt will be made to chronicle the deeds of this dealer in human flesh. Those stories fresh from the lips of one who had just escaped, were painful in the extreme, but in the very nature of things some of the statements are too revolting to be published. In lieu of this fact, except the above allusions to the trader's business, this sketch will only refer to Robert's condition as a slave, and finally as a traveler on the Underground Rail Road.

Robert was a man of medium size, dark mulatto, of more than ordinary intelligence. His duties had been confined to the house, and not to the slave pen. As a general thing, he had managed, doubtless through much shrewdness, to avoid very severe outrages from the trader. On the whole, he had fared "about as well" as the generality of slaves.

Yet, in order to free himself from his "miserable" life, he was willing, as he declared, to suffer almost any sacrifice. Indeed, his conduct proved the sincerity of this declaration, as he had actually been concealed five months in a place in the city, where he could not possibly avoid daily suffering of the most trying kind. His resolve to be free was all this while maturing. The trader had threatened to sell Robert, and to prevent it Robert (thus) "took out." Successfully did he elude the keen scent and grasp of the hunters, who made diligent efforts to recapture him. Although a young man—only about twenty-eight years of age, his health was by no means good. His system had evidently been considerably shattered by Slavery, and symptoms of consumption, together with chronic rheumatism, were making rapid headway against the physical man. Under his various ills, he declared, as did many others from the land of bondage, that his faith in God afforded him comfort and hope. He was obliged to leave his wife, Eliza, in bonds, not knowing whether they should ever meet again on earth, but he was somewhat hopeful that the way would open for her escape also.

After reaching Philadelphia, where his arrival had long been anticipated by the Vigilance Committee, his immediate wants were met, and in due order he was forwarded to New Bedford, where, he was led to feel, he would be happy in freedom.

Scarcely had he been in New Bedford one month, before his prayers and hopes were realized with regard to the deliverance of his wife. On hearing of the good news of her coming he wrote as follows—

NEW BEDFORD, Nov. 3, 1859.

DEAR SIR:—i embrace this opertunity to inform you that i received your letter with pleasure, i am enjoying good health and hope that these few lines will find you enjoying the same blessing. i rejoise to hear from you i feel very much indetted to you for not writing before but i have been so bissy that is the cause, i rejoise to heare of the arrival of my wife, and hope she is not sick from the roling of the sea and if she is not, pleas to send her on here Monday with a six baral warlian and a rifall to gard her up to my residance i thank you kindly for the good that you have don for me. Give my respects to Mrs. Still, tell her i want to see her very bad and you also i would come but i am afraid yet to venture, i received your letter the second, but about the first of spring i hope to pay you a visit or next summer. i am getting something to do every day. i will write on her arrivall and tell you more. Mr. R. White sends his love to you and your famerly and says that he is very much indetted to you for his not writing and all so he desires to know wheather his cloths has arived yet or not, and if they are please to express them on to him or if at preasant by Mrs. Donar. Not any more at preasent. i remain your affectionate brother, WILLIAM DONAR.

By the same arrival, and similarly secreted, Elizabeth Frances, alias Ellen Saunders, had the good luck to reach Philadelphia. She was a single young woman, about twenty-two, with as pleasant a countenance as one would wish to see. Her manners were equally agreeable. Perhaps her joy over her achieved victory added somewhat to her personal appearance. She had, however, belonged to the more favored class of slaves. She had neither been over-worked nor badly abused. Elizabeth was the property of a lady a few shades lighter than herself, (Elizabeth was a mulatto) by the name of Sarah Shephard, of Norfolk. In order the more effectually to profit by Elizabeth's labor, the mistress resorted to the plan of hiring her out for a given sum per month. Against this usage Elizabeth urged no complaint. Indeed the only very serious charge she brought was to the effect, that her mistress sold her mother away from her far South, when she was a child only ten years old. She had also sold a brother and sister to a foreign southern market. The reflections consequent upon the course that her mistress had thus pursued, awakened Elizabeth to much study relative to freedom, and by the time that she had reached womanhood she had very decided convictions touching her duty with regard to escaping. Thus growing to hate slavery in every way and manner, she was prepared to make a desperate effort to be free. Having saved thirty-five dollars by rigid economy, she was willing to give every cent of it (although it was all she possessed), to be aided from Norfolk to Philadelphia. After reaching the city, having suffered severely while coming, she was invited to remain until somewhat recruited. In the healthy air of freedom she was soon fully restored, and ready to take her departure for New Bedford, which place she reached without difficulty and was cordially welcomed. The following letter, expressive of her obligations for aid received, was forwarded soon after her arrival in New Bedford:

NEW BEDFORD, Mass., October 16th, 1854.

MR. STILL:—Dear Sir—I now take my pen in my hand to inform you of my health which is good at present all except a cold I have got but I hope when these few lines reach you you may be enjoying good health. I arrived in New Bedford Thursday morning safely and what little I have seen of the city I like it very much my friends were very glad to see me. I found my sister very well. Give my love to Mrs. Still and also your dear little children. I am now out at service. I do not think of going to Canada now. I think I shall remain in this city this winter. Please tell Mrs. Still I have not met any person who has treated me any kinder than she did since I left. I consider you both to have been true friends to me. I hope you will think me the same to you. I feel very thankful to you indeed. It might been supposed, out of sight out of mind, but it is not so. I never forget my friends. Give my love to Florence. If you come to this city I would be very happy to see you. Kiss your dear little children for me. Please to answer this as soon as possible, so that I may know you received this. No more at present. I still remain your friend,

ELLEN SAUNDERS.

ELIZA McCOY—the wife of Robert McCoy, whose narrative has just been given—and who was left to wait in hope when her husband escaped—soon followed him to freedom. It is a source of great satisfaction to be able to present her narrative in so close proximity to her husband's. He arrived about the first of October— she about the first of November, following. From her lips testimony of much weight and interest was listened to by several friends relative to her sufferings as a slave—on the auction-block, and in a place of concealment seven months, waiting and praying for an opportunity to escape. But it was thought sufficient to record merely a very brief outline of her active slave life, which consisted of the following noticeable features.

Eliza had been owned by Andrew Sigany, of Norfolk—age about thirty-eight—mulatto, and a woman whose appearance would readily command attention and respect anywhere outside of the barbarism of Slavery. She stated that her experience as a sufferer in cruel hands had been very trying, and that in fretting under hardships, she had "always wanted to be free." Her language was unmistakable on this point. Neither mistress nor servant was satisfied with each other; the mistress was so "queer" and "hard to please," that Eliza became heartily sick of trying to please her—an angel would have failed with such a woman. So, while matters were getting no better, but, on the contrary, were growing worse and worse, Eliza thought she would seek a more pleasant atmosphere in the North. In fact she felt that it would afford her no little relief to allow her place to be occupied by another. When she went into close quarters of concealment, she fully understood what was meant and all the liabilities thereto. She had pluck enough to endure unto the end without murmuring. The martyrs in olden times who dwelt in "dens and caves of the earth," could hardly have fared worse than some of these way-worn travelers.

After the rest, needed by one who had suffered so severely until her arrival in Philadelphia, she was forwarded to her anxiously waiting husband in New Bedford, where she was gladly received.

From the frequent arrivals from Virginia, especially in steamers, it may be thought that no very stringent laws or regulations existed by which offenders, who might aid the Underground Rail Road, could be severely punished—that the slave-holders were lenient, indifferent and unguarded as to how this property took wings and escaped. In order to enlighten the reader with regard to this subject, it seems necessary, in this connection, to publish at least one of the many statutes from the slave laws of the South bearing directly on the aid and escape of slaves by vessels. The following enactment is given as passed by the Legislature of Virginia in 1856:

THE PROTECTION OF SLAVE PROPERTY IN VIRGINIA.

A Bill Providing Additional Protection for the Slave Property of Citizens of This Commonwealth.

(1.) Be it enacted, by the General Assembly, that it shall not be lawful for any vessel, of any size or description, whatever, owned in whole, or in part, by any citizen or resident of another State, and about to sail or steam for any port or place in this State, for any port or place north of and beyond the capes of Virginia, to depart from the waters of this commonwealth, until said vessel has undergone the inspection hereinafter provided for in this act, and received a certificate to that effect. If any such vessel shall depart from the State without such certificate of inspection, the captain or owner thereof, shall forfeit and pay the sum of five hundred dollars, to be recovered by any person who will sue for the same, in any court of record in this State, in the name of the Governor of the Commonwealth. Pending said suit, the vessel of said captain or owner shall not leave the State until bond be given by the captain or owner, or other person for him, payable to the Governor, with two or three sureties satisfactory to the court, in the penalty of one thousand dollars, for the payment of the forfeit or fine, together with the cost and expenses incurred in enforcing the same; and in default of such bond, the vessel shall be held liable. Provided that nothing contained in this section, shall apply to vessels belonging to the United States Government, or vessels, American or foreign, bound direct to any foreign country other than the British American Provinces.

(2.) The pilots licensed under the laws of Virginia, and while attached to a vessel regularly employed as a pilot boat, are hereby constituted inspectors to execute this act, so far as the same may be applicable to the Chesapeake Bay, and the waters tributary thereto, within the jurisdiction of this State, together with such other inspectors as may be appointed by virtue of this act.

(3.) The branch or license issued to a pilot according to the provisions of the 92d chapter of Code, shall be sufficient evidence that he is authorized and empowered to act as inspector as aforesaid.

(4.) It shall be the duty of the inspector, or other person authorized to act under this law, to examine and search all vessels hereinbefore described, to see that no slave or person held to service or labor in this State, or person charged with the commission of any crime within the State, shall be concealed on board said vessel. Such inspection shall be made within twelve hours of the time of departure of such vessel from the waters of Virginia, and may be made in any bay, river, creek, or other water-course of the State, provided, however, that steamers plying as regular packets, between ports in Virginia and those north of, and outside of the capes of Virginia, shall be inspected at the port of departure nearest Old Point Comfort.

(5.) A vessel so inspected and getting under way, with intent to leave the waters of the State, if she returns to an anchorage above Back River Point, or within Old Point Comfort, shall be again inspected and charged as if an original case. If such vessel be driven back by stress of weather to seek a harbor, she shall be exempt from payment of a second fee, unless she holds intercourse with the shore.

(6.) If, after searching the vessel, the inspector see no just cause to detain her, he shall give to the captain a certificate to that effect. If, however, upon such inspection, or in any other manner, any slave or person held to service or labor, or any person charged with any crime, be found on board of any vessel whatever, for the purpose aforesaid, or said vessel be detected in the act of leaving this commonwealth with any such slave or person on board, or otherwise violating the provisions of this act, he shall attach said vessel, and arrest all persons on board, to be delivered up to the sergeant or sheriff of the nearest port in this commonwealth, to be dealt with according to law.

(7.) If any inspector or other officer be opposed, or shall have reason to suspect that he will be opposed or obstructed in the discharge of any duty required of him under this act, he shall have power to summon and command the force of any county or corporation to aid him in the discharge of such duty, and every person who shall resist, obstruct, or refuse to aid any inspector or other officer in the discharge of such duty, shall be deemed guilty of a misdemeanor, and, upon conviction thereof, shall be fined and imprisoned as in other cases of misdemeanor.

(8.) For every inspection of a vessel under this law, the inspector, or other officer shall be entitled to demand and receive the sum of five dollars; for the payment of which such vessel shall be liable, and the inspector or other officer may seize and hold her until the same is paid, together with all charges incurred in taking care of the vessel, as well as in enforcing the payment of the same. Provided, that steam packets trading regularly between the waters of Virginia and ports north of and beyond the capes of Virginia, shall pay not more than five dollars for each inspection under the provisions of this act; provided, however, that for every inspection of a vessel engaged in the coal trade, the inspector shall not receive a greater sum than two dollars.

(9.) Any inspector or other person apprehending a slave in the act of escaping from the state, on board a vessel trading to or belonging to a non-slave-holding state, or who shall give information that will lead to the recovery of any slave, as aforesaid, shall be entitled to a reward of One Hundred Dollars, to be paid by the owner of such slave, or by the fiduciary having charge of the estate to which such slave belongs; and if the vessel be forfeited under the provisions of this act, he shall be entitled to one-half of the proceeds arising from the sale of the vessel; and if the same amounts to one hundred dollars, he shall not receive from the owner the above reward of one hundred dollars.

(10.) An inspector permitting a slave to escape for the want of proper exertion, or by neglect in the discharge of his duty, shall be fined One Hundred Dollars; or if for like causes he permit a vessel, which the law requires him to inspect, to leave the state without inspection, he shall be fined not less than twenty, nor more than fifty dollars, to be recovered by warrant by any person who will proceed against him.

(11.) No pilot acting under the authority of the laws of the state, shall pilot out of the jurisdiction of this state any such vessel as is described in this act, which has not obtained and exhibited to him the certificate of inspection hereby required; and if any pilot shall so offend, he shall forfeit and pay not less than twenty, or more than fifty dollars, to be recovered in the mode prescribed in the next preceding section of this act.

(12.) The courts of the several counties or corporations situated on the Chesapeake Bay, or its tributaries, by an order entered on record, may appoint one or more inspectors, at such place or places within their respective districts as they may deem necessary, to prevent the escape or for the recapture of slaves attempting to escape beyond the limits of the state, and to search or otherwise examine all vessels trading to such counties or corporations. The expenses in such cases to be provided for by a levy on negroes now taxed by law; but no inspection by county or corporation officers thus appointed, shall supersede the inspection of such vessels by pilots and other inspectors, as specially provided for in this act.

(13.) It shall be lawful for the county court of any county, upon the application of five or more slave-holders, residents of the counties where the application is made, by an order of record, to designate one or more police stations in their respective counties, and a captain and three or more other persons as a police patrol on each station, for the recapture of fugitive slaves; which patrol shall be in service at such times, and such stations as the court shall direct by their order aforesaid; and the said court shall allow a reasonable compensation, to be paid to the members of such patrol; and for that purpose, the said court may from time to time direct a levy on negroes now taxed by law, at such rate per capita as the court may think sufficient, to be collected and accounted for by the sheriff as other county levies, and to be called, "The fugitive slave tax." The owner of each fugitive slave in the act of escaping beyond the limits of the commonwealth, to a non-slave-holding state, and captured by the patrol aforesaid, shall pay for each slave over fifteen, and under forty-five years old, a reward of One Hundred dollars; for each slave over five, and under fifteen years old, the sum of sixty dollars; and for all others, the sum of forty dollars. Which reward shall be divided equally among the members of the patrol retaking the slave and actually on duty at the time; and to secure the payment of said reward, the said patrol may retain possession and use of the slave until the reward is paid or secured to them.

(14.) The executive of this State may appoint one or more inspectors for the Rappahannock and Potomac rivers, if he shall deem it expedient, for the due execution of this act. The inspectors so appointed to perform the same duties, and to be invested with the same powers in their respective districts, and receive the same fees, as pilots acting as inspectors in other parts of the State. A vessel subject to inspection under this law, departing from any of the above-named counties or rivers on her voyage to sea, shall be exempted from the payment of a fee for a second inspection by another officer, if provided with a certificate from the proper inspecting officer of that district; but if, after proceeding on her voyage, she returns to the port or place of departure, or enters any other port, river, or roadstead in the State, the said vessel shall be again inspected, and pay a fee of five dollars, as if she had undergone no previous examination and received no previous certificate. If driven by stress of weather to seek a harbor, and she has no intercourse with the shore, then, and in that case, no second fee shall be paid by said vessel.

(15.) For the better execution of the provisions of this act, in regard to the inspection, of vessels, the executive is hereby authorized and directed to appoint a chief inspector, to reside at Norfolk, whose duty it shall be, to direct and superintend the police, agents, or inspectors above referred to. He shall keep a record of all vessels engaged in the piloting business, together with a list of such persons as may be employed as pilots and inspectors under this law. The owner or owners of each boat shall make a monthly report to him, of all vessels inspected by persons attached to said pilot boats, the names of such vessels, the owner or owners thereof, and the places where owned or licensed, and where trading to or from, and the business in which they are engaged, together with a list of their crews. Any inspector failing to make his report to the chief inspector, shall pay a fine of twenty dollars for each such failure, which fine shall be recovered by warrant, before a justice of the county or corporation. The chief inspector may direct the time and station for the cruise of each pilot boat, and perform such other duty as the Governor may designate, not inconsistent with the other provisions of this act. He shall make a quarterly return to the executive of all the transactions of his department, reporting to him any failure or refusal on the part of inspectors to discharge the duty assigned to them, and the Governor, for sufficient cause, may suspend or remove from office any delinquent inspector. The chief inspector shall receive as his compensation, ten per cent, on all the fees and fines received by the inspectors acting under his authority, and may be removed at the pleasure of the executive.

(16.) All fees and forfeitures imposed by this act, and not otherwise specially provided for, shall go one half to the informer, and the other be paid into the treasury of the State, to constitute a fund, to be called the "fugitive slave fund," and to be used for the payment of rewards awarded by the Governor, for the apprehension of runaway slaves, and to pay other expenses incident to the execution of this law, together with such other purposes as may hereafter be determined on by the General Assembly.

(17.) This act shall be in force from its passage.

ESCAPING IN A CHEST.

$150 REWARD. Ran away from the subscriber, on Sunday night, 27th inst., my NEGRO GIRL, Lear Green, about 18 years of age, black complexion, round-featured, good-looking and ordinary size; she had on and with her when she left, a tan-colored silk bonnet, a dark plaid silk dress, a light mouslin delaine, also one watered silk cape and one tan colored cape. I have reason to be confident that she was persuaded off by a negro man named Wm. Adams, black, quick spoken, 5 feet 10 inches high, a large scar on one side of his face, running down in a ridge by the corner of his mouth, about 4 inches long, barber by trade, but works mostly about taverns, opening oysters, &c. He has been missing about a week; he had been heard to say he was going to marry the above girl and ship to New York, where it is said his mother resides. The above reward will be paid if said girl is taken out of the State of Maryland and delivered to me; or fifty dollars if taken in the State of Maryland. JAMES NOBLE,
m26-3t. No. 153 Broadway, Baltimore.

Lear Green, so particularly advertised in the "Baltimore Sun" by "James Noble," won for herself a strong claim to a high place among the heroic women of the nineteenth century. In regard to description and age the advertisement is tolerably accurate, although her master might have added, that her countenance was one of peculiar modesty and grace. Instead of being "black," she was of a "dark-brown color." Of her bondage she made the following statement: She was owned by "James Noble, a Butter Dealer" of Baltimore. He fell heir to Lear by the will of his wife's mother, Mrs. Rachel Howard, by whom she had previously been owned. Lear was but a mere child when she came into the hands of Noble's family. She, therefore, remembered but little of her old mistress. Her young mistress, however, had made a lasting impression upon her mind; for she was very exacting and oppressive in regard to the tasks she was daily in the habit of laying upon Lear's shoulders, with no disposition whatever to allow her any liberties. At least Lear was never indulged in this respect. In this situation a young man by the name of William Adams proposed marriage to her. This offer she was inclined to accept, but disliked the idea of being encumbered with the chains of slavery and the duties of a family at the same time.

After a full consultation with her mother and also her intended upon the matter, she decided that she must be free in order to fill the station of a wife and mother. For a time dangers and difficulties in the way of escape seemed utterly to set at defiance all hope of success. Whilst every pulse was beating strong for liberty, only one chance seemed to be left, the trial of which required as much courage as it would to endure the cutting off the right arm or plucking out the right eye. An old chest of substantial make, such as sailors commonly use, was procured. A quilt, a pillow, and a few articles of raiment, with a small quantity of food and a bottle of water were put in it, and Lear placed therein; strong ropes were fastened around the chest and she was safely stowed amongst the ordinary freight on one of the Erricson line of steamers. Her intended's mother, who was a free woman, agreed to come as a passenger on the same boat. How could she refuse? The prescribed rules of the Company assigned colored passengers to the deck. In this instance it was exactly where this guardian and mother desired to be—as near the chest as possible. Once or twice, during the silent watches of the night, she was drawn irresistibly to the chest, and could not refrain from venturing to untie the rope and raise the lid a little, to see if the poor child still lived, and at the same time to give her a breath of fresh air. Without uttering a whisper, that frightful moment, this office was successfully performed. That the silent prayers of this oppressed young woman, together with her faithful protector's, were momentarily ascending to the ear of the good God above, there can be no question. Nor is it to be doubted for a moment but that some ministering angel aided the mother to unfasten the rope, and at the same time nerved the heart of poor Lear to endure the trying ordeal of her perilous situation. She declared that she had no fear.

After she had passed eighteen hours in the chest, the steamer arrived at the wharf in Philadelphia, and in due time the living freight was brought off the boat, and at first was delivered at a house in Barley street, occupied by particular friends of the mother. Subsequently chest and freight were removed to the residence of the writer, in whose family she remained several days under the protection and care of the Vigilance Committee.

Such hungering and thirsting for liberty, as was evinced by Lear Green, made the efforts of the most ardent friends, who were in the habit of aiding fugitives, seem feeble in the extreme. Of all the heroes in Canada, or out of it, who have purchased their liberty by downright bravery, through perils the most hazardous, none deserve more praise than Lear Green.

She remained for a time in this family, and was then forwarded to Elmira. In this place she was married to William Adams, who has been previously alluded to. They never went to Canada, but took up their permanent abode in Elmira. The brief space of about three years only was allotted her in which to enjoy freedom, as death came and terminated her career. About the time of this sad occurrence, her mother-in-law died in this city. The impressions made by both mother and daughter can never be effaced. The chest in which Lear escaped has been preserved by the writer as a rare trophy, and her photograph taken, while in the chest, is an excellent likeness of her and, at the same time, a fitting memorial.

ISAAC WILLIAMS, HENRY BANKS, AND KIT NICKLESS.

Months in a Cave,—Shot by Slave-Hunters.

Rarely were three travelers from the house of bondage received at the Philadelphia station whose narratives were more interesting than those of the above-named individuals. Before escaping they had encountered difficulties of the most trying nature. No better material for dramatic effect could be found than might have been gathered from the incidents of their lives and travels. But all that we can venture to introduce here is the brief account recorded at the time of their sojourn at the Philadelphia station when on their way to Canada in 1854. The three journeyed together. They had been slaves together in the same neighborhood. Two of them had shared the same den and cave in the woods, and had been shot, captured, and confined in the same prison; had broken out of prison and again escaped; consequently their hearts were thoroughly cemented in the hope of reaching freedom together.

Isaac was a stout-made young man, about twenty-six years of age, possessing a good degree of physical and mental ability. Indeed his intelligence forbade his submission to the requirements of Slavery, rendered him unhappy and led him to seek his freedom. He owed services to D. Fitchhugh up to within a short time before he escaped. Against Fitchhugh he made grave charges, said that he was a "hard, bad man." It is but fair to add that Isaac was similarly regarded by his master, so both were dissatisfied with each other. But the master had the advantage of Isaac, he could sell him. Isaac, however, could turn the table on his master, by running off. But the master moved quickly and sold Isaac to Dr. James, a negro trader. The trader designed making a good speculation out of his investment: Isaac determined that he should be disappointed; indeed that he should lose every dollar that he paid for him. So while the doctor was planning where and how he could get the best price for him, Isaac was planning how and where he might safely get beyond his reach. The time for planning and acting with Isaac was, however, exceedingly short. He was daily expecting to be called upon to take his departure for the South. In this situation he made known his condition to a friend of his who was in a precisely similar situation; had lately been sold just as Isaac had to the same trader James. So no argument was needed to convince his friend and fellow-servant that if they meant to be free they would have to set off immediately.

That night Henry Banks and Isaac Williams started for the woods together, preferring to live among reptiles and wild animals, rather than be any longer at the disposal of Dr. James. For two weeks they successfully escaped their pursuers. The woods, however, were being hunted in every direction, and one day the pursuers came upon them, shot them both, and carried them to King George's Co. jail. The jail being an old building had weak places in it; but the prisoners concluded to make no attempt to break out while suffering badly from their wounds. So they remained one month in confinement. All the while their brave spirits under suffering grew more and more daring. Again they decided to strike for freedom, but where to go, save to the woods, they had not the slightest idea. Of course they had heard, as most slaves had, of cave life, and pretty well understood all the measures which had to be resorted to for security when entering upon so hazardous an undertaking. They concluded, however, that they could not make their condition any worse, let circumstances be what they might in this respect. Having discovered how they could break jail, they were not long in accomplishing their purpose, and were out and off to the woods again. This time they went far into the forest, and there they dug a cave, and with great pains had every thing so completely arranged as to conceal the spot entirely. In this den they stayed three months. Now and then they would manage to secure a pig. A friend also would occasionally serve them with a meal. Their sufferings at best were fearful; but great as they were, the thought of returning to Slavery never occurred to them, and the longer they stayed in the woods, the greater was their determination to be free. In the belief that their owner had about given them up they resolved to take the North Star for a pilot, and try in this way to reach free land.

Kit, an old friend in time of need, having proved true to them in their cave, was consulted. He fully appreciated their heroism, and determined that he would join them in the undertaking, as he was badly treated by his master, who was called General Washington, a common farmer, hard drinker, and brutal fighter, which Kit's poor back fully evinced by the marks it bore. Of course Isaac and Henry were only too willing to have him accompany them.

In leaving their respective homes they broke kindred ties of the tenderest nature. Isaac had a wife, Eliza, and three children, Isaac, Estella, and Ellen, all owned by Fitchhugh. Henry was only nineteen, single, but left parents, brothers, and sisters, all owned by different slave-holders. Kit had a wife, Matilda, and three children, Sarah Ann, Jane Frances, and Ellen, slaves.

"PETE MATTHEWS," ALIAS SAMUEL SPARROWS.

"I Might as Well Be in the Penitentiary, &C."

Up to the age of thirty-five "Pete" had worn the yoke steadily, if not patiently under William S. Matthews, of Oak Hall, near Temper-anceville, in the State of Virginia. Pete said that his "master was not a hard man," but the man to whom he "was hired, George Mat-thews, was a very cruel man." "I might as well be in the penitentiary as in his hands," was his declaration.

One day, a short while before Pete "took out," an ox broke into the truck patch, and helped himself to choice delicacies, to the full extent of his capacious stomach, making sad havoc with the vegeta-bles generally. Peter's attention being directed to the ox, he turned him out, and gave him what he considered proper chastisement, according to the mischief he had done. At this liberty taken by Pete, the master became furious. "He got his gun and threatened to shoot him," "Open your mouth if you dare, and I will pat the whole load into you," said the enraged master. "He took out a large dirk-knife, and attempted to stab me, but I kept out of his way," said Pete. Nev-ertheless the violence of the master did not abate until he had beaten Pete over the head and body till he was weary, inflicting se-vere injuries. A great change was at once wrought in Pete's mind. He was now ready to adopt any plan that might hold out the least encouragement to escape. Having capital to the amount of four dollars only, he felt that he could not do much towards employing a conductor, but he had a good pair of legs, and a heart stout enough to whip two or three slave-catchers, with the help of a pistol. Hap-pening to know a man who had a pistol for sale, he went to him and told him that he wished to purchase it. For one dollar the pistol became Pete's property. He had but three dollars left, but he was determined to make that amount answer his purposes under the circumstances. The last cruel beating maddened him almost to desperation, especially when he remembered how he had been compelled to work hard night and day, under Matthews. Then, too, Peter had a wife, whom his master prevented him from visiting; this was not among the least offences with which Pete charged his master. Fully bent on leaving, the following Sunday was fixed by him on which to commence his journey.

The time arrived and Pete bade farewell to Slavery, resolved to follow the North Star, with his pistol in hand ready for action. After traveling about two hundred miles from home he unexpectedly had an opportunity of using his pistol. To his astonishment he suddenly came face to face with a former master, whom he had not seen for a long time. Pete desired no friendly intercourse with him whatever; but he perceived that his old master recognized him and was bent upon stopping him. Pete held on to his pistol, but moved as fast as his wearied limbs would allow him, in an opposite direction. As he was running, Pete cautiously cast his eye over his shoulder, to see what had become of his old master, when to his amazement, he found that a regular chase was being made after him. Need of redoubling his pace was quite obvious. In this hour of peril, Pete's legs saved him.

After this signal leg-victory, Pete had more confidence in his "understandings," than he had in his old pistol, although he held on to it until he reached Philadelphia, where he left it in the possession of the Secretary of the Committee. Considering it worth saving simply as a relic of the Underground Rail Road, it was carefully laid aside. Pete was now christened Samuel Sparrows. Mr. Sparrows had the rust of Slavery washed off as clean as possible and the Committee furnishing him with clean clothes, a ticket, and letters of introduction, started him on Canada-ward, looking quite respectable. And doubtless he felt even more so than he looked; free air had a powerful effect on such passengers as Samuel Sparrows.

The unpleasantness which grew out of the mischief done by the ox on George Matthews' farm took place the first of October, 1855. Pete may be described as a man of unmixed blood, well-made, and intelligent.

"MOSES" ARRIVES WITH SIX PASSENGERS.

"Not Allowed to Seek a Master;"—"Very Devilish;"—Father "Leaves Two Little Sons;"—"Used Hard;"—"Feared Falling into the Hands of Young Heirs," Etc. John Chase, Alias Daniel Floyd; Benjamin Ross, Alias James Stewart; Henry Ross, Alias Levin Stewart; Peter Jackson, Alias Staunch Tilghman; Jane Kane, Alias Catharine Kane, and Robert Ross.

The coming of these passengers was heralded by Thomas Garrett as follows:

THOMAS GARRETT'S LETTER.

————

WILMINGTON, 12 mo. 29th, 1854.

ESTEEMED FRIEND, J. MILLER MCKIM:—We made arrangements last night, and sent away Harriet Tubman, with six men and one woman to Allen Agnew's, to be forwarded across the country to the city. Harriet, and one of the men had worn their shoes off their feet, and I gave them two dollars to help fit them out, and directed a carriage to be hired at my expense, to take them out, but do not yet know the expense. I now have two more from the lowest county in Maryland, on the Peninsula, upwards of one hundred miles. I will try to get one of our trusty colored men to take them to-morrow morning to the Anti-slavery office. You can then pass them on.

THOMAS GARRETT.

HARRIET TUBMAN had been their "Moses," but not in the sense that Andrew Johnson was the "Moses of the colored people." She had faithfully gone down into Egypt, and had delivered these six bondmen by her own heroism. Harriet was a woman of no pretensions, indeed, a more ordinary specimen of humanity could hardly be found among the most unfortunate-looking farm hands of the South. Yet, in point of courage, shrewdness and disinterested exertions to rescue her fellow-men, by making personal visits to Maryland among the slaves, she was without her equal.

Her success was wonderful. Time and again she made successful visits to Maryland on the Underground Rail Road, and would be absent for weeks at a time, running daily risks while making preparations for herself and passengers. Great fears were entertained for her safety, but she seemed wholly devoid of personal fear. The idea of being captured by slave-hunters or slave-holders, seemed never to enter her mind. She was apparently proof against all adversaries. While she thus manifested such utter personal indifference, she was much more watchful with regard to those she was piloting. Half of her time, she had the appearance of one asleep, and would actually sit down by the road-side and go fast asleep when on her errands of mercy through the South, yet, she would not suffer one of her party to whimper once, about "giving out and going back," however wearied they might be from hard travel day and night. She had a very short and pointed rule or law of her own, which implied death to any who talked of giving out and going back. Thus, in an emergency she would give all to understand that "times were very critical and therefore no foolishness would be indulged in on the road." That several who were rather weak-kneed and faint-hearted were greatly invigorated by Harriet's blunt and positive manner and threat of extreme measures, there could be no doubt.

After having once enlisted, "they had to go through or die." Of course Harriet was supreme, and her followers generally had full faith in her, and would back up any word she might utter. So when she said to them that "a live runaway could do great harm by going back, but that a dead one could tell no secrets," she was sure to have obedience. Therefore, none had to die as traitors on the "middle passage." It is obvious enough, however, that her success in going into Maryland as she did, was attributable to her adventurous spirit and utter disregard of consequences. Her like it is probable was never known before or since. On examining the six passengers who came by this arrival they were thus recorded:

December 29th, 1854—John is twenty years of age, chestnut color, of spare build and smart. He fled from a farmer, by the name of John Campbell Henry, who resided at Cambridge, Dorchester Co., Maryland. On being interrogated relative to the character of his master, John gave no very amiable account of him. He testified that he was a "hard man" and that he "owned about one hundred and forty slaves and sometimes he would sell," etc. John was one of the slaves who were "hired out." He "desired to have the privilege of hunting his own master." His desire was not granted. Instead of meekly submitting, John felt wronged, and made this his reason for running away. This looked pretty spirited on the part of one so young as John. The Committee's respect for him was not a little increased, when they heard him express himself.

Benjamin was twenty-eight years of age, chestnut color, medium size, and shrewd. He was the so-called property of Eliza Ann Brodins, who lived near Buckstown, in Maryland. Ben did not hesitate to say, in unqualified terms, that his mistress was "very devilish." He considered his charges, proved by the fact that three slaves (himself one of them) were required to work hard and fare meagerly, to support his mistress' family in idleness and luxury. The Committee paid due attention to his ex parte statement, and was obliged to conclude that his argument, clothed in common and homely language, was forcible, if not eloquent, and that he was well worthy of aid. Benjamin left his parents besides one sister, Mary Ann Williamson, who wanted to come away on the Underground Rail Road.

Henry left his wife, Harriet Ann, to be known in future by the name of "Sophia Brown." He was a fellow-servant of Ben's, and one of the supports of Eliza A. Brodins.

Henry was only twenty-two, but had quite an insight into matters and things going on among slaves and slave-holders generally, in country life. He was the father of two small children, whom he had to leave behind.

Peter was owned by George Wenthrop, a farmer, living near Cambridge, Md. In answer to the question, how he had been used, he said "hard." Not a pleasant thought did he entertain respecting his master, save that he was no longer to demand the sweat of Peter's brow. Peter left parents, who were free; he was born before they were emancipated, consequently, he was retained in bondage.

Jane, aged twenty-two, instead of regretting that she had unadvisedly left a kind mistress and indulgent master, who had afforded her necessary comforts, affirmed that her master, "Rash Jones, was the worst man in the country." The Committee were at first disposed to doubt her sweeping statement, but when they heard particularly how she had been treated, they thought Catharine had good ground for all that she said. Personal abuse and hard usage, were the common lot of poor slave girls.

Robert was thirty-five years of age, of a chestnut color, and well made. His report was similar to that of many others. He had been provided with plenty of hard drudgery—hewing of wood and drawing of water, and had hardly been treated as well as a gentleman would treat a dumb brute. His feelings, therefore, on leaving his old master and home, were those of an individual who had been unjustly in prison for a dozen years and had at last regained his liberty.

The civilization, religion, and customs under which Robert and his companions had raised, were, he thought, "very wicked." Although these travelers were all of the field-hand order, they were, nevertheless, very promising, and they anticipated better days in Canada. Good advice was proffered them on the subject of temperance, industry, education, etc. Clothing, food and money were also given them to meet their wants, and they were sent on their way rejoicing.

SLAVE-HOLDER IN MARYLAND WITH THREE COLORED WIVES.

James Griffin Alias Thomas Brown.

James was a tiller of the soil under the yoke of Joshua Hitch, who lived on a farm about seventeen miles from Baltimore. James spoke rather favorably of him; indeed, it was through a direct act of kindness on the part of his master that he procured the opportunity to make good his escape. It appeared from his story, that his master's affairs had become particularly embarrassed, and the Sheriff was making frequent visits to his house. This sign was interpreted to mean that James, if not others, would have to be sold before long. The master was much puzzled to decide which way to turn. He owned but three other adult slaves besides James, and they were females. One of them was his chief housekeeper, and with them all his social relations were of such a nature as to lead James and others to think and say that they "were all his wives." Or to use James's own language, "he had three slave women; two were sisters, and he lived with them all as his wives; two of them he was very fond of," and desired to keep them from being sold if possible. The third, he concluded he could not save, she would have to be sold. In this dilemma, he was good enough to allow James a few days' holiday, for the purpose of finding him a good master. Expressing his satisfaction and gratification, James, armed with full authority from his master to select a choice specimen, started for Baltimore.

On reaching Baltimore, however, James carefully steered clear of all slave-holders, and shrewdly turned his attention to the matter of getting an Underground Rail Road ticket for Canada. After making as much inquiry as he felt was safe, he came to the conclusion to walk of nights for a long distance. He examined his feet and legs, found that they were in good order, and his faith and hope strong enough to remove a mountain. Besides several days still remained in which he was permitted to look for a new master, and these he decided could be profitably spent in making his way towards Canada. So off he started, at no doubt a very diligent pace, for at the end of the first night's journey, he had made much headway, but at the expense of his feet.

His faith was stronger than ever. So he rested next day in the woods, concealed, of course, and the next evening started with fresh courage and renewed perseverance. Finally, he reached Columbia, Pennsylvania, and there he had the happiness to learn, that the mountain which at first had tried his faith so severely, was removed, and friendly hands were reached out and a more speedy and comfortable mode of travel advised. He was directed to the Vigilance Committee in Philadelphia, from whom he received friendly aid, and all necessary information respecting Canada and how to get there.

James was thirty-one years of age, rather a fine-looking man, of a chestnut color, and quite intelligent. He had been a married man, but for two years before his escape, he had been a widower—that is, his wife had been sold away from him to North Carolina, and in that space of time he had received only three letters from her; he had given up all hope of ever seeing her again. He had two little boys living in Baltimore, whom he was obliged to leave. Their names were Edward and William. What became of them afterwards was never known at the Philadelphia station.

James's master was a man of about fifty years of age—who had never been lawfully married, yet had a number of children on his place who were of great concern to him in the midst of other pressing embarrassments. Of course, the Committee never learned how matters were settled after James left, but, in all probability, his wives, Nancy and Mary (sisters), and Lizzie, with all the children, had to be sold.

OWEN AND OTHO TAYLOR'S FLIGHT WITH HORSES, ETC.

Three Brothers, Two of Them with Wives and Children.

About the latter part of March, 1856, Owen Taylor and his wife, Mary Ann, and their little son, Edward, together with a brother and his wife and two children, and a third brother, Benjamin, arrived from near Clear Springs, nine miles from Hagerstown, Maryland. They all left their home, or rather escaped from the prison-house, on Easter Sunday, and came *via* Harrisburg, where they were assisted and directed to the Vigilance Committee in Philadelphia. A more interesting party had not reached the Committee for a long time.

The three brothers were intelligent, and heroic, and, in the resolve to obtain freedom, not only for themselves, but for their wives and children desperately in earnest. They had counted well the cost of this struggle for liberty, and had fully made up their minds that if interfered with by slave-catchers, somebody would have to bite the dust. That they had pledged themselves never to surrender alive, was obvious. Their travel-worn appearance, their attachment for each other, the joy that the tokens of friendship afforded them, the description they gave of incidents on the road, made an impression not soon to be effaced.

In the presence of a group like this Sumner's great and eloquent speech on the Barbarism of Slavery, seemed almost cold and dead,—the mute appeals of these little ones in their mother's arms—the unlettered language of these young mothers, striving to save their offspring from the doom of Slavery—the resolute and manly bearing of these brothers expressed in words full of love of liberty, and of the determination to resist Slavery to the death, in defence of their wives and children—this was Sumner's speech enacted before our eyes.

Owen was about thirty-one years of age, but had experienced a deal of trouble. He had been married twice, and both wives were believed to be living. The first one, with their little child, had been sold in the Baltimore market, about three years before, the mother was sent to Louisiana, the child to South Carolina. Father, mother, and child, parted with no hope of ever seeing each other again in this world. After Owen's wife was sent South, he sent her his likeness and a dress; the latter was received, and she was greatly delighted with it, but he never heard of her having received his likeness. He likewise wrote to her, but he was not sure that she received his letters. Finally, he came to the conclusion that as she was forever dead to him, he would do well to marry again. Accordingly he took to himself another partner, the one who now accompanied him on the Underground Rail Road.

Omitting other interesting incidents, a reference to his handiwork will suffice to show the ability of Owen. Owen was a born mechanic, and his master practically tested his skill in various ways; sometimes in the blacksmith shop—at other times as a wheelwright—again at making brushes and brooms, and at leisure times he would try his hand in all these crafts. This Jack-of-all-trades was, of course, very valuable to his master. Indeed his place was hard to fill.

Henry Fiery, a farmer, "about sixty-four years of age, a stout, crusty old fellow," was the owner of Owen and his two brothers. Besides slaves, the old man was in possession of a wife, whose name was Martha, and seven children, who were pretty well grown up. One of the sons owned Owen's wife and two children. Owen declared, that they had been worked hard, while few privileges had been allowed them. Clothing of the poorest texture was only sparingly furnished. Nothing like Sunday raiment was ever given them; for these comforts they were compelled to do overwork of nights. For a long time the idea of escape had been uppermost in the minds of this party. The first of January, past, was the time "solemnly" fixed upon to "took out," but for some reason or other (not found on the record book), their strategical minds did not see the way altogether clear, and they deferred starting until Easter Sunday.

On that memorable evening, the men boldly harnessed two of Mr. Fiery's steeds and placing their wives and children in the carriage, started off *via* Hagerstown, in a direct line for Chambersburg, Pennsylvania, at a rate that allowed no grass to grow under the horses' feet. In this manner they made good time, reached Chambersburg safely, and ventured up to a hotel where they put up their horses. Here they bade their faithful beasts good-bye and "took out" for Harrisburg by another mode of travel, the cars. On their arrival they naturally fell into the hands of the Committee, who hurried them off to Philadelphia, apprising the Committee there of their approach by a dispatch sent ahead. Probably they had scarcely reached Philadelphia ere the Fierys were in hot haste after them, as far as Harrisburg, if not farther.

It hardly need be hinted, that the community in which the Fierys lived was deeply agitated for days after, as indeed it was along the entire route to Chambersburg, in consequence of this bold and successful movement. The horses were easily captured at the hotel, where they were left, but, of course, they were mute as to what had become of their drivers. The furious Fierys probably got wind of the fact, that they had made their way to Harrisburg. At any rate they made very diligent search at this point. While here prosecuting his hunting operations, Fiery managed to open communication with at least one member of the Harrisburg Committee, to whom his grievances were made known, but derived little satisfaction.

After the experience of a few weeks, the pursuers came to the conclusion, that there was no likelihood of recovering them through these agencies, or through the Fugitive Slave Law. In their despair, therefore, they resorted to another "dodge." All at once they became "sort-o'-friendly"—indeed more than half disposed to emancipate. The member of the Committee in Harrisburg had, it is probable, frequently left room for their great delusion, if he did not even go so far as to feed their hopes with plausible suggestions, that some assistance might be afforded by which an amicable settlement might be made between masters and slaves.

234 of William Still

The following extract, from the Committee's letter, relative to this matter, is open to this inference, and may serve to throw some light on the subject:

HARRISBURG, April 28, '56.

Friend Still:—Your last came to hand in due season, and I am happy to hear of the safe arrival of those gents.

I have before me the Power of Attorney of Mr. John S. Fiery, son of Mr. Henry Fiery, of Washington county, Md., the owner of those three men, two women and three children, who arrived in your town on the 24th or 25th of March. He graciously condescends to liberate the oldest in a year, and the remainder in proportional time, if they will come back; or to sell them their time for $1300. He is sick of the job, and is ready to make any conditions. Now, if you personally can get word to them and get them to send him a letter, in my charge, informing him of their whereabouts and prospects, I think it will be the best answer I can make him. He will return here in a week or two, to know what can be done. He offers $500 to see them.

Or if you can send me word where they are, I will endeavor to write to them for his special satisfaction; or if you cannot do either, send me your latest information, for I intend to make him spend a few more dollars, and if possible get a little sicker of this bad job. Do try and send him a few bitter pills for his weak nerves and disturbed mind.

Yours in great haste, Jos. C. Bustill.

A subsequent letter from Mr. Bustill contains, besides other interesting Underground Rail Road matter, an item relative to the feeling of disappointment experienced by Mr. Fiery on learning that his property was in Canada.

HARRISBURG, May 26, '56.

Friend Still:—I embrace the opportunity presented by the visit of our friend, John F. Williams, to drop you a few lines in relation to our future operations.

The Lightning Train was put on the Road on last Monday, and as the traveling season has commenced and this is the Southern route for Niagara Falls, I have concluded not to send by way of Auburn, except in cases of great danger; but hereafter we will use the Lightning Train, which leaves here at 1-½ and arrives in your city at 5 o'clock in the morning, and I will telegraph about 5-½ o'clock in the afternoon, so it may reach you before you close. These four are the only ones that have come since my last. The woman has been here some time waiting for her child and her beau, which she expects here about the first of June. If possible, please keep a knowledge of her whereabouts, to enable me to inform him if he comes.

I have nothing more to send you, except that John Fiery has visited us again and much to his chagrin received the information of their being in Canada.

Yours as ever, Jos. C. Bustill.

Whilst the Fierys were working like beavers to re-enslave these brave fugitives, the latter were daily drinking in more and more of the spirit of freedom and were busy with schemes for the deliverance of other near kin left behind under the galling yoke.

Several very interesting letters were received from Otho Taylor, relative to a raid he designed making expressly to effect the escape of his family. The two subjoined must suffice, (others, much longer, cannot now be produced, they have probably been loaned and not returned.)

APRIL 15th, 1857.

SIR—We arrived here safely. Mr. Syrus and his lady is well situated. They have a place for the year round 15 dollars per month. We are all well and hope that you are all the same. Now I wish to know whether you would please to send me some money to go after those people. Send it here if you please.

Yours truly, OTHO TAYLOR.
WILLIAM STILL.

ST. CATHARINES, Jan. 26, 1857.

MR. WM. STILL:—Dear Sir—I write at this time in behalf of Otho Taylor. He is very anxious to go and get his family at Clear Spring, Washington county, Md. He would like to know if the Society there would furnish him the means to go after them from Philadelphia, that you will be running no risk in doing this. If the Society can do this, he would not be absent from P. more than three days.

He is so anxious to get his family from slavery that he is willing to do almost anything to get them to Canada. You may possibly recollect him—he was at your place last August. I think he can be trusted. If you can do something for him, he has the means to take him to your place.

Please let me know immediately if you can do this. Respectfully yours,

M.A.H. WILSON.

Such appeals came very frequently from Canada, causing much sadness, as but little encouragement could be held out to such projects. In the first place, the danger attendant upon such expeditions was so fearful, and in the second place, our funds were so inadequate for this kind of work, that, in most cases, such appeals had to be refused. Of course, there were those whose continual coming, like the poor widow in the Gospel, could not be denied.

HEAVY REWARD.

THREE HUNDRED DOLLARS REWARD.—Ran away from the subscriber, residing near Bladensburg, Prince George's county, Maryland, on Saturday night, the 22d of March, 1856, my negro man, Tom Matthews, aged about 25 years, about 5 feet 9 or 10 inches high, dark copper color, full suit of bushy hair, broad face, with high cheek bones, broad and square shoulders, stands and walks very erect, though quite a sluggard in action, except in a dance, at which he is hard to beat. He wore away a black coat and brown pantaloons. I will give the above reward if taken and brought home, or secured in jail, so that I get him.

E.A. JONES, near Bladensburg, Md.

As Mr. Jones may be unaware which way his man Tom traveled, this item may inform him that his name was entered on the Underground Rail Road book April 4th, 1856, at which date he appeared to be in good health and full of hope for a safe sojourn in Canada. He was destitute, of course, just as anybody else would have been, if robbers had stripped him of every dollar of his earnings; but he felt pretty sure, that he could take care of himself in her Majesty's dominion.

The Committee, encouraged by his efforts, reached him a helping hand and sent him on to swell the goodly number in the promised land—Canada.

On the same day that Tom arrived, the Committee had the pleasure of taking JAMES JONES by the hand. He was owned by Dr. William Stewart, of King George's Court House, Maryland. He was not, however, in the service of his master at the time of his escape but was hired out in Alexandria. For some reason, not noticed in the book, James became dissatisfied, changed his name to Henry Rider, got an Underground Rail Road pass and left the Dr. and his other associations in Maryland. He was one of the well-cared for "articles," and was of very near kin to the white people, at least a half-brother (mulatto, of course). He was thirty-two years of age, medium size, hard-featured and raw-boned, but "no marks about him."

James looked as if he had had pretty good health, still the Committee thought that he would have much better in Canada. After hearing a full description of that country and of the great number of fugitives there from Maryland and other parts of the South, "Jim" felt that that was just the place he wanted to find, and was soon off with a free ticket, a letter of introduction, etc.

THE FUGITIVE SLAVE BILL OF 1850.

"An Act Respecting Fugitives from Justice, and Persons Escaping from the Service of Their Masters."

Be it enacted by the Senate and House of Representatives of the United States of America in Congress assembled:

That the persons who have been, or may hereafter be appointed commissioners, in virtue of any Act of Congress, by the circuit courts of the United States, and who, in consequence of such appointment, are authorized to exercise the powers that any justice of the peace or other magistrate of any of the United States, may exercise in respect to offenders for any crime or offence against the United States, by arresting, imprisoning, or bailing the same under and by virtue of the thirty-third section of the act of the twenty-fourth of September, seventeen hundred and eighty-nine, entitled, "An act to establish the judicial courts of the United States," shall be, and are hereby authorized and required to exercise and discharge all the powers and duties conferred by this act.

SEC. 2. And be it further enacted: That the superior court of each organized territory of the United States, shall have the same power to appoint commissioners to take acknowledgments of bail and affidavit, and to take depositions of witnesses in civil causes, which is now possessed by the circuit courts of the United States, and all commissioners, who shall hereafter be appointed for such purposes, by the superior court of any organized territory of the United States, shall possess all the powers, and exercise all the duties conferred by law, upon the commissioners appointed by the circuit courts of the United States for similar purposes, and shall, moreover, exercise and discharge all the powers and duties conferred by this act.

SEC. 3. And be it further enacted: That the circuit courts of the United States, and the superior courts of each organized territory of the United States, shall, from time to time, enlarge the number of Commissioners, with a view to afford reasonable facilities to reclaim fugitives from labor, and to the prompt discharge of the duties imposed by this act.

SEC. 4. And be it further enacted, that the commissioners above named, shall have concurrent jurisdiction with the judges of the circuit and district courts of the United States, in their respective circuits and districts within the several States, and the judges of the superior courts of the Territories severally and collectively, in term time and vacation; and shall grant certificates to such claimants, upon satisfactory proof being made, with authority to take and remove such fugitives from service or labor, under the restrictions herein contained, to the State or territory from which such persons may have escaped or fled.

SEC. 5. And be it further enacted: That it shall be the duty of all marshals and deputy marshals, to obey and execute all warrants and precepts issued under the provisions of this act, when to them directed; and should any marshal or deputy marshal refuse to receive such warrant or other process when tendered, or to use all proper means diligently to execute the same, he shall, on conviction thereof, be fined in the sum of one thousand dollars to the use of such claimant, on the motion of such claimant by the circuit or district court for the district of such marshal; and after arrest of such fugitive by the marshal, or his deputy, or whilst at any time in his custody, under the provisions of this act, should such fugitive escape, whether with or without the assent of such marshal or his deputy, such marshal shall be liable, on his official bond, to be prosecuted, for the benefit of such claimant, for the full value of the service or labor of said fugitive in the State, Territory or district whence he escaped; and the better to enable the said commissioners, when thus appointed, to execute their duties faithfully and efficiently, in conformity with the requirements of the Constitution of the United States, and of this act, they are hereby authorized and empowered, within their counties respectively, to appoint in writing under their hands, any one or more suitable persons, from time to time, to execute all such warrants and other process as may be issued by them in the lawful performance of their respective duties, with an authority to such commissioners, or the persons to be appointed by them, to execute process as aforesaid, to summon and call to their aid the bystanders or posse comitatus, of the proper county, when necessary to insure a faithful observance of the clause of the Constitution referred to, in conformity with the provisions of this act; and all good citizens are hereby commanded to aid and assist in the prompt and efficient execution of this law, whenever their services may be required, as aforesaid, for that purpose; and said warrants shall run and be executed by said officers anywhere in the State within which they are issued.

SEC. 6. And be it further enacted, That when a person held to service or labor in any State or Territory of the United States, has heretofore, or shall hereafter escape into another State or Territory of the United States, the person or persons to whom such service or labor may be due, or his, her or their agent or attorney, duly authorized, by power of attorney, in writing, acknowledged and certified under the seal of some legal office or court of the State or Territory, in which the same may be executed, may pursue and reclaim such fugitive person, either by procuring a warrant from some one of the courts, judges, or commissioners aforesaid, of the proper circuit, district or county, for the apprehension of such fugitive from service or labor, or by seizing and arresting such fugitive, where the same can be done without process, and by taking, or causing such person to be taken, forthwith, before such court, judge or commissioner, whose duty it shall be to hear and determine the case of such claimant in a summary manner, and upon satisfactory proof being made, by deposition or affidavit, in writing, to be taken and certified by such court, judge or commissioner, or by other satisfactory testimony, duly taken and certified by some court, magistrate, justice of the peace, or other legal officer authorized to administer an oath and take depositions under the laws of the State or Territory from which such person owing service or labor may have escaped, with a certificate of such magistrate, or other authority, as aforesaid, with the seal of the proper court or officer thereto attached, which seal shall be sufficient to establish the competency of the proof, and with proof also, by affidavit, of the identity of the person whose service or labor is claimed to be due, as aforesaid, that the person so arrested does in fact owe service or labor to the person or persons claiming him or her, in the State or Territory from which such fugitive may have escaped, as aforesaid, and that said person escaped, to make out and deliver to such claimant, his or her agent or attorney, a certificate setting forth the substantial facts as to the service or labor due from such fugitive to the claimant, and of his or her escape from the State or Territory in which such service or labor was due, to the State or Territory, in which he or she was arrested, with authority to such claimant, or his or her agent or attorney, to use such reasonable force and restraint as may be necessary, under the circumstances of the case, to take and remove such fugitive person back to the State or Territory from whence he or she may have escaped, as aforesaid. In no trial or hearing, under this act, shall the testimony of such alleged fugitives be admitted in evidence, and the certificates in this and the first section mentioned, shall be conclusive of the right of the person or persons in whose favor granted to remove such fugitives to the State or Territory from which they escaped, and shall prevent all molestation of said person or persons by any process issued by any court, judge, magistrate, or other person whomsoever.

SEC. 7. And be it further enacted, That any person who shall knowingly and willfully obstruct, hinder, or prevent such claimant, his agent, or attorney, or any person or persons lawfully assisting him, her or them from arresting such a fugitive from service or labor, either with or without process, as aforesaid, or shall rescue, or attempt to rescue, such fugitive from service or labor, or from the custody of such claimant, his or her agent, or attorney, or other person or persons lawfully assisting, as aforesaid, when so arrested, pursuant to the authority herein given and declared, or shall aid, abet, or assist such person, so owing service or labor, as aforesaid, directly or indirectly, to escape from such claimant, his agent or attorney, or other person or persons legally authorized, as aforesaid, or shall harbor or conceal such fugitive, so as to prevent the discovery and arrest of such person, after notice or knowledge of the fact that such person was a fugitive from service or labor, as aforesaid, shall, for either of said offences, be subject to a fine not exceeding one thousand dollars, and imprisonment not exceeding six months, by indictment and conviction before the District Court of the United States, for the district in which such offence may have been committed, or before the proper court of criminal jurisdiction, if committed within any one of the organized Territories of the United States; and shall, moreover, forfeit and pay, by way of civil damages, to the party injured by such illegal conduct, the sum of one thousand dollars for each fugitive so lost, as aforesaid, to be recovered by action of debt in any of the District or Territorial Courts aforesaid, within whose jurisdiction the said offence may have been committed.

SEC. 8. And be it further enacted, That the Marshals, their deputies, and the clerks of the said districts and territorial courts, shall be paid for their services the like fees as may be allowed to them for similar services in other cases; and where such services are rendered exclusively in the arrest, custody, and delivery of the fugitives to the claimant, his or her agent, or attorney, or where such supposed fugitive may be discharged out of custody from the want of sufficient proof, as aforesaid, then such fees are to be paid in the whole by such complainant, his agent or attorney, and in all cases where the proceedings are before a Commissioner, he shall be entitled to a fee of ten dollars in full for his services in each case, upon the delivery of the said certificate to the claimant, his or her agent or attorney; or a fee of five dollars in cases where proof shall not, in the opinion of said Commissioner, warrant such certificate and delivery, inclusive of all services incident to such arrest and examination, to be paid in either case, by the claimant, his or her agent or attorney. The person or persons authorized to execute the process to be issued by such Commissioners for the arrest and detention of fugitives from service or labor, as aforesaid, shall also be entitled to a fee of five dollars each for each person he or they may arrest and take before any such Commissioners, as aforesaid, at the instance and request of such claimant, with such other fees as may be deemed reasonable by such Commissioner for such other additional services as may be necessarily performed by him or them; such as attending to the examination, keeping the fugitive in custody, and providing him with food and lodgings during his detention, and until the final determination of such Commissioner; and in general for performing such other duties as may be required by such claimant, his or her attorney or agent or commissioner in the premises; such fees to be made up in conformity with the fees usually charged by the officers of the courts of justice within the proper district or county as far as may be practicable, and paid by such claimants, their agents or attorneys, whether such supposed fugitive from service or labor be ordered to be delivered to such claimants by the final determination of such Commissioners or not.

SEC. 9. And be it further enacted, That upon affidavit made by the claimant of such fugitive, his agent or attorney, after such certificate has been issued, that he has reason to apprehend that such fugitive will be rescued by force from his or their possession before he can be taken beyond the limits of the State in which the arrest is made, it shall be the duty of the officer making the arrest to retain such fugitive in his custody, and to remove him to the State whence he fled, and there to deliver him to said claimant, his agent or attorney. And to this end the officer aforesaid is hereby authorized and required to employ so many persons as he may deem necessary, to overcome such force, and to retain them in his service so long as circumstances may require; the said officer and his assistants, while so employed, to receive the same compensation, and to be allowed the same expenses as are now allowed by law for the transportation of criminals, to be certified by the judge of the district within which the arrest is made, and paid out of the treasury of the United States.

SEC. 10. And be it further enacted, That when any person held to service or labor in any State or Territory, or in the District of Columbia, shall escape therefrom, the party to whom such service or labor shall be due, his, her, or their agent, or attorney may apply to any court of record therein, or judge thereof in vacation, and make such satisfactory proof to such court or judge in vacation, of the escape aforesaid, and that the person escaping owed service or labor to such party. Thereupon the court shall cause a record to be made of the matters so proved, and also a personal description of the person so escaping, with such convenient certainty as may be; and a transcript of such record, authenticated by the attestation of the clerk, and of the seal of said court being produced in any other State, Territory or District in which the person so escaping may be found, and being exhibited to any judge, commissioner, or other officer authorized by the law of the United States to cause persons escaping from, service or labor to be delivered up, shall be held and taken to be full and conclusive evidence of the fact of escape, and that the service or labor of the person escaping is due to the party in such record mentioned. And upon the production, by the said party, of other and further evidence, if necessary, either oral or by affidavit, in addition to what is contained in said record of the identity of the person escaping, he or she shall be delivered up to the claimant. And said court, commissioners, judge, or other persons authorized by this act to grant certificates to claimants of fugitives, shall, upon the production of the record and other evidence aforesaid, grant to such claimant a certificate of his right to take any such person, identified and proved to be owing service or labor as aforesaid, which certificate shall authorize such claimant to seize, or arrest, and transport such person to the State or Territory from which he escaped: Provided, That nothing herein contained shall be construed as requiring the production of a transcript of such record as evidence as aforesaid, but in its absence, the claim shall be heard and determined upon other satisfactory proofs competent in law.

THE SLAVE-HUNTING TRAGEDY IN LANCASTER COUNTY, IN SEPTEMBER, 1851.

"Treason at Christiana."

Having inserted the Fugitive Slave Bill in these records of the Underground Rail Road, one or two slave cases will doubtless suffice to illustrate the effect of its passage on the public mind, and the colored people in particular. The deepest feelings of loathing, contempt and opposition were manifested by the opponents of Slavery on every hand. Anti-slavery papers, lecturers, preachers, etc., arrayed themselves boldly against it on the ground of its inhumanity and violation of the laws of God.

On the other hand, the slave-holders South, and their pro-slavery adherents in the North demanded the most abject obedience from all parties, regardless of conscience or obligation to God. In order to compel such obedience, as well as to prove the practicability of the law, unbounded zeal daily marked the attempt on the part of slave-holders and slave-catchers to refasten the fetters on the limbs of fugitives in different parts of the North, whither they had escaped.

In this dark hour, when colored men's rights were so insecure, as a matter of self-defence, they felt called upon to arm themselves and resist all kidnapping intruders, although clothed with the authority of wicked law. Among the most exciting cases tending to justify this course, the following may be named:

James Hamlet was the first slave case who was summarily arrested under the Fugitive Slave Law, and sent back to bondage from New York.

William and Ellen Craft were hotly pursued to Boston by hunters from Georgia.

Adam Gibson, a free colored man, residing in Philadelphia, was arrested, delivered into the hands of his alleged claimants, by commissioner Edward D. Ingraham, and hurried into Slavery. Euphemia Williams (the mother of six living children),—her case excited much interest and sympathy.

Shadrach was arrested and rescued in Boston.

Hannah Dellum and her child were returned to Slavery from Philadelphia.

Thomas Hall and his wife were pounced upon at midnight in Chester county, beaten and dragged off to Slavery, etc.

And, as if gloating over their repeated successes, and utterly regardless of all caution, about one year after the passage of this nefarious bill, a party of slave-hunters arranged for a grand capture at Christiana.

One year from the passage of the law, at a time when alarm and excitement were running high, the most decided stand was taken at Christiana, in the State of Pennsylvania, to defeat the law, and defend freedom. Fortunately for the fugitives the plans of the slave-hunters and officials leaked out while arrangements were making in Philadelphia for the capture, and, information being sent to the Anti-slavery office, a messenger was at once dispatched to Christiana to put all persons supposed to be in danger on their guard.

Among those thus notified, were brave hearts, who did not believe in running away from slave-catchers. They resolved to stand up for the right of self-defence. They loved liberty and hated Slavery, and when the slave-catchers arrived, they were prepared for them. Of the contest, on that bloody morning, we have copied a report, carefully written at the time, by C.M. Burleigh, editor of the "Pennsylvania Freeman," who visited the scene of battle, immediately after it was over, and doubtless obtained as faithful an account of all the facts in the case, as could then be had:

———

"Last Thursday morning, (the 11th inst.), a peaceful neighborhood in the borders of Lancaster county, was made the scene of a bloody battle, resulting from an attempt to capture seven colored men as fugitive slaves. As the reports of the affray which came to us were contradictory, and having good reason to believe that those of the daily press were grossly one-sided and unfair, we repaired to the scene of the tragedy, and, by patient inquiry and careful examination, endeavored to learn the real facts. To do this, from the varying and conflicting statements which we encountered, scarcely two of which agreed in every point, was not easy; but we believe the account we give below, as the result of these inquiries, is substantially correct.

Very early on the 11th inst. a party of slave-hunters went into a neighborhood about two miles west of Christiana, near the eastern border of Lancaster county, in pursuit of fugitive slaves. The party consisted of Edward Gorsuch, his son, Dickerson Gorsuch, his nephew, Dr. Pearce, Nicholas Hutchins, and others, all from Baltimore county, Md., and one Henry H. Kline, a notorious slave-catching constable from Philadelphia, who had been deputized by Commissioner Ingraham for this business. At about day-dawn they were discovered lying in an ambush near the house of one William Parker, a colored man, by an inmate of the house, who had started for his work. He fled back to the house, pursued by the slave-hunters, who entered the lower part of the house, but were unable to force their way into the upper part, to which the family had retired. A horn was blown from an upper window; two shots were fired, both, as we believe, though we are not certain, by the assailants, one at the colored man who fled into the house, and the other at the inmates, through the window. No one was wounded by either. A parley ensued. The slave-holder demanded his slaves, who he said were concealed in the house. The colored men presented themselves successively at the window, and asked if they were the slaves claimed; Gorsuch said, that neither of them was his slave. They told him that they were the only colored men in the house, and were determined never to be taken alive as slaves. Soon the colored people of the neighborhood, alarmed by the horn, began to gather, armed with guns, axes, corn-cutters, or clubs. Mutual threatenings were uttered by the two parties. The slave-holders told the blacks that resistance would be useless, as they had a party of thirty men in the woods near by. The blacks warned them again to leave, as they would die before they would go into Slavery.

From an hour to an hour and a half passed in these parleyings, angry conversations, and threats; the blacks increasing by new arrivals, until they probably numbered from thirty to fifty, most of them armed in some way. About this time, Castner Hanaway, a white man, and a Friend, who resided in the neighborhood, rode up, and was soon followed by Elijah Lewis, another Friend, a merchant, in Cooperville, both gentlemen highly esteemed as worthy and peaceable citizens. As they came up, Kline, the deputy marshal, ordered them to aid him, as a United States officer, to capture the fugitive slaves. They refused of course, as would any man not utterly destitute of honor, humanity, and moral principle, and warned the assailants that it was madness for them to attempt to capture fugitive slaves there, or even to remain, and begged them if they wished to save their own lives, to leave the ground. Kline replied, 'Do you really think so?' 'Yes,' was the answer, 'the sooner you leave, the better, if you would prevent bloodshed.' Kline then left the ground, retiring into a very safe distance into a cornfield, and toward the woods. The blacks were so exasperated by his threats, that, but for the interposition of the two white Friends, it is very doubtful whether he would have escaped without injury. Messrs. Hanaway and Lewis both exerted their influence to dissuade the colored people from violence, and would probably have succeeded in restraining them, had not the assailing party fired upon them. Young Gorsuch asked his father to leave, but the old man refused, declaring, as it is said and believed, that he would 'go to hell, or have his slaves.'

Finding they could do nothing further, Hanaway and Lewis both started to leave, again counselling the slave-hunters to go away, and the colored people to peace, but had gone but a few rods, when one of the inmates of the house attempted to come out at the door. Gorsuch presented his revolver, ordering him back. The colored man replied, 'You had better go away, if you don't want to get hurt,' and at the same time pushed him aside and passed out. Maddened at this, and stimulated by the question of his nephew, whether he would 'take such an insult from a d——d nigger,' Gorsuch fired at the colored man, and was followed by his son and nephew, who both fired their revolvers. The fire was returned by the blacks, who made a rush upon them at the same time. Gorsuch and his son fell, the one dead the other wounded. The rest of the party after firing their revolvers, fled precipitately through the corn and to the woods, pursued by some of the blacks. One was wounded, the rest escaped unhurt. Kline, the deputy marshal, who now boasts of his miraculous escape from a volley of musket-balls, had kept at a safe distance, though urged by young Gorsuch to stand by his father and protect him, when he refused to leave the ground. He of course came off unscathed. Several colored men were wounded, but none severely. Some had their hats or their clothes perforated with bullets; others had flesh wounds. They said that the Lord protected them, and they shook the bullets from their clothes. One man found several shot in his boot, which seemed to have spent their force before reaching him, and did not even break the skin. The slave-holders having fled, several neighbors, mostly Friends and anti-slavery men, gathered to succor the wounded and take charge of the dead. We are told that Parker himself protected the wounded man from his excited comrades, and brought water and a bed from his own house for the invalid, thus showing that he was as magnanimous to his fallen enemy as he was brave in the defence of his own liberty. The young man was then removed to a neighboring house, where the family received him with the tenderest kindness and paid him every attention, though they told him in Quaker phrase, that 'they had no unity with his cruel business,' and were very sorry to see him engaged in it. He was much affected by their kindness, and we are told, expressed his regret that he had been thus engaged, and his determination, if his life was spared, never again to make a similar attempt. His wounds are very severe, and it is feared mortal. All attempts to procure assistance to capture the fugitive slaves failed, the people in the neighborhood either not relishing the business of slave-catching, or at least, not choosing to risk their lives in it. There was a very great reluctance felt to going even to remove the body and the wounded man, until several abolitionists and Friends had collected for that object, when others found courage to follow on. The excitement caused by this most melancholy affair is very great among all classes. The abolitionists, of course, mourn the occurrence, while they see in it a legitimate fruit of the Fugitive Slave Law, just such a harvest of blood as they had long feared that the law would produce, and which they had earnestly labored to prevent. We believe that they alone, of all classes of the nation, are free from responsibility for its occurrence, having wisely foreseen the danger, and faithfully labored to avert it by removing its causes, and preventing the inhuman policy which has hurried on the bloody convulsion.

The enemies of the colored people, are making this the occasion of fresh injuries, and a more bitter ferocity toward that defenceless people, and of new misrepresentation and calumnies against the abolitionists.

The colored people, though the great body of them had no connection with this affair, are hunted like partridges upon the mountains, by the relentless horde which has been poured forth upon them, under the pretense of arresting the parties concerned in the fight. When we reached Christiana, on Friday afternoon, we found that the Deputy-Attorney Thompson, of Lancaster, was there, and had issued warrants, upon the depositions of Kline and others, for the arrest of all suspected persons. A company of police were scouring the neighborhood in search of colored people, several of whom were seized while at their work near by, and brought in.

Castner Hanaway and Elijah Lewis, hearing that warrants were issued against them, came to Christiana, and voluntarily gave themselves up, calm and strong in the confidence of their innocence. They, together with the arrested colored men, were sent to Lancaster jail that night.

The next morning we visited the ground of the battle, and the family where young Gorsuch now lives, and while there, we saw a deposition which he had just made, that he believed no white persons were engaged in the affray, beside his own party. As he was on the ground during the whole controversy, and deputy Marshall Kline had discreetly run off into the corn-field, before the fighting began, the hireling slave-catcher's eager and confident testimony against our white friends, will, we think, weigh lightly with impartial men.

On returning to Christiana, we found that the United States Marshal from the city, had arrived at that place, accompanied by Commissioner Ingraham, Mr. Jones, a special commissioner of the United States, from Washington, the U.S. District Attorney Ashmead, with forty-five U.S. Marines from the Navy Yard, and a posse of about forty of the City Marshal's police, together with a large body of special constables, eager for such a manhunt, from Columbia and Lancaster and other places. This crowd divided into parties, of from ten to twenty-five, and scoured the country, in every direction, for miles around, ransacking the houses of the colored people, and captured every colored man they could find, with several colored women, and two other white men. Never did our heart bleed with deeper pity for the peeled and persecuted colored people, than when we saw this troop let loose upon them, and witnessed the terror and distress which its approach excited in families, wholly innocent of the charges laid against them."

———

On the other hand, a few extracts from the editorials of some of the leading papers, will suffice to show the state of public feeling at that time, and the dreadful opposition abolitionists and fugitives had to contend with.

From one of the leading daily journals of Philadelphia, we copy as follows:

"There can be no difference of opinion concerning the shocking affair which occurred at Christiana, on Thursday, the resisting of a law of Congress by a band of armed negroes, whereby the majesty of the Government was defied and life taken in one and the same act. There is something more than a mere ordinary, something more than even a murderous, riot in all this. It is an act of insurrection, we might, considering the peculiar class and condition of the guilty parties, almost call it a servile insurrection—if not also one of treason. Fifty, eighty, or a hundred persons, whether white or black, who are deliberately in arms for the purpose of resisting the law, even the law for the recovery of fugitive slaves, are in the attitude of levying war against the United States; and doubly heavy becomes the crime of murder in such a case, and doubly serious the accountability of all who have any connection with the act as advisers, suggesters, countenancers, or accessories in any way whatever."

In those days, the paper from which this extract is taken, represented the Whig party and the more moderate and respectable class of citizens.

The following is an extract from a leading democratic organ of Philadelphia:

"We will not, however, insult the reader by arguing that which has not been heretofore doubted, and which is not doubted now, by ten honest men in the State, and that is that the abolitionists are implicated in the Christiana murder. All the ascertained facts go to show that they were the real, if not the chief instigators. White men are known to harbor fugitives, in the neighborhood of Christiana, and these white men are known to be abolitionists, known to be opposed to the Fugitive Slave Law, and *known* to be the warm friends of William F. Johnston, (Governor of the State of Pennsylvania). And, as if to clinch the argument, no less than three white men are now in the Lancaster prison, and were arrested as accomplices in the dreadful affair on the morning of the eleventh. And one of these white men was committed on a charge of high treason, on Saturday last, by United States Commissioner Ingraham."

Another daily paper of opposite politics thus spake:

"The unwarrantable outrage committed last week, at Christiana, Lancaster county, is a foul stain upon the fair name and fame of our State. We are pleased to see that the officers of the Federal and State Governments are upon the tracks of those who were engaged in the riot, and that several arrests have been made.

We do not wish to see the poor misled blacks who participated in the affair, suffer to any great extent, for they were but tools. The men who are really chargeable with treason against the United States Government, and with the death of Mr. Gorsuch, an estimable citizen of Maryland, are unquestionably *white*, with hearts black enough to incite them to the commission of any crime equal in atrocity to that committed in Lancaster county. Pennsylvania has now but one course to pursue, and that is to aid, and warmly aid, the United States in bringing to condign punishment, every man engaged in the riot. She owes it to herself and to the Union. Let her in this resolve, be just and fearless."

From a leading neutral daily paper the following is taken: "One would suppose from the advice of forcible resistance, so familiarly given by the abolitionists, that they are quite unaware that there is any such crime as treason recognized by the Constitution, or punished with death by the laws of the United States. We would remind them, that not only is there such a crime, but that there is a solemn decision of the Supreme Court, that all who are concerned in a conspiracy which ripens into treason, whether present or absent from the scene of actual violence, are involved in the same liabilities as the immediate actors. If they engage in the conspiracy and stimulate the treason, they may keep their bodies from the affray without saving their necks from a halter.

It would be very much to the advantage of society, if an example could be made of some of these persistent agitators, who excite the ignorant and reckless to treasonable violence, from which they themselves shrink, but who are, not only in morals, but in law, equally guilty and equally amenable to punishment with the victims of their inflammatory counsels."

A number of the most influential citizens represented the occurrence to the Governor as follows:

"To the Governor of Pennsylvania:

The undersigned, citizens of Pennsylvania, respectfully represent:

That citizens of a neighboring State have been cruelly assassinated by a band of armed outlaws at a place not more than three hours' journey distant from the seat of Government and from the commercial metropolis of the State:

That this insurrectionary movement in one of the most populous parts of the State has been so far successful as to overawe the local ministers of justice and paralyze the power of the law:

That your memorialists are not aware that 'any military force' has been sent to the seat of insurrection, or that the civil authority has been strengthened by the adoption of any measures suited to the momentous crisis.

They, therefore, respectfully request the chief executive magistrate of Pennsylvania to take into consideration the necessity of vindicating the outraged laws, and sustaining the dignity of the Commonwealth on this important and melancholy occasion."

Under this high pressure of public excitement, threatening and alarm breathed so freely on every hand, that fugitive slaves and their friends in this region of Pennsylvania at least, were compelled to pass through an hour of dreadful darkness—an ordeal extremely trying. The authorities of the United States, as well as the authorities of the State of Pennsylvania and Maryland, were diligently making arrests wherever a suspected party could be found, who happened to belong in the neighborhood of Christiana.

In a very short time the following persons were in custody: J. Castner Hanaway, Elijah Lewis, Joseph Scarlett, Samuel Kendig, Henry Spins, George Williams, Charles Hunter, Wilson Jones, Francis Harkins, Benjamin Thomson, William Brown (No. 1), William Brown (No. 2), John Halliday, Elizabeth Mosey, John Morgan, Joseph Berry, John Norton, Denis Smith, Harvey Scott, Susan Clark, Tansy Brown, Eliza Brown, Eliza Parker, Hannah Pinckney, Robert Johnson, Miller Thompson, Isaiah Clark, and Jonathan Black.

These were not all, but sufficed for a beginning; at least it made an interesting entertainment for the first day's examination; and although there were two or three non-resistant Quakers, and a number of poor defenceless colored women among those thus taken as prisoners, still it seemed utterly impossible for the exasperated defenders of Slavery to divest themselves of the idea, that this heroic deed, in self-defence, on the part of men who felt that their liberties were in danger, was anything less than actually levying war against the United States.

Accordingly, therefore, the hearing gravely took place at Lancaster. On the side of the Commonwealth, the following distinguished counsel appeared on examination: Hon. John L. Thompson, District Attorney; Wm. B. Faulney, Esq.; Thos. E. Franklin, Esq.,

Attorney-General of Lancaster county; George L. Ashmead, Esq., of Philadelphia, representative of the United States authorities; and Hon. Robert Brent, Attorney-General of Maryland.

For the defence—Hon. Thaddeus Stevens, Reah Frazer, Messrs. Ford, Cline, and Dickey, Esquires.

From a report of the first day's hearing we copy a short extract, as follows:

"The excitement at Christiana, during yesterday, was very great. Several hundred persons were present, and the deepest feeling was manifested against the perpetrators of the outrage. At two o'clock yesterday afternoon, the United States Marshal, Mr. Roberts, United States District Attorney, J.H. Ashmead, Esq., Mr. Commissioner Ingraham, and Recorder Lee, accompanied by the United States Marines, returned to the city. Lieut. Johnson, and officers Lewis S. Brest, Samuel Mitchell, Charles McCully, Samuel Neff, Jacob Albright, Robert McEwen, and—Perkenpine, by direction of the United States Marshal, had charge of the following named prisoners, who were safely lodged in Moyamensing prison, accompanied by the Marines:—Joseph Scarlett, (white), William Brown, Ezekiel Thompson, Isaiah Clarkson, Daniel Caulsberry, Benjamin Pendergrass, Elijah Clark, George W.H. Scott, Miller Thompson, and Samuel Hanson, all colored. The last three were placed in the debtors' apartment, and the others in the criminal apartment of the Moyamensing prison to await their trial for treason, &c."

In alluding to the second day's doings, the Philadelphia Ledger thus represented matters at the field of battle:

"The intelligence received last evening, represents the country for miles around, to be in as much excitement as at any time since the horrible deed was committed. The officers sent there at the instance of the proper authorities are making diligent search in every direction, and securing every person against whom the least suspicion is attached. The police force from this city, amounting to about sixty men, are under the marshalship of Lieut. Ellis. Just as the cars started east, in the afternoon, five more prisoners who were secured at a place called the Welsh Mountains, twelve miles distant, were brought into Christiana. They were placed in custody until such time as a hearing will take place."

Although the government had summoned its ablest legal talent and the popular sentiment was as a hundred to one against William Parker and his brave comrades who had made the slave-hunter "bite the dust," most nobly did Thaddeus Stevens prove that he was not to be cowed, that he believed in the stirring sentiment so much applauded by the American people, "Give me liberty, or give me death," not only for the white man but for all men. Thus standing upon such great and invulnerable principles, it was soon discovered that one could chase a thousand, and two put ten thousand to flight in latter as well as in former times.

At first even the friends of freedom thought that the killing of Gorsuch was not only wrong, but unfortunate for the cause. Scarcely a week passed, however, before the matter was looked upon in a far different light, and it was pretty generally thought that, if the Lord had not a direct hand in it, the cause of Freedom at least would be greatly benefited thereby.

And just in proportion as the masses cried, Treason! Treason! the hosts of freedom from one end of the land to the other were awakened to sympathize with the slave. Thousands were soon aroused to show sympathy who had hitherto been dormant. Hundreds visited the prisoners in their cells to greet, cheer, and offer them aid and counsel in their hour of sore trial.

The friends of freedom remained calm even while the pro-slavery party were fiercely raging and gloating over the prospect, as they evidently thought of the satisfaction to be derived from teaching the abolitionists a lesson from the scaffold, which would in future prevent Underground Rail Road passengers from killing their masters when in pursuit of them.

Through the efforts of the authorities three white men, and twenty-seven colored had been safely lodged in Moyamensing prison, under the charge of treason. The authorities, however, had utterly failed to catch the hero, William Parker, as he had been sent to Canada, *via* the Underground Rail Road, and was thus "sitting under his own vine and fig tree, where none dared to molest, or make him afraid."

As an act of simple justice it may here be stated that the abolitionists and prisoners found a true friend and ally at least in one United States official, who, by the way, figured prominently in making arrests, etc., namely: the United States Marshal, A.E. Roberts. In all his intercourse with the prisoners and their friends, he plainly showed that all his sympathies were on the side of Freedom, and not with the popular pro-slavery sentiment which clamored so loudly against traitors and abolitionists.

Two of his prisoners had been identified in the jail as fugitive slaves by their owners. When the trial came on these two individuals were among the missing. How they escaped was unknown; the Marshal, however, was strongly suspected of being a friend of the Underground Rail Road, and to add now, that those suspicions were founded on fact, will, doubtless, do him no damage.

In order to draw the contrast between Freedom and Slavery, simply with a view of showing how the powers that were acted and judged in the days of the reign of the Fugitive Slave Law, unquestionably nothing better could be found to meet the requirements of this issue than the charge of Judge Kane, coupled with the indictment of the Grand Jury. In the light of the Emancipation and the Fifteenth Amendment, they are too transparent to need a single word of comment. Judge and jury having found the accused chargeable with Treason, nothing remained, so far as the men were concerned, but to bide their time as best they could in prison. Most of them were married, and had wives and children clinging to them in this hour of fearful looking for of judgment.

THE LAW OF TREASON, AS LAID DOWN BY JUDGE KANE.

The following charge to the Grand Jury of the United States District Court, in reference to the Slave-hunting affray in Lancaster county, and preparatory to their finding bills of indictment against the prisoners, was delivered on Monday, September 28, by Judge Kane:

"Gentlemen of the Grand Jury:—It has been represented to me, that since we met last, circumstances have occurred in one of the neighboring counties in our District, which should call for your prompt scrutiny, and perhaps for the energetic action of the Court. It is said, that a citizen of the State of Maryland, who had come into Pennsylvania to reclaim a fugitive from labor, was forcibly obstructed in the attempt by a body of armed men, assaulted, beaten and murdered; that some members of his family, who had accompanied him in the pursuit, were at the same time, and by the same party maltreated and grievously wounded; and that an officer of justice, constituted under the authority of this Court, who sought to arrest the fugitive, was impeded and repelled by menaces and violence, while proclaiming his character, and exhibiting his warrant. It is said, too, that the time and manner of these outrages, their asserted object, the denunciations by which they were preceded, and the simultaneous action of most of the guilty parties, evinced a combined purpose forcibly to resist and make nugatory a constitutional provision, and the statutes enacted in pursuance of it: and it is added, in confirmation of this, that for some months back, gatherings of people, strangers, as well as citizens, have been held from time to time in the vicinity of the place of the recent outbreaks, at which exhortations were made and pledges interchanged to hold the law for the recovery of fugitive slaves as of no validity, and to defy its execution. Such are some of the representations that have been made in my hearing, and in regard to which, it has become your duty, as the Grand Inquest of the District, to make legal inquiry. Personally, I know nothing of the facts, or the evidence relating to them. As a member of the Court, before which the accused persons may hereafter be arraigned and tried, I have sought to keep my mind altogether free from any impressions of their guilt or innocence, and even from an extra-judicial knowledge of the circumstances which must determine the legal character of the offence that has thus been perpetrated. It is due to the great interests of public justice, no less than to the parties implicated in a criminal charge, that their cause should be in no wise and in no degree pre-judged. And in referring, therefore, to the representations which have been made to me, I have no other object than to point you to the reasons for my addressing you at this advanced period of our sessions, and to enable you to apply with more facility and certainty the principles and rules of law, which I shall proceed to lay before you.

If the circumstances, to which I have adverted, have in fact taken place, they involve the highest crime known to our laws. Treason against the United States is defined by the Constitution, Art. 3, Sec. 3, cl. 1, to consist in "levying war against them, or adher-ing to their enemies, giving them aid and comfort." This definition is borrowed from the ancient Law of England, Stat. 25, Edw. 3, Stat. 5, Chap. 2, and its terms must be understood, of course, in the sense which they bore in that law, and which obtained here when the Constitution was adopted. The expression, "levying war," so regarded, embraces not merely the act of formal or declared war, but any combination forcibly to prevent or oppose the execution or enforcement of a provision of the Constitution, or of a public Statute, if accompanied or followed by an act of forcible opposi-tion in pursuance of such combination. This, in substance, has been the interpretation given to these words by the English Judges, and it has been uniformly and fully recognized and adopted in the Courts of the United States. (See Foster, Hale, and Hawkins, and the opinions of Iredell, Patterson, Chase, Marshall, and Washing-ton, J.J., of the Supreme Court, and of Peters, D.J., in U.S. vs. Vijol, U.S. vs. Mitchell, U.S. vs. Fries, U.S. vs. Bollman and Swartwout, and U.S. vs. Burr).

The definition, as you will observe, includes two particulars, both of them indispensable elements of the offence. There must have been a combination or conspiring together to oppose the law by force, and some actual force must have been exerted, or the crime of treason is not consummated. The highest, or at least the direct proof of the combination may be found in the declared pur-poses of the individual party before the actual outbreak; or it may be derived from the proceedings of meetings, in which he took part

openly; or which he either prompted, or made effective by his countenance or sanction,—commending, counselling and instigating
forcible resistance to the law. I speak, of course, of a conspiring to
resist a law, not the more limited purpose to violate it, or to prevent
its application and enforcement in a particular case, or against a
particular individual. The combination must be directed against the
law itself. But such direct proof of this element of the offence is not
legally necessary to establish its existence. The concert of purpose
may be deduced from the concerted action itself, or it may be inferred from facts occurring at the time, or afterwards, as well as
before. Besides this, there must be some act of violence, as the result
or consequence of the combining.

But here again, it is not necessary to prove that the individual
accused was a direct, personal actor in the violence. If he was present, directing, aiding, abetting, counselling, or countenancing it, he
is in law guilty of the forcible act. Nor is even his personal presence
indispensable. Though he be absent at the time of its actual perpe-
tration, yet, if he directed the act, devised, or knowingly furnished
the means for carrying it into effect, instigated others to perform it,
he shares their guilt.

In treason there are no accessories. There has been, I fear, an erroneous impression on this subject, among a portion of our people.
If it has been thought safe, to counsel and instigate others to acts of
forcible oppugnation to the provisions of a statute, to inflame the
minds of the ignorant by appeals to passion, and denunciations of
the law as oppressive, unjust, revolting to the conscience, and not
binding on the actions of men, to represent the constitution of the
land as a compact of iniquity, which it were meritorious to violate
or subvert, the mistake has been a grievous one; and they who have
fallen into it may rejoice, if peradventure their appeals and their
counsels have been hitherto without effect. The supremacy of the
constitution, in all its provisions, is at the very basis of our existence
as a nation. He, whose conscience, or whose theories of political or
individual right, forbid him to support and maintain it in its fullest
integrity, may relieve himself from the duties of citizenship, by di-
vesting himself of its rights. But while he remains within our bor-

ders, he is to remember, that successfully to instigate treason, is to commit it. I shall not be supposed to imply in these remarks, that I have doubts of the law-abiding character of our people. No one can know them well, without the most entire reliance on their fidelity to the constitution. Some of them may differ from the mass, as to the rightfulness or the wisdom of this or the other provision that is found in the federal compact, they may be divided in sentiment as to the policy of a particular statute, or of some provision in a statute; but it is their honest purpose to stand by the engagements, all the engagements, which bind them to their brethren of the other States. They have but one country; they recognize no law of higher social obligation than its constitution and the laws made in pursuance of it; they recognize no higher appeal than to the tribunals it has appointed; they cherish no patriotism that looks beyond the union of the States. That there are men here, as elsewhere, whom a misguided zeal impels to violations of law; that there are others who are controlled by false sympathies, and some who yield too readily and too fully to sympathies not always false, or if false, yet pardonable, and become criminal by yielding, that we have, not only in our jails and almshouses, but segregated here and there in detached portions of the State, ignorant men, many of them without political rights, degraded in social position, and instinctive of revolt, all this is true. It is proved by the daily record of our police courts, and by the ineffective labors of those good men among us, who seek to detach want from temptation, passion from violence, and ignorance from crime.

But it should not be supposed that any of these represent the sentiment of Pennsylvania, and it would be to wrong our people sorely, to include them in the same category of personal, social, or political morals. It is declared in the article of the constitution, which I have already cited, that 'no person shall be convicted of treason, unless on the testimony of two witnesses to the same overt act, or on confession in open court.' This and the corresponding language in the act of Congress of the 30th of April, 1790, seem to refer to the proofs on the trial, and not to the preliminary hearing before the committing magistrate, or the proceeding before the grand inquest. There can be no conviction until after arraignment on bill found. The previous action in the case is not a trial, and cannot convict, whatever be the evidence or the number of witnesses. I understand this to have been the opinion entertained by Chief Justice Marshall, 1 Burr's Trial, 195, and though it differs from that expressed by Judge Iredell on the indictment of Fries, (1 Whart. Am. St. Tr. 480), I feel authorized to recommend it to you, as within the terms of the Constitution, and involving no injustice to the accused. I have only to add that treason against the United States, may be committed by any one resident or sojourning within its territory, and under the protection of its laws, whether he be a citizen or an alien. (Fost. C.L. 183, 5.—1 Hale 59, 60, 62. 1 Hawk. ch. 17, § 5, Kel. 38).

Besides the crime of treason, which I have thus noticed, there are offences of minor grades, against the Constitution and the State, some or other of which may be apparently established by the evidence that will come before you. These are embraced in the act of Congress, on the 30th of Sept., 1790, Ch. 9, Sec. 22, on the subject of obstructing or resisting the service of legal process,—the act of the 2d of March, 1831, Chap. 99, Sec. 2, which secures the jurors, witnesses, and officers of our Courts in the fearless, free, and impartial administration of their respective functions,—and the act of the 18th of September, 1850, Ch. 60, which relates more particularly to the rescue, or attempted rescue of a fugitive from labor. These Acts were made the subject of a charge to the Grand Jury of this Court in November last, of which I shall direct a copy to be laid before you; and I do not deem it necessary to repeat their provisions at this time.

Gentlemen of the Grand Jury: You are about to enter upon a most grave and momentous duty. You will be careful in performing it, not to permit your indignation against crime, or your just appreciation of its perilous consequences, to influence your judgment of the guilt of those who may be charged before you with its commission. But you will be careful, also, that no misguided charity shall persuade you to withhold the guilty from the retributions of justice. You will inquire whether an offence has been committed, what was its legal character, and who were the offenders,—and this done, and this only, you will make your presentments according to the evidence and the law. Your inquiries will not be restricted to the conduct of the people belonging to our own State. If in the progress of them, you shall find, that men have been among us, who, under whatever mask of conscience or of peace, have labored to incite others to treasonable violence, and who, after arranging the elements of the mischief, have withdrawn themselves to await the explosion they had contrived, you will feel yourselves bound to present the fact to the Court,—and however distant may be the place in which the offenders may have sought refuge, we give you the pledge of the law, that its far-reaching energies shall be exerted to bring them up for trial,—if guilty, to punishment. The offence of treason is not triable in this Court; but by an act of Congress, passed on the 8th of August, 1845, Chap. 98, it is made lawful for the Grand Jury, empanelled and sworn in the District Court, to take cognizance of all the indictments for crimes against the United States within the jurisdiction of either of the Federal Courts of the District. There being no Grand Jury in attendance at this time in the Circuit Court, to pass upon the accusations I have referred to in the first instance, it has fallen to my lot to assume the responsible office of expounding to you the law in regard to them. I have the satisfaction of knowing, that if the views I have expressed are in any respect erroneous, they must undergo the revision of my learned brother of the Supreme Court, who presides in this Circuit, before they can operate to the serious prejudice of any one; and that if they are doubtful even, provision exists for their re-examination in the highest tribunal of the country."

On the strength of Judge Kane's carefully-drawn up charge the Grand Jury found true bills of indictment against forty of the Christiana offenders, charged with treason. James Jackson, an aged member of the Society of Friends (a Quaker), and a well-known non-resistant abolitionist, was of this number. With his name the blanks were filled up; the same form (with regard to these bills) was employed in the case of each one of the accused. The following is a

COPY OF THE INDICTMENT.

———

The Grand Inquest of the United States of America, inquiring for the Eastern District of Pennsylvania, on their oaths and affirmations, respectfully do present, that James Jackson, yeoman of the District aforesaid, owing allegiance to the United States of America, wickedly devising and intending the peace and tranquility of said United States, to disturb, and prevent the execution of the laws thereof within the same, to wit, a law of the United States, entitled "An act respecting fugitives from justice and persons escaping from the service of their masters," approved February twelfth, one thousand seven hundred and ninety-three, and also a law of the United States, entitled "An act to amend, and supplementary to, the act entitled, An act respecting fugitives from justice and persons escaping from the service of their masters, approved February the twelfth, one thousand seven hundred and ninety-three," which latter supplementary act was approved September eighteenth, one thousand eight hundred and fifty, on the eleventh day of September, in the year of our Lord, one thousand eight hundred and fifty-one, in the county of Lancaster, in the State of Pennsylvania and District aforesaid, and within the jurisdiction of this Court, wickedly and traitorously did intend to levy war against the United States within the same. And to fulfill and bring to effect the said traitorous intention of him, the said James Jackson, he, the said James Jackson afterward, to wit, on the day and year aforesaid, in the State, District and County aforesaid, and within the jurisdiction of this Court, with a great multitude of persons, whose names, to this Inquest are as yet unknown, to a great number, to wit, to the number of one hundred persons and upwards, armed and arrayed in a warlike manner, that is to say, with guns, swords, and other warlike weapons, as well offensive as defensive, being then and there unlawfully and traitorously assembled, did traitorously assemble and combine against the said United States, and then and there, with force and arms, wickedly and traitorously, and with the wicked and traitorous intention to oppose and prevent, by means of intimidation and violence, the execution of the said laws of the United States within the same, did array and dispose themselves in a warlike and hostile manner against the said United States, and then and there, with force and arms, in pursuance of such their traitorous intention, he, the said James Jackson, with the said persons so as aforesaid, wickedly and traitorously did levy war against the United States.

And further, to fulfill and bring to effect the said traitorous intention of him, the said James Jackson, and in pursuance and in execution of the said wicked and traitorous combination to oppose, resist and prevent the said laws of the United States from being carried into execution, he, the said James Jackson, afterwards, to wit, on the day and year first aforesaid, in the State, District and county aforesaid, and within the jurisdiction aforesaid, with the said persons whose names to this Inquest are as yet unknown, did, wickedly and traitorously assemble against the said United States, with the avowed intention by force of arms and intimidation to prevent the execution of the said laws of the United States within the same; and in pursuance and execution of such their wicked and traitorous combination, he, the said James Jackson, then and there with force and arms, with the said persons to a great number, to wit, the number of one hundred persons and upwards, armed and arrayed in a warlike manner, that is to say, with guns, swords, and other warlike weapons, as well offensive as defensive, being then and there, unlawfully and traitorously assembled, did wickedly, knowingly, and traitorously resist and oppose one Henry H. Kline, an officer, duly appointed by Edward D. Ingraham, Esq., a commissioner, duly appointed by the Circuit Court of the United States, for the said district, in the execution of the duty of the office of the said Kline, he, the said Kline, being appointed by the said Edward Ingraham, Esq., by writing under his hand, to execute warrants and other process issued by him, the said Ingraham, in the performance of his duties as Commissioner, under the said laws of the United States, and then and there, with force and arms, with the said great multitude of persons, so as, aforesaid, unlawfully and traitorously assembled, and armed and arrayed in manner as aforesaid, he, the said, James Jackson, wickedly and traitorously did oppose and resist, and prevent the said Kline, from executing the lawful process to him directed and delivered by the said commissioner against sundry persons, then residents of said county, who had been legally charged before the said commissioner as being persons held to service or labor in the State of Maryland, and owing such service or labor to a certain Edward Gorsuch, under the laws of the said State of Maryland, had escaped therefrom, into the said Eastern district of Pennsylvania; which process, duly issued by the said commissioner, the said Kline then and there had in his possession, and was then and there proceeding to execute, as by law he was bound to do; and so the grand inquest, upon their respective oaths and affirmations aforesaid, do say, that the said James Jackson, in manner aforesaid, as much as in him lay, wickedly and traitorously did prevent, by means of force and intimidation, the execution of the said laws of the United States, in the said State and District. And further, to fulfill and bring to effect, the said traitorous intention of him, the said James Jackson, and in further pursuance, and in the execution of the said wicked and traitorous combination to expose, resist, and prevent the execution of the said laws of the said United States, in the State and District aforesaid, he, the said James Jackson, afterwards, to wit, on the day and year first aforesaid, in the State, county, and district aforesaid, and within the jurisdiction of this court, with the said persons whose names to the grand inquest aforesaid, are as yet unknown, did, wickedly and traitorously assemble against the said United States with the avowed intention, by means of force and intimidation, to prevent the execution of the said laws of the United States in the State and district aforesaid, and in pursuance and execution of such, their wicked and traitorous combination and intention, then and there to the State, district, and county aforesaid, and within the jurisdiction of this court, with force and arms, with a great multitude of persons, to wit, the number of one hundred persons and upwards, armed and arrayed in a warlike manner, that is to say, with guns, swords, and other warlike weapons, as well offensive as defensive, being then and there unlawfully and traitorously assembled, he, the said James Jackson, did, knowingly, and unlawfully assault the said Henry H. Kline, he, the said Kline, being an officer appointed by writing, under the hand of the said Edward D. Ingraham, Esq., a commissioner under said laws, to execute warrants and other process, issued by the said commissioner in the performance of his duties as such; and he, the said James Jackson, did, then and there, traitorously, with force and arms, against the will of the said Kline, liberate and take out of his custody, persons by him before that time arrested, and in his lawful custody, then and there being, by virtue of lawful process against them issued by the said commissioner, they being legally charged with being persons held to service or labor in the State of Maryland, and owing such service or labor to a certain Edward Gorsuch, under the laws of the said State of Maryland, who had escaped therefrom into the said district; and so the grand inquest aforesaid, upon their oaths and affirmations, aforesaid, do say, that he, the said James Jackson, as much as in him lay, did, then and there, in pursuance and in execution of the said wicked and traitorous combination and intention, wickedly and traitorously, by means of force and intimidation, prevent the execution of the said laws of the United States, in the said State and district.

And further to fulfill and bring to effect, the said traitorous intention of him, the said James Jackson, and in pursuance and in execution of the said wicked and traitorous combination to oppose, resist and prevent the said laws of the United States from being carried into execution, he, the said James Jackson, afterwards, to wit, on the day and year first aforesaid, and on divers other days, both before and afterwards in the State and district aforesaid, and within the jurisdiction of this court, with the said persons to this inquest as yet unknown, maliciously and traitorously did meet, conspire, consult, and agree among themselves, further to oppose, resist, and prevent, by means of force and intimidation, the execution of the said laws herein before specified.

And further to fulfill, perfect, and bring to effect the said traitorous intention of him the said James Jackson, and in pursuance and execution of the said wicked and traitorous combination to oppose and resist the said laws of the United States from being carried into execution, in the State and district aforesaid, he, the said James Jackson, together with the other persons whose names are to this inquest as yet unknown, on the day and year first aforesaid, and on divers other days and times, as well before and after, at the district aforesaid, within the jurisdiction of said court, with force and arms, maliciously and traitorously did prepare and compose, and did then and there maliciously and traitorously cause and procure to be prepared and composed, divers books, pamphlets, letters, declarations, resolutions, addresses, papers and writings, and did then and there maliciously and traitorously publish and disperse and cause to be published and dispersed, divers other books and pamphlets, letters, declarations, resolutions, addresses, papers and writings; the said books, pamphlets, letters, declarations, resolutions, addresses, papers and writings, so respectively prepared, composed, published and dispersed, as last aforesaid, containing therein, amongst other things, incitements, encouragements, and exhortations, to move, induce and persuade persons held to service in any of the United States, by the laws thereof, who had escaped into the said district, as well as other persons, citizens of said district, to resist, oppose, and prevent, by violence and intimidation, the execution of the said laws, and also containing therein, instructions and directions how and upon what occasion, the traitorous purposes last aforesaid, should and might be carried into effect, contrary to the form of the act of Congress in such case made and provided, and against the peace and dignity of the United States.

JOHN W. ASHMEAD,
Attorney of the U.S. for the Eastern District of Pennsylvania.

———

The abolitionists were leaving no stone unturned in order to triumphantly meet the case in Court. During the interim many tokens of kindness and marks of Christian benevolence were extended to the prisoners by their friends and sympathizers; among these none deserve more honorable mention than the noble act of Thomas L. Kane (son of Judge Kane, and now General), in tendering all the prisoners a sumptuous Thanksgiving dinner, consisting of turkey, etc., pound cake, etc., etc. The dinner for the white prisoners, Messrs. Hanaway, Davis, and Scarlett, was served in appropriate style in the room of Mr. Morrison, one of the keepers. The U.S. Marshal, A.E. Roberts, Esq., several of the keepers, and Mr. Hanes, one of the prison officers, dined with the prisoners as their guests. Mayor Charles Gilpin was also present and accepted an invitation to test the quality of the luxuries, thus significantly indicating that he was not the enemy of Freedom.

Mrs. Martha Hanaway, the wife of the "traitor" of that name, and who had spent most of her time with her husband since his incarceration, served each of the twenty-seven colored "traitors" with a plate of the delicacies, and the supply being greater than the demand, the balance was served to outsiders in other cells on the same corridor.

The pro-slavery party were very indignant over the matter, and the Hon. Mr. Brent thought it incumbent upon him to bring this high-handed procedure to the notice of the Court, where he received a few crumbs of sympathy, from the pro-slavery side, of course. But the dinner had been so handsomely arranged, and coming from the source that it did, it had a very telling effect. Long before this, however, Mr. T.L. Kane had given abundant evidence that he approved of the Underground Rail Road, and was a decided opponent of the Fugitive Slave Law; in short, that he believed in freedom for all men, irrespective of race or color.

Castnor Hanaway was first to be tried; over him, therefore, the great contest was to be made. For the defence of this particular case, the abolitionists selected J.M. Read, Thaddeus Stevens, Joseph S. Lewis and Theodore Cuyler, Esqs. On the side of the Fugitive Slave Law, and against the "traitors," were U.S. District Attorney, John W. Ashmead, Hon. James Cooper, James R. Ludlow, Esq., and Robert G. Brent, Attorney General of Maryland. Mr. Brent was allowed to act as "overseer" in conducting matters on the side of the Fugitive Slave Law. On this infamous enactment, combined with a corrupted popular sentiment, the pro-slavery side depended for success. The abolitionists viewed matters in the light of freedom and humanity, and hopefully relied upon the justice of their cause and the power of truth to overcome and swallow up all the Pharaoh's rods of serpents as fast as they might be thrown down.

The prisoners having lain in their cells nearly three months, the time for their trial arrived. Monday morning, November 24th, the contest began. The first three days were occupied in procuring jurors. The pro-slavery side desired none but such as believed in the Fugitive Slave law and in "Treason" as expounded in the Judge's charge and the finding of the Grand Jury.

The counsel for the "Traitors" carefully weighed the jurors, and when found wanting challenged them; in so doing, they managed to get rid of most all of that special class upon whom the prosecution depended for a conviction. The jury having been sworn in, the battle commenced in good earnest, and continued unabated for nearly two weeks. It is needless to say, that the examinations and arguments would fill volumes, and were of the most deeply interesting nature.

No attempt can here be made to recite the particulars of the trial other than by a mere reference. It was, doubtless, the most important trial that ever took place in this country relative to the Underground Rail Road passengers, and in its results more good was brought out of evil than can easily be estimated. The pro-slavery theories of treason were utterly demolished, and not a particle of room was left the advocates of the peculiar institution to hope, that slave-hunters in future, in quest of fugitives, would be any more safe than Gorsuch. The tide of public sentiment changed— Hanaway, and the other "traitors," began to be looked upon as having been greatly injured, and justly entitled to public sympathy and honor, while confusion of face, disappointment and chagrin were plainly visible throughout the demoralized ranks of the enemy. Hanaway was victorious.

An effort was next made to convict Thompson, one of the colored "traitors." To defend the colored prisoners, the old Abolition Society had retained Thaddeus Stevens, David Paul Brown, William S. Pierce, and Robert P. Kane, Esqs., (son of Judge Kane). Stevens, Brown and Pierce were well-known veterans, defenders of the slave wherever and whenever called upon so to do. In the present case, they were prepared for a gallant stand and a long siege against opposing forces. Likewise, R.P. Kane, Esq., although a young volunteer in the anti-slavery war, brought to the work great zeal, high attainments, large sympathy and true pluck, while, in view of all the circumstances, the committee of arrangements felt very much gratified to have him in their ranks.

By this time, however, the sandy foundations of "overseer" Brent and Co., (on the part of slavery), had been so completely swept away by the Hon. J.M. Read and Co., on the side of freedom, that there was but little chance left to deal heavy blows upon the defeated advocates of the Fugitive Slave Law. Thompson was pronounced "not guilty." The other prisoners, of course, shared the same good luck. The victory was then complete, equally as much so as at Christiana. Underground Rail Road stock arose rapidly and a feeling of universal rejoicing pervaded the friends of freedom from one end of the country to the other.

Especially were slave-holders taught the wholesome lesson, that the Fugitive Slave Law was no guarantee against "red hot shot," nor the charges of U.S. Judges and the findings of Grand Juries, together with the superior learning of counsel from slave-holding Maryland, any guarantee that "traitors" would be hung. In every respect, the Underground Rail Road made capital by the treason. Slave-holders from Maryland especially were far less disposed to hunt their runaway property than they had hitherto been. The Deputy Marshal likewise considered the business of catching slaves very unsafe.

WILLIAM AND ELLEN CRAFT.

*Female Slave in Male Attire, Fleeing as
a Planter, with Her Husband as Her Body Servant.*

A quarter of a century ago, William and Ellen Craft were slaves in the State of Georgia. With them, as with thousands of others, the desire to be free was very strong. For this jewel they were willing to make any sacrifice, or to endure any amount of suffering. In this state of mind they commenced planning. After thinking of various ways that might be tried, it occurred to William and Ellen, that one might act the part of master and the other the part of servant.

Ellen being fair enough to pass for white, of necessity would have to be transformed into a young planter for the time being. All that was needed, however, to make this important change was that she should be dressed elegantly in a fashionable suit of male attire, and have her hair cut in the style usually worn by young planters. Her profusion of dark hair offered a fine opportunity for the change. So far this plan looked very tempting. But it occurred to them that Ellen was beardless. After some mature reflection, they came to the conclusion that this difficulty could be very readily obviated by having the face muffled up as though the young planter was suffering badly with the face or toothache; thus they got rid of this trouble. Straightway, upon further reflection, several other very serious difficulties stared them in the face. For instance, in traveling, they knew that they would be under the necessity of stopping repeatedly at hotels, and that the custom of registering would have to be conformed to, unless some very good excuse could be given for not doing so.

Here they again, thought much over matters, and wisely concluded that the young man had better assume the attitude of a gentleman very much indisposed. He must have his right arm placed

carefully in a sling; that would be a sufficient excuse for not registering, etc. Then he must be a little lame, with a nice cane in the left
hand; he must have large green spectacles over his eyes, and withal
he must be very hard of hearing and dependent on his faithful servant (as was no uncommon thing with slave-holders), to look after
all his wants.

William was just the man to act this part. To begin with, he was
very "likely-looking;" smart, active and exceedingly attentive to his
young master—indeed he was almost eyes, ears, hands and feet for
him. William knew that this would please the slave-holders. The
young planter would have nothing to do but hold himself subject to
his ailments and put on a bold air of superiority; he was not to deign
to notice anybody. If, while traveling, gentlemen, either politely or
rudely, should venture to scrape acquaintance with the young
planter, in his deafness he was to remain mute; the servant was to
explain. In every instance when this occurred, as it actually did, the
servant was fully equal to the emergency—none dreaming of the
disguises in which the Underground Rail Road passengers were
traveling.

They stopped at a first-class hotel in Charleston, where the
young planter and his body servant were treated, as the house was
wont to treat the chivalry. They stopped also at a similar hotel in
Richmond, and with like results.

They knew that they must pass through Baltimore, but they did
not know the obstacles that they would have to surmount in the
Monumental City. They proceeded to the depot in the usual manner, and the servant asked for tickets for his master and self. Of
course the master could have a ticket, but "bonds will have to be
entered before you can get a ticket," said the ticket master. "It is the
rule of this office to require bonds for all negroes applying for tickets to go North, and none but gentlemen of well-known responsibility will be taken," further explained the ticket master.

The servant replied, that he knew "nothing about that"—that he
was "simply traveling with his young master to take care of him—he
being in a very delicate state of health, so much so, that fears were
entertained that he might not be able to hold out to reach Philadel-

phia, where he was hastening for medical treatment," and ended his reply by saying, "my master can't be detained." Without further parley, the ticket master very obligingly waived the old "rule," and furnished the requisite tickets. The mountain being thus removed, the young planter and his faithful servant were safely in the cars for the city of Brotherly Love.

Scarcely had they arrived on free soil when the rheumatism departed—the right arm was unslung—the toothache was gone—the beardless face was unmuffled—the deaf heard and spoke—the blind saw—and the lame leaped as an hart, and in the presence of a few astonished friends of the slave, the facts of this unparalleled Underground Rail Road feat were fully established by the most unquestionable evidence.

The constant strain and pressure on Ellen's nerves, however, had tried her severely, so much so, that for days afterwards, she was physically very much prostrated, although joy and gladness beamed from her eyes, which bespoke inexpressible delight within.

Never can the writer forget the impression made by their arrival. Even now, after a lapse of nearly a quarter of a century, it is easy to picture them in a private room, surrounded by a few friends—Ellen in her fine suit of black, with her cloak and high-heeled boots, looking, in every respect, like a young gentleman; in an hour after having dropped her male attire, and assumed the habiliments of her sex the feminine only was visible in every line and feature of her structure.

Her husband, William, was thoroughly colored, but was a man of marked natural abilities, of good manners, and full of pluck, and possessed of perceptive faculties very large.

It was necessary, however, in those days, that they should seek a permanent residence, where their freedom would be more secure than in Philadelphia; therefore they were advised to go to headquarters, directly to Boston. There they would be safe, it was supposed, as it had then been about a generation since a fugitive had been taken back from the old Bay State, and through the incessant labors of William Lloyd Garrison, the great pioneer, and his faithful coadjutors, it was conceded that another fugitive slave case could never be tolerated on the free soil of Massachusetts. So to Boston they went.

On arriving, the warm hearts of abolitionists welcomed them heartily, and greeted and cheered them without let or hindrance. They did not pretend to keep their coming a secret, or hide it under a bushel; the story of their escape was heralded broadcast over the country—North and South, and indeed over the civilized world. For two years or more, not the slightest fear was entertained that they were not just as safe in Boston as if they had gone to Canada. But the day the Fugitive Bill passed, even the bravest abolitionist began to fear that a fugitive slave was no longer safe anywhere under the stars and stripes, North or South, and that William and Ellen Craft were liable to be captured at any moment by Georgia slave hunters. Many abolitionists counselled resistance to the death at all hazards. Instead of running to Canada, fugitives generally armed themselves and thus said, "Give me liberty or give me death."

William and Ellen Craft believed that it was their duty, as citizens of Massachusetts, to observe a more legal and civilized mode of conforming to the marriage rite than had been permitted them in slavery, and as Theodore Parker had shown himself a very warm friend of their's, they agreed to have their wedding over again according to the laws of a free State. After performing the ceremony, the renowned and fearless advocate of equal rights (Theodore Parker), presented William with a revolver and a dirk-knife, counselling him to use them manfully in defence of his wife and himself, if ever an attempt should be made by his owners or anybody else to re-enslave them.

But, notwithstanding all the published declarations made by abolitionists and fugitives, to the effect, that slave-holders and slave-catchers in visiting Massachusetts in pursuit of their runaway property, would be met by just such weapons as Theodore Parker presented William with, to the surprise of all Boston, the owners of William and Ellen actually had the effrontery to attempt their recapture under the Fugitive Slave Law. How it was done, and the results, taken from the *Old Liberator*, (William Lloyd Garrison's organ), we copy as follows:

From the "Liberator," Nov. 1, 1850.

SLAVE-HUNTERS IN BOSTON.

Our city, for a week past, has been thrown into a state of intense excitement by the appearance of two prowling villains, named Hughes and Knight, from Macon, Georgia, for the purpose of seizing William and Ellen Craft, under the infernal Fugitive Slave Bill, and carrying them back to the hell of Slavery. Since the day of '76, there has not been such a popular demonstration on the side of human freedom in this region. The humane and patriotic contagion has infected all classes. Scarcely any other subject has been talked about in the streets, or in the social circle. On Thursday, of last week, warrants for the arrest of William and Ellen were issued by Judge Levi Woodbury, but no officer has yet been found ready or bold enough to serve them. In the meantime, the Vigilance Committee, appointed at the Faneuil Hall meeting, has not been idle. Their number has been increased to upwards of a hundred "good men and true," including some thirty or forty members of the bar; and they have been in constant session, devising every legal method to baffle the pursuing bloodhounds, and relieve the city of their hateful presence. On Saturday placards were posted up in all directions, announcing the arrival of these slave-hunters, and describing their persons. On the same day, Hughes and Knight were arrested on the charge of slander against William Craft. The Chronotype says, the damages being laid at $10,000; bail was demanded in the same sum, and was promptly furnished. By whom? is the question. An immense crowd was assembled in front of the Sheriff's office, while the bail matter was being arranged. The reporters were not admitted. It was only known that Watson Freeman, Esq., who once declared his readiness to hang any number of negroes remarkably cheap, came in, saying that the arrest was a shame, all a humbug, the trick of the damned abolitionists, and proclaimed his readiness to stand bail. John H. Pearson was also sent for, and came—the same John H. Pearson, merchant and Southern packet agent, who immortalized himself by sending back, on the 10th of September, 1846, in the bark Niagara, a poor fugitive slave, who came secreted in the brig Ottoman, from New Orleans—being himself judge, jury and executioner, to consign a fellow-being to a life of bondage—in obedience to the law of a slave State, and in violation of the law of his own. This same John H. Pearson, not contented with his previous infamy, was on hand. There is a story that the slave-hunters have been his table-guests also, and whether he bailed them or not, we don't know. What we know is, that soon after Pearson came out from the back room, where he and Knight and the Sheriff had been closeted, the Sheriff said that Knight was bailed—he would not say by whom. Knight being looked after, was not to be found. He had slipped out through a back door, and thus cheated the crowd of the pleasure of greeting him—possibly with that rough and ready affection which Barclay's brewers bestowed upon Haynau. The escape was very fortunate every way. Hughes and Knight have since been twice arrested and put under bonds of $10,000 (making $30,000 in all), charged with a conspiracy to kidnap and abduct William Craft, a peaceable citizen of Massachusetts, etc. Bail was entered by Hamilton Willis, of Willis & Co., 25 State street, and Patrick Riley, U.S. Deputy Marshal.

The following (says the Chronotype), is a *verbatim et literatim* copy of the letter sent by Knight to Craft, to entice him to the U.S. Hotel, in order to kidnap him. It shows, that the school-master owes Knight more "service and labor" than it is possible for Craft to:

BOSTON, Oct. 22, 1850, 11 Oclk P.M.

Wm. Craft—Sir—I have to leave so Eirley in the moring that I cold not call according to promis, so if you want me to carry a letter home with me, you must bring it to the United States Hotel to morrow and leave it in box 44, or come your self to morro eavening after tea and bring it. let me no if you come your self by sending a note to box 44 U.S. Hotel so that I may know whether to wate after tea or not by the Bearer. If your wife wants to see me you cold bring her with you if you come your self.

JOHN KNIGHT.

P.S. I shall leave for home eirley a Thursday moring. J.K.

At a meeting of colored people, held in Belknap Street Church, on Friday evening, the following resolutions were unanimously adopted:

Resolved, That God willed us free; man willed us slaves. We will as God wills; God's will be done.

Resolved, That our oft repeated determination to resist oppression is the same now as ever, and we pledge ourselves, at all hazards, to resist unto death any attempt upon our liberties.

Resolved, That as South Carolina seizes and imprisons colored seamen from the North, under the plea that it is to prevent insurrection and rebellion among her colored population, the authorities of this State, and city in particular, be requested to lay hold of, and put in prison, immediately, any and all fugitive slave-hunters who may be found among us, upon the same ground, and for similar reasons.

Spirited addresses, of a most emphatic type, were made by Messrs. Remond, of Salem, Roberts, Nell, and Allen, of Boston, and Davis, of Plymouth. Individuals and highly respectable committees of gentlemen have repeatedly waited upon these Georgia miscreants, to persuade them to make a speedy departure from the city. After promising to do so, and repeatedly falsifying their word, it is said that they left on Wednesday afternoon, in the express train for New York, and thus (says the Chronotype), they have "gone off with their ears full of fleas, to fire the solemn word for the dissolution of the Union!"

Telegraphic intelligence is received, that President Fillmore has announced his determination to sustain the Fugitive Slave Bill, at all hazards. Let him try! The fugitives, as well as the colored people generally, seem determined to carry out the spirit of the resolutions to their fullest extent.

Ellen first received information that the slave-hunters from Georgia were after her through Mrs. Geo. S. Hilliard, of Boston, who had been a good friend to her from the day of her arrival from slavery. How Mrs. Hilliard obtained the information, the impression it made on Ellen, and where she was secreted, the following extract of a letter written by Mrs. Hilliard, touching the memorable event, will be found deeply interesting:

"In regard to William and Ellen Craft, it is true that we received her at our house when the first warrant under the act of eighteen hundred and fifty was issued.

Dr. Bowditch called upon us to say, that the warrant must be for William and Ellen, as they were the only fugitives here known to have come from Georgia, and the Dr. asked what we could do. I went to the house of the Rev. F.T. Gray, on Mt. Vernon street, where Ellen was working with Miss Dean, an upholsteress, a friend of ours, who had told us she would teach Ellen her trade. I proposed to Ellen to come and do some work for me, intending not to alarm her. My manner, which I supposed to be indifferent and calm, *betrayed* me, and she threw herself into my arms, sobbing and weeping. She, however, recovered her composure as soon as we reached the street, and was *very firm* ever after.

My husband wished her, by all means, to be brought to our house, and to remain under his protection, saying 'I am perfectly willing to meet the penalty, should she be found here, but will never give her up.' The penalty, you remember, was six months' imprisonment and a thousand dollars fine. William Craft went, after a time, to Lewis Hayden. He was at first, as Dr. Bowditch told us, 'barricaded in his shop on Cambridge street.' I saw him there, and he said, 'Ellen must not be left at your house.' 'Why? William,' said I, 'do you think we would give her up?' 'Never,' said he, 'but Mr. Hilliard is not only our friend, but he is a U.S. Commissioner, and should Ellen be found in his house, he must resign his office, as well as incur the penalty of the law, and I will not subject a friend to such a punishment for the sake of our safety.' Was not this noble, when you think how small was the penalty that any one could receive for aiding slaves to escape, compared to the fate which threatened them in case they were captured? William C. made the same objection to having his wife taken to Mr. Ellis Gray Loring's, he also being a friend and a Commissioner."

———

This deed of humanity and Christian charity is worthy to be commemorated and classed with the act of the good Samaritan, as the same spirit is shown in both cases. Often was Mrs. Hilliard's house an asylum for fugitive slaves.

After the hunters had left the city in dismay, and the storm of excitement had partially subsided, the friends of William and Ellen concluded that they had better seek a country where they would not be in daily fear of slave-catchers, backed by the Government of the United States. They were, therefore, advised to go to Great Britain. Outfits were liberally provided for them, passages procured, and they took their departure for a habitation in a foreign land.

Much might be told concerning the warm reception they met with from the friends of humanity on every hand, during a stay in England of nearly a score of years, but we feel obliged to make the following extract suffice:

EXTRACT OF A LETTER FROM WM. FARMER, ESQ., OF LONDON, TO WM. LLOYD GARRISON, JUNE 26, 1851—"FUGITIVE SLAVES AT THE GREAT EXHIBITION."

Fortunately, we have, at the present moment, in the British Metropolis, some specimens of what were once American "chattels personal," in the persons of William and Ellen Craft, and William W. Brown, and their friends resolved that they should be exhibited under the world's huge glass case, in order that the world might form its opinion of the alleged mental inferiority of the African race, and their fitness or unfitness for freedom. A small party of anti-slavery friends was accordingly formed to accompany the fugitives through the Exhibition. Mr. and Mrs. Estlin, of Bristol, and a lady friend, Mr. and Mrs. Richard Webb, of Dublin, and a son and daughter, Mr. McDonnell, (a most influential member of the Executive Committee of the National Reform Association—one of our unostentatious, but highly efficient workers for reform in this country, and whose public and private acts, if you were acquainted with, you would feel the same esteem and affection for him as is felt towards him by Mr. Thompson, myself and many others)—these ladies and gentlemen, together with myself, met at Mr. Thompson's house, and, in company with Mrs. Thompson, and Miss Amelia Thompson, the Crafts and Brown, proceeded from thence to the Exhibition. Saturday was selected, as a day upon which the largest number of the aristocracy and wealthy classes attend the Crystal Palace, and the company was, on this occasion, the most distinguished that had been gathered together within its walls since its opening day. Some fifteen thousand, mostly of the upper classes, were there congregated, including the Queen, Prince Albert, and the royal children, the anti-slavery Duchess of Sutherland, (by whom the fugitives were evidently favorably regarded), the Duke of Wellington, the Bishops of Winchester and St. Asaph, a large number of peers, peeresses, members of Parliament, merchants and bankers, and distinguished men from almost all parts of the world, surpassing, in variety of tongue, character and costume, the description of the population of Jerusalem on the day of Pentecost—a season of which it is hoped the Great Exhibition will prove a type, in the copious outpouring of the holy spirit of brotherly union, and the consequent diffusion, throughout the world, of the anti-slavery gospel of good will to all men.

In addition to the American exhibitors, it so happened that the American visitors were particularly numerous, among whom the experienced eyes of Brown and the Crafts enabled them to detect slave-holders by dozens. Mr. McDonnell escorted Mrs. Craft, and Mrs. Thompson; Miss Thompson, at her own request, took the arm of Wm. Wells Brown, whose companion she elected to be for the day; Wm. Craft walked with Miss Amelia Thompson and myself. This arrangement was purposely made in order that there might be no appearance of patronizing the fugitives, but that it might be shown that we regarded them as our equals, and honored them for their heroic escape from Slavery. Quite contrary to the feeling of ordinary visitors, the American department was our chief attraction. Upon arriving at Powers' Greek Slave, our glorious anti-slavery friend, Punch's 'Virginia Slave' was produced. I hope you have seen this production of our great humorous moralist. It is an admirably-drawn figure of a female slave in chains, with the inscription beneath, 'The Virginia Slave, a companion for Powers' Greek Slave.' The comparison of the two soon drew a small crowd, including several Americans, around and near us. Although they refrained from any audible expression of feeling, the object of the comparison was evidently understood and keenly felt. It would not have been prudent in us to have challenged, in words, an antislavery discussion in the World's Convention; but everything that we could with propriety do was done to induce them to break silence upon the subject. We had no intention, verbally, of taking the initiative in such a discussion; we confined ourselves to speaking at them, in order that they might be led to speak to us; but our efforts were of no avail. The gauntlet, which was unmistakably thrown down by our party, the Americans were too wary to take up. We spoke among each other of the wrongs of Slavery; it was in vain. We discoursed freely upon the iniquity of a professedly Christian Republic holding three millions of its population in cruel and degrading bondage; you might as well have preached to the winds. Wm. Wells Brown took 'Punch's Virginia Slave' and deposited it within the enclosure by the 'Greek Slave,' saying audibly, 'As an American fugitive slave, I place this 'Virginia Slave' by the side of the 'Greek Slave,' as its most fitting companion.' Not a word, or reply, or remonstrance from Yankee or Southerner. We had not, however, proceeded many steps from the place before the 'Virginia Slave' was removed. We returned to the statue, and stood near the American by whom it had been taken up, to give him an opportunity of making any remarks he chose upon the matter. Whatever were his feelings, his policy was to keep his lips closed. If he had felt that the act was wrongful, would he not have appealed to the sense of justice of the British bystanders, who are always ready to resist an insult offered to a foreigner in this country? If it was an insult, why not resent it, as became high-spirited Americans? But no; the chivalry of the South tamely allowed itself to be plucked by the beard; the garrulity of the North permitted itself to be silenced by three fugitive slaves. . . . We promenaded the Exhibition between six and seven hours, and visited nearly every portion of the vast edifice. Among the thousands whom we met in our perambulations, who dreamed of any impropriety in a gentleman of character and standing, like Mr. McDonnell, walking arm-in-arm with a colored woman; or an elegant and accomplished young lady, like Miss Thompson, (daughter of the Hon. George Thompson, M.C.), becoming the promenading companion of a colored man? Did the English peers or peeresses? Not the most aristocratic among them. Did the representatives of any other country have their notions of propriety shocked by the matter? None but Americans. To see the arm of a beautiful English young lady passed through that of 'a nigger,' taking ices and other refreshments with him, upon terms of the most perfect equality, certainly was enough to 'rile,' and evidently did 'rile' the slave-holders who beheld it; but there was no help for it. Even the New York Broadway bullies would not have dared to utter a word of insult, much less lift a finger against Wm. Wells Brown, when walking with his fair companion in the World's Exhibition. It was a circumstance not to be forgotten by these Southern Bloodhounds. Probably, for the first time in their lives, they felt themselves thoroughly muzzled; they dared not even to bark, much less bite. Like the meanest curs, they had to sneak through the Crystal Palace, unnoticed and uncared for; while the victims who had been rescued from their jaws, were warmly greeted by visitors from all parts of the country.

* * * * *

Brown and the Crafts have paid several other visits to the Great Exhibition, in one of which, Wm. Craft succeeded in getting some Southerners "out" upon the Fugitive Slave Bill, respecting which a discussion was held between them in the American department. Finding themselves worsted at every point, they were compelled to have recourse to lying, and unblushingly denied that the bill contained the provisions which Craft alleged it did. Craft took care to inform them who and what he was. He told them that there had been too much information upon that measure diffused in England for lying to conceal them. He has subsequently met the same parties, who, with contemptible hypocrisy, treated "the nigger" with great respect.

In England the Crafts were highly respected. While under her British Majesty's protection, Ellen became the mother of several children, (having had none under the stars and stripes). These they spared no pains in educating for usefulness in the world. Some two years since William and Ellen returned with two of their children to the United States, and after visiting Boston and other places, William concluded to visit Georgia, his old home, with a view of seeing what inducement war had opened up to enterprise, as he had felt a desire to remove his family thither, if encouraged. Indeed he was prepared to purchase a plantation, if he found matters satisfactory. This visit evidently furnished the needed encouragement, judging from the fact that he did purchase a plantation somewhere in the neighborhood of Savannah, and is at present living there with his family.

The portraits of William and Ellen represent them at the present stage of life, (as citizens of the U.S.)—of course they have greatly changed in appearance from what they were when they first fled from Georgia. Obviously the Fugitive Slave Law in its crusade against William and Ellen Craft, reaped no advantages, but on the contrary, liberty was greatly the gainer.

ARRIVAL FROM DELAWARE, 1857.

John Wright and Wife, Elizabeth Ann,
and Charles Connor.

This party arrived from Sussex county. John was about thirty years of age, ordinary size, full black and clear-headed. In physical appearance he would have readily passed for a superior laborer. The keenness of his eyes and quickness of his perception, however, would doubtless have rendered him an object of suspicion in some parts of the South. The truth was that the love of liberty was clearly indicated in his expressive countenance. William S. Phillips, a farmer, had been "sucking" John's blood, and keeping him poor and ignorant for the last eight years at least; before that, Phillips' father had defrauded him of his hire.

Under the father and son John had found plenty of hard work and bad usage, severe and repeated floggings not excepted. Old master and mistress and young master and mistress, including the entire family, belonged to what was known as the "Farmer church," at Portsville. Outwardly they were good Christians. "Occasionally," John said, "the old man would have family prayers," and to use John's own words, "in company he would try to moralize, but out of company was as great a rowdy as ever was." In further describing his old master, he said that he was a large man, with a red face and blunt nose, and was very quick and fiery in his temper; would drink and swear—and even his wife, with all hands, would have to run when he was "raised."

Of his young master he said: "He was quite a long-bodied, thin-faced man, weighing over one hundred and fifty pounds. In temper just like his father, though he did not drink—that is all the good quality that I can recommend in him." John said also that his master, on one occasion, in a most terribly angry mood, threatened that he would "wade up to his knees in his (John's) blood." It so happened that John's blood was up pretty high just at that time; he gave his master to understand that he would rather go South (be sold) than submit to the scourging which was imminent. John's pluck probably had the effect of allaying the master's fire; at any rate the storm subsided after awhile, and until the day that he took the Underground Rail Road car the servant managed to put up with his master. As John's wife was on the eve of being sold he was prompted to leave some time sooner than he otherwise would have done.

THE WIFE'S STATEMENT

She was thirty-two years of age, of good physical proportions, and a promising-looking person, above the ordinary class of slaves belonging to Delaware. She was owned by Jane Cooper, who lived near Laurel, in Sussex county. She had been more accustomed to field labor than house-work; ploughing, fencing, driving team, grubbing, cutting wood, etc., were well understood by her. During "feeding times" she had to assist in the house. In this respect, she had harder times than the men. Her mistress was also in the habit of hiring Elizabeth out by the day to wash. On these occasions she was required to rise early enough to milk the cows, get breakfast, and feed the hogs before sunrise, so that she might be at her day's washing in good time.

It is plainly to be seen, that Elizabeth had not met with the "ease" and kindness which many claimed for the slave. Elizabeth was sensible of the wrongs inflicted by her Delaware mistress, and painted her in very vivid colors. Her mistress was a widow, "quite old," but "very frisky," and "wore a wig to hide her gray hairs." At the death of her husband, the slaves believed, from what they had heard their master say, that they would be freed, each at the age of thirty. But no will was found, which caused Elizabeth, as well as the rest of the slaves, to distrust the mistress more than ever, as they suspected that she knew something of its disappearance.

Her mistress belonged to the Presbyterian Church, but would have "family prayers only when the minister would stop;" Elizabeth thought that she took greater pains to please the minister than her Maker. Elizabeth had no faith in such religion.

Both Elizabeth and her husband were members of the Methodist Church. Neither had ever been permitted to learn to read or write, but they were naturally very smart. John left his mother and one sister in bondage. One of his brothers fled to Canada fifteen years before their escape. His name was Abraham.

Charles Connor, the third person in the party, was twenty-seven years of age—fast color, and a tough-looking "article," who would have brought twelve hundred dollars or more in the hands of a Baltimore trader. The man from whom Charles fled was known by the name of John Chipman, and was described as "a fleshy man, with rank beard and quick temper, very hard—commonly kept full of liquor, though he would not get so drunk that he could not go about." For a long time Charles had been the main dependence on his master's place, as he only owned two other slaves. Charles particularly remarked, that no weather was too bad for them to be kept at work in the field. Charles was a fair specimen of the "corn-field hand," but thought that he could take care of himself in Canada.

ARRIVAL FROM NEW ORLEANS, 1857.

James Conner, Shot in Different Parts of the Body.

James stated to the Committee that he was about forty-three years of age, that he was born a slave in Nelson county, Ky., and that he was first owned by a widow lady by the name of Ruth Head. "She (mistress) was like a mother to me," said Jim. "I was about sixteen years old when she died; the estate was settled and I was sold South to a man named Vincent Turner, a planter, and about the worst man, I expect, that ever the sun shined on. His slaves he fairly murdered; two hundred lashes were merely a promise for him. He owned about three hundred slaves. I lived with Turner until he died. After his death I still lived on the plantation with his widow, Mrs. Virginia Turner." About twelve years ago (prior to Jim's escape) she was married to a Mr. Charles Parlange, "a poor man, though a very smart man, bad-hearted, and very barbarous."

Before her second marriage cotton had always been cultivated, but a few years later sugar had taken the place of cotton, and had become the principal thing raised in that part of the country. Under the change sugar was raised and the slaves were made to experience harder times than ever; they were allowed to have only from three to three and a half pounds of pork a week, with a peck of meal; nothing else was allowed. They commenced work in the morning, just when they could barely see; they quit work in the evening when they could not see to work longer.

Mistress was a large, portly woman, good-looking, and pretty well liked by her slaves. The place where the plantation was located was at Point Copee, on Falls River, about one hundred and fifty miles from New Orleans. She also owned property and about twenty slaves in the city of New Orleans.

"I lived there and hired my time for awhile. I saw some hard times on the plantation. Many a time I have seen slaves whipped almost to death—well, I tell you I have seen them whipped to death. A slave named Sam was whipped to death tied to the ground. Joe, another slave, was whipped to death by the overseer: running away was the crime.

"Four times I was shot. Once, before I would be taken, all hands, young and old on the plantation were on the chase after me. I was strongly armed with an axe, tomahawk, and butcher knife. I expected to be killed on the spot, but I got to the woods and stayed two days. At night I went back to the plantation and got something to eat. While going back to the woods I was shot in the thigh, legs, back and head, was badly wounded, my mind was to die rather than be taken. I ran a half mile after I was shot, but was taken. I have shot in me now. Feel here on my head, feel my back, feel buck shot in my thigh. I shall carry shot in me to my grave. I have been shot four different times. I was shot twice by a fellow servant; it was my master's orders. Another time by the overseer. Shooting was no uncommon thing in Louisiana. At one time I was allowed to raise hogs. I had twenty-five taken from me without being allowed the first copper.

"My mistress promised me at another time forty dollars for gathering honey, but when I went to her, she said, by and by, but the by and by never came. In 1853 my freedom was promised; for five years before this time I had been overseer; during four years of this time a visit was made to France by my owners, but on their return my freedom was not given me. My mistress thought I had made enough money to buy myself. They asked eleven hundred and fifty dollars for me. I told them that I hadn't the money. Then they said if I would go with them to Virginia after a number of slaves they wished to purchase, and would be a good boy, they would give me my freedom on the return of the trip. We started on the 8th of June, 1857. I made fair promises wishing to travel, and they placed all confidence in me. I was to carry the slaves back from Virginia.

"They came as far as Baltimore, and they began to talk of coming farther North, to Philadelphia. They talked very good to me, and told me that if they brought me with them to a free State that I must not leave them; talked a good deal about giving me my freedom, as had been promised before starting, etc. I let on to them that I had no wish to go North; that Baltimore was as far North as I wished to see, and that I had rather be going home than going North. I told them that I was tired of this country. In speaking of coming North, they made mention of the Alleghany mountains. I told them that I would like to see that, but nothing more. They hated the North, and I made believe that I did too. Mistress said, that if I behaved myself I could go with them to France, when they went again, after they returned home—as they intended to go again.

"So they decided to take me with them to Philadelphia, for a short visit, before going into Virginia to buy up their drove of slaves for Louisiana. My heart leaped for joy when I found we were going to a free State; but I did not let my owners know my feelings.

"We reached Philadelphia and went to the Girard Hotel, and there I made up my mind that they should go back without me. I saw a colored man who talked with me, and told me about the Committee. He brought me to the anti-slavery office," etc., etc., etc.

The Committee told Jim that he could go free immediately, without saying a word to anybody, as the simple fact of his master's bringing him into the State was sufficient to establish his freedom before the Courts. At the same time the Committee assured him if he were willing to have his master arrested and brought before one of the Judges of the city to show cause why he held him a slave in Pennsylvania, contrary to the laws of the State, that he should lack neither friends nor money to aid him in the matter; and, moreover, his freedom would be publicly proclaimed.

Jim thought well of both ways, but preferred not to meet his "kind-hearted" master and mistress in Court, as he was not quite sure that he would have the courage to face them and stand by his charges.

This was not strange. Indeed not only slaves cowed before the eye of slave-holders. Did not even Northern men, superior in education and wealth, fear to say their souls were their own in the same presence?

Jim, therefore, concluded to throw himself upon the protection of the Committee and take an Underground Rail Road ticket, and thereby spare himself and his master and mistress the disagreeableness of meeting under such strange circumstances. The Committee arranged matters for him to the satisfaction of all concerned, and gave him a passport for her British majesty's possession, Canada.

The unvarnished facts, as they were then recorded substantially from the lips of Jim, and as they are here reproduced, comprise only a very meagre part of his sadly interesting story. At the time Jim left his master and mistress so unceremoniously in Philadelphia, some excitement existed at the attempt of his master to recover him through the Police of Philadelphia, under the charge that he (Jim) had been stealing, as may be seen from the following letter which appeared in the "National Anti-Slavery Standard:"

ANOTHER SLAVE HUNT IN PHILADELPHIA.

Philadelphia, Monday, July 27, 1857.

Yesterday afternoon a rumor was afloat that a negro man named Jim, who had accompanied his master (Mr. Charles Parlange), from New Orleans to this city, had left his master for the purpose of tasting the sweets of freedom. It was alleged by Mr. Parlange that the said "Jim" had taken with him two tin boxes, one of which contained money. Mr. Parlange went, on his way to New York, *via* the Camden and Amboy Railroad, and upon his arrival at the Walnut street wharf, with two ladies, "Jim" was missing. Mr. Parlange immediately made application to a Mr. Wallace, who is a Police officer stationed at the Walnut street depot. Mr. Wallace got into a carriage with Mr. Parlange and the two ladies, and, as Mr. Wallace stated, drove back to the Girard House, where "Jim" had not been heard of since he had left for the Walnut street wharf.

A story was then set afloat to the effect, that a negro of certain, but very particular description (such as a Louisiana nigger-driver only can give), had stolen two boxes as stated above. A notice signed "Clarke," was received at the Police Telegraph Office by the operator (David Wunderly) containing a full description of Jim, also offering a reward of $100 for his capture. This notice was telegraphed to all the wards in every section. This morning Mr. Wunderly found fault with the reporters using the information, and, in presence of some four or five persons, said the notice signed "Clarke," was a private paper, and no reporter had a right to look at it; at the same time asserting, that if he knew where the nigger was he would give him up, as $100 did not come along every day. The policeman, Wallace, expressed the utmost fear lest the name of Mr. Parlange should transpire, and stated, that he was an intimate friend of his. It does not seem that the matter was communicated to the wards by any official authority whatever, and who the "Clarke" is, whose name was signed to the notice, has not yet transpired. Some of the papers noticed it briefly this morning, which has set several of the officers on their tips. There is little doubt, that "Jim" has merely exercised his own judgment about remaining with his master any longer, and took this opportunity to betake himself to freedom. It is assumed, that he was to precede his master to Walnut street wharf with the baggage; but, singular enough to say, no complaint has been made about the baggage being missed, simply the two tin boxes, and particularly the one containing money. This is, doubtless, a ruse to engage the services of the Philadelphia police in the interesting game of nigger hunting. Mr. Parlange, if he is sojourning in your city, will doubtless be glad to learn that the matter of his man "Jim" and the two tin boxes has received ample publicity. W.H.

Rev. Hiram Wilson, the Underground Rail Road agent at St. Catharines, C.W., duly announced his safe arrival as follows:

BUFFALO, Aug. 12th, 1857.

MY DEAR FRIEND—WM. STILL:—I take the liberty to inform you, that I had the pleasure of seeing a man of sable brand at my house in St. C. yesterday, by name of James Connor, lately from New Orleans, more recently from the city of Brotherly love, where he took French leave of his French master. He desired me to inform you of his safe arrival in the glorious land of Freedom, and to send his kind regards to you and to Mr. Williamson; also to another person, (the name I have forgotten). Poor Malinda Smith, with her two little girls and young babe is with us doing well.

Affectionately yours, HIRAM WILSON.

ARRIVAL FROM WASHINGTON, D.C.

Harrison Cary.

The passenger bearing this name who applied to the Committee for assistance, was a mulatto of medium size, with a prepossessing countenance, and a very smart talker. With only a moderate education he might have raised himself to the "top round of the ladder," as a representative of the down-trodden slave. Seeking, as usual, to learn his history, the subjoined questions and answers were the result of the interview:

Q. "How old are you?"
A. "Twenty-eight years of age this coming March."
Q. "To whom did you belong?"
A. "Mrs. Jane E. Ashley."
Q. "What kind of a woman was she?"
A. "She was a very clever woman; never said anything out of the way."
Q. "How many servants had she?"
A. "She had no other servants."
Q. "Did you live with her?"
A. "No. I hired my time for twenty-two dollars a month."
Q. "How could you make so much money?"
A. "I was a bricklayer by trade, and ranked among the first in the city."

As Harrison talked so intelligently, the member of the Committee who was examining him, was anxious to know how he came to be so knowing, the fact that he could read being very evident.

Harrison proceeded to explain how he was led to acquire the art both of reading and writing: "Slaves caught out of an evening without passes from their master or mistress, were invariably arrested, and if they were unable to raise money to buy themselves off, they were taken and locked up in a place known as the 'cage,' and in the morning the owner was notified, and after paying the fine the unfortunate prisoner had to go to meet his fate at the hands of his owner."

Often he or she found himself or herself sentenced to take thirty-nine or more lashes before atonement could be made for the violated law, and the fine sustained by the enraged owner.

Harrison having strong aversion to both of the "wholesome regulations" of the peculiar institution above alluded to, saw that the only remedy that he could avail himself of was to learn to write his own passes. In possessing himself of this prize he knew that the law against slaves being taught, would have to be broken, nevertheless he was so anxious to succeed, that he was determined to run the risk. Consequently he grasped the boon with but very little difficulty or assistance. Valuing his prize highly, he improved more and more until he could write his own passes satisfactorily. The "cage" he denounced as a perfect "hog hole," and added, "it was more than I could bear."

He also spoke with equal warmth on the pass custom, "the idea of working hard all day and then being obliged to have a pass," etc.,—his feelings sternly revolted against. Yet he uttered not a disrespectful word against the individual to whom he belonged. Once he had been sold, but for what was not noted on the record book.

His mother had been sold several times. His brother, William Henry Gary, escaped from Washington, D.C., when quite a youth. What became of him it was not for Harrison to tell, but he supposed that he had made his way to a free State, or Canada, and he hoped to find him. He had no knowledge of any other relatives.

In further conversation with him, relative to his being a single man, he said, that he had resolved not to entangle himself with a family until he had obtained his freedom.

He had found it pretty hard to meet his monthly hire, consequently he was on the look-out to better his condition as soon as a favorable opportunity might offer. Harrison's mistress had a son named John James Ashley, who was then a minor. On arriving at majority, according to the will of this lad's father, he was to have possession of Harrison as his portion. Harrison had no idea of having to work for his support—he thought that, if John could not take care of himself when he grew up to be a man, there was a place for all such in the poor-house.

Harrison was also moved by another consideration. His mistress' sister had been trying to influence the mistress to sell him; thus considering himself in danger, he made up his mind that the time had come for him to change his habitation, so he resolved to try his fortune on the Underground Rail Road.

ARRIVAL FROM MARYLAND.

Christopher Green and Wife, Ann Maria, and Son Nathan.

Christopher had a heavy debt charged against Clayton Wright, a commission merchant, of Baltimore, who claimed him as his property, and was in the habit of hiring him out to farmers in the country, and of taking all his hire except a single dollar, which was allotted him every holiday.

The last item in his charge against Wright, suggested certain questions: "How have you been used?" was the first query. "Sometimes right smart, and then again bad enough for it," said Christopher. Again he was asked, "What kind of a man was your master?" "He was only tolerable, I can't say much good for him. I got tired of working and they getting my labor and I getting nothing for my labor." At the time of his escape, he was employed in the service of a man by the name of Cook. Christopher described him as "a dissatisfied man, who couldn't be pleased at nothing and his wife was like him."

This passenger was quite black, medium size, and in point of intellect, about on a par with ordinary field hands. His wife, Ann, in point of go-ahead-ativeness, seemed in advance of him. Indeed, she first prompted her husband to escape.

Ann bore witness against one James Pipper, a farmer, whom she had served as a slave, and from whom she fled, saying that "he was as mean a man as ever walked—a dark-complected old man, with gray hair." With great emphasis she thus continued her testimony: "He tried to work me to death, and treated me as mean as he could, without killing me; he done so much I couldn't tell to save my life. I wish I had as many dollars as he has whipped me with sticks and other things. His wife will do tolerable." "I left because he was going to sell me and my son to Georgia; for years he had been threatening; since the boys ran away, last spring, he was harder than ever. One was my brother, Perry, and the other was a young man by the name of Jim." "David, my master, drank all he could get, poured it down, and when drunk, would cuss, and tear, and rip, and beat. He lives near the nine bridges, in Queen Ann county."

Ann was certainly a forcible narrator, and was in every way a wideawake woman, about thirty-seven years of age. Among other questions they were asked if they could read, etc. "Read," said Ann. "I would like to see anybody (slave) that could read our way; to see you with a book in your hand they would almost cut your throat."

Ann had one child only, a son, twenty years of age, who came in company with his parents. This son belonged to the said Pipper already described. When they started from the land of bondage they had large hopes, but not much knowledge of the way; however, they managed to get safely on the Underground Rail Road track, and by perseverance they reached the Committee and were aided in the usual manner.

ARRIVAL FROM ALEXANDRIA.

William Triplett and Thomas Harper.

Ran away from the subscriber, on Saturday night, 22d instant, WIL-LIAM TRIPLETT, a dark mulatto, with whiskers and mustache, 23 to 26 years of age; lately had a burn on the instep of his right foot, but perhaps well enough to wear a boot or shoe. He took with him very excellent clothing, both summer and winter, consisting of a brown suit in cloth, summer coats striped, check cap, silk hat, &c. $50 reward will be paid if taken within thirty miles of Alexandria or in the State of Virginia, and $150 and necessary expenses if taken out of the State and secured so that I get him again. He is the property of Mrs. A.B. Fairfax, of Alexandria, and is likely to make his way to Cincinnati, where he has friends, named Hamilton and Hopes, now living.

ROBT. W. WHEAT.

William, answering to the above description, arrived safely in company with Thomas Harper, about six days after the date of their departure from the house of bondage.

Mrs. A.B. Fairfax was the loser of this "article." William spoke rather favorably of her. He said he did not leave because he was treated badly, but simply because he wanted to own himself—to be free. He also said that he wanted to be able to take care of his family if he should see fit to marry.

As to Slavery, he could see no justice in the system; he therefore made up his mind no longer to yield submission thereto. Being a smart "chattel," he reasoned well on the question of Slavery, and showed very conclusively that even under the kindest mistress it had no charms for him—that at best, it was robbery and an outrage.

Thomas Harper, his comrade, fled from John Cowling, who also lived near Alexandria. His great trouble was, that he had a wife and family, but could do nothing for them. He thought that it was hard to see them in want and abused when he was not at liberty to aid or protect them. He grew very unhappy, but could see no remedy except in flight.

Cowling, his master, was an Englishman by birth, and followed black-smithing for a living. He was a man in humble circumstances, trying to increase his small fortune by slave-labor.

He allowed Thomas to hire himself for one hundred dollars a year, which amount he was required to raise, sick or well. He did not complain, however, of having received any personal abuse from his black-smith master. It was the system which was daily grinding the life out of him, that caused him to suffer, and likewise escape. By trade Thomas was also a blacksmith. He left a wife and three children.

ARRIVAL FROM NORFOLK, VA.

Abram Wooders.

Although slave-holders had spared no pains to keep Abram in the dark and to make him love his yoke, he proved by his actions, that he had no faith in their doctrines. Nor did he want for language in which to state the reasons for his actions. He was just in the prime of life, thirty-five years of age, chestnut color, common size, with a scar over the left eye, and another on the upper lip.

Like many others, he talked in a simple, earnest manner, and in answer to queries as to how he had fared, the following is his statement:

"I was held as the property of the late Taylor Sewell, but when I escaped I was in the service of W.C. Williams, a commission merchant. My old master was a very severe man, but he was always very kind to me. He had a great many more colored folks, was very severe amongst them, would get mad and sell right away. He was a drinking man, dissipated and a gambler, a real sportsman. He lived on Newell Creek, about twelve miles from Norfolk. For the last eight years I was hired to W.C. Williams, for $150 a year—if I had all that money, it might do me some good. I left because I wanted to enjoy myself some. I felt if I staid and got old no one would care for me, I wouldn't be of no account to nobody."

"But are not the old slaves well cared for by their masters?" a member of the Committee here remarked. "Take care of them! no!" Abram replied with much earnestness, and then went on to explain how such property was left to perish. Said Abram, "There was an old man named Ike, who belonged to the same estate that I did, he was treated like a dog; after they could get no more work out of him, they said, 'let him die, he is of no service; there is no use of getting a doctor for him.' Accordingly there could be no other fate for the old man but to suffer and die with creepers in his legs."

It was sickening to hear him narrate instances of similar suffering in the case of old slaves. Abram left two sisters and one brother in bondage.

ARRIVAL FROM NORTH CAROLINA, 1857.

Harry Grimes, George Upsher, and Edward Lewis. Feet Slit for Running Away, Flogged, Stabbed, Stayed in the Hollow of a Big Poplar Tree, Visited by a Snake, Abode in a Cave.

The coming of the passengers here noticed was announced in the subjoined letter from Thomas Garrett:

WILMINGTON, 11th Mo. 25th, 1857.

RESPECTED FRIEND, WILLIAM STILL:—I write to inform thee, that Captain Fountain has arrived this evening from the South with three men, one of which is nearly naked, and very lousy. He has been in the swamps of Carolina for eighteen months past. One of the others has been some time out. I would send them on to-night, but will have to provide two of them with some clothes before they can be sent by rail road. I have forgotten the number of thy house. As most likely all are more or less lousy, having been compelled to sleep together, I thought best to write thee so that thee may get a suitable place to take them to, and meet them at Broad and Prime streets on the arrival of the cars, about II o'clock to-morrow evening. I have engaged one of our men to take them to his house, and go to Philadelphia with them to-morrow evening. Johnson who will accompany them is a man in whom we can confide. Please send me the number of thy house when thee writes. THOMAS GARRETT.

This epistle from the old friend of the fugitive, Thomas Garrett, excited unusual interest. Preparation was immediately made to give the fugitives a kind reception, and at the same time to destroy their plagues, root and branch, without mercy.

They arrived according to appointment. The cleansing process was carried into effect most thoroughly, and no vermin were left to tell the tale of suffering they had caused. Straightway the passengers were made comfortable in every way, and the spirit of freedom seemed to be burning like "fire shut up in the bones." The appearance alone of these men indicated their manhood, and wonderful natural ability. The examining Committee were very desirous of hearing their story without a moment's delay.

As Harry, from having suffered most, was the hero of this party, and withal was an intelligent man, he was first called upon to make his statement as to how times had been with him in the prison house, from his youth up. He was about forty-six years of age, according to his reckoning, full six feet high, and in muscular appearance was very rugged, and in his countenance were evident marks of firmness. He said that he was born a slave in North Carolina, and had been sold three times. He was first sold when a child three years of age, the second time when he was thirteen years old, and the third and last time he was sold to Jesse Moore, from whom he fled. Prior to his coming into the hands of Moore he had not experienced any very hard usage, at least nothing more severe than fell to the common lot of slave-boys, therefore the period of his early youth was deemed of too little interest to record in detail. In fact time only could be afforded for noticing very briefly some of the more remarkable events of his bondage. The examining Committee confined their interrogations to his last taskmaster.

"How did Moore come by you?" was one of the inquiries. "He bought me," said Harry, "of a man by the name of Taylor, nine or ten years ago; he was as bad as he could be, couldn't be any worse to be alive. He was about fifty years of age, when I left him, a right red-looking man, big bellied old fellow, weighs about two hundred and forty pounds. He drinks hard, he is just like a rattlesnake, just as cross and crabbed when he speaks, seems like he could go through you. He flogged Richmond for not ploughing the corn good, that was what he pretended to whip him for. Richmond ran away, was away four months, as nigh as I can guess, then they cotched him, then struck him a hundred lashes, and then they split both feet to the bone, and split both his insteps, and then master took his knife and stuck it into him in many places; after he done him that way, he put him into the barn to shucking corn. For a long time he was not able to work; when he did partly recover, he was set to work again."

We ceased to record anything further concerning Richmond, although not a fourth part of what Harry narrated was put upon paper. The account was too sickening and the desire to hear Harry's account of himself too great to admit of further delay; so Harry confined himself to the sufferings and adventures which had marked his own life. Briefly he gave the following facts: "I have been treated bad. One day we were grubbing and master said we didn't do work enough. 'How came there was no more work done that day?' said master to me. I told him I did work. In a more stormy manner he 'peated the question. I then spoke up and said: 'Massa, I don't know what to say.' At once massa plunged his knife into my neck causing me to stagger. Massa was drunk. He then drove me down to the black folk's houses (cabins of the slaves). He then got his gun, called the overseer, and told him to get some ropes. While he was gone I said, 'Massa, now you are going to tie me up and cut me all to pieces for nothing. I would just as leave you would take your gun and shoot me down as to tie me up and cut me all to pieces for nothing.' In a great rage he said 'go.' I jumped, and he put up his gun and snapped both barrels at me. He then set his dogs on me, but as I had been in the habit of making much of them, feeding them, &c. they would not follow me, and I kept on straight to the woods. My master and the overseer cotched the horses and tried to run me down, but as the dogs would not follow me they couldn't make nothing of it. It was the last of August a year ago. The devil was into him, and he flogged and beat four of the slaves, one man and three of the women, and said if he could only get hold of me he wouldn't strike me, 'nary-a-lick,' but would tie me to a tree and empty both barrels into me.

In the woods I lived on nothing, you may say, and something too. I had bread, and roasting ears, and 'taters. I stayed in the hollow of a big poplar tree for seven months; the other part of the time I stayed in a cave. I suffered mighty bad with the cold and for something to eat. Once I got me some charcoal and made me a fire in my tree to warm me, and it liked to killed me, so I had to take the fire out. One time a snake come to the tree, poked its head in the hollow and was coming in, and I took my axe and chopped him in two. It was a poplar leaf moccasin, the poisonest kind of a snake we have. While in the woods all my thoughts was how to get away to a free country."

Subsequently, in going back over his past history, he referred to the fact, that on an occasion long before the cave and tree existence, already noticed, when suffering under this brutal master, he sought protection in the woods and abode twenty-seven months in a cave, before he surrendered himself, or was captured. His offence, in this instance, was simply because he desired to see his wife, and "stole" away from his master's plantation and went a distance of five miles, to where she lived, to see her. For this grave crime his master threatened to give him a hundred lashes, and to shoot him; in order to avoid this punishment, he escaped to the woods, etc. The lapse of a dozen years and recent struggles for an existence, made him think lightly of his former troubles and he would, doubtless, have failed to recall his earlier conflicts but for the desire manifested by the Committee to get all the information out of him they could.

He was next asked, "Had you a wife and family?" "Yes, sir," he answered, "I had a wife and eight children, belonged to the widow Slade." Harry gave the names of his wife and children as follows: Wife, Susan, and children, Oliver, Sabey, Washington, Daniel, Jonas, Harriet, Moses and Rosetta, the last named he had never seen. "Between my mistress and my master there was not much difference."

Of his comrades time admitted of writing out only very brief sketches, as follows:

EDWARD LEWIS.

$100 REWARD.—Ran away from the subscriber, on the 7th of November, negro slave, EDGAR. He is 36 years old, 6 feet high, of dark brown complexion, very high forehead, is a little bald, and is inclined to stoop in the shoulders. Edgar says he was raised in Norfolk county, has worked about Norfolk several years. I bought him at the Auction house of Messrs. Pulham & Davis, the 20th of July, 1856. The bill of sale was signed by W.Y. Milmer for Jas. A. Bilisoly, administrator of G.W. Chambers, dec'd. He told one of my negroes he was going to Norfolk to sell some plunder he had there, then go to Richmond, steal his wife, get on board a boat about Norfolk, and go to a free State. He can read and write well, and I have no doubt he has provided himself with papers of some kind. He may have purchased the papers of some free negro. I will give the above reward of One Hundred Dollars to any person who will arrest and confine him, so I can get him.

C.H. GAY.

My Post office is Laurel, N.C. no. 21.

The above advertisement, which was cut from a Southern paper, brought light in regard to one of the passengers at least. It was not often that a slave was so fortunate as to get such a long sketch of himself in a newspaper. The description is so highly complimentary, that we simply endorse it as it stands. The sketch as taken for the record book is here transcribed as follows:

"Edward reported himself from Franklin county, N.C., where, according to statement, a common farmer by the name of Carter Gay owned him, under whose oppression his life was rendered most unhappy, who stinted him daily for food and barely allowed him clothing enough to cover his nakedness, who neither showed justice nor mercy to any under his control, the 'weaker vessels' not excepted; therefore Edward was convinced that it was in vain to hope for comfort under such a master. Moreover, his appetite for liquor, combined with a high temper, rendered him a being hard to please, but easy to excite to a terrible degree. Scarcely had Edward lived two years with this man (Gay) when he felt that he had lived with him long enough. Two years previous to his coming into the hands of Gay, he and his wife were both sold; the wife one day and he the next. She brought eleven hundred and twenty-five dollars, and he eight hundred and thirty-five dollars; thus they were sold and resold as a matter of speculation, and husband and wife were parted."

After the fugitives had been well cared for by the Committee, they were forwarded on North; but for some reason they were led to stop short of Canada, readily finding employment and going to work to take care of themselves. How they were received and in what way they were situated, the subjoined letter from Edward will explain:

SKANEATELES, Dec. 17, 1857.

DEAR SIR:—As I promised to let you hear from me as soon as I found a home, I will now fulfill my promise to you and say that I am alive and well and have found a stopping place for the winter.

When we arrived at Syracuse we found Mr. Loguen ready to receive us, and as times are rather hard in Canada he thought best for us not to go there, so he sent us about twenty miles west of Syracuse to Skaneateles, where George Upshur and myself soon found work. Henry Grimes is at work in Garden about eight miles from this place. If you should chance to hear any of my friends inquiring for me, please direct them to Skaneateles, Onondaga county, N.Y.

If you can inform me of the whereabouts of Miss Alice Jones I shall be very much obliged to you, until I can pay you better. I forgot to ask you about her when I was at your house. She escaped about two years ago.

Please not to forget to inquire of my wife, Rachel Land, and if you should hear of her, let me know immediately, George Upshur and myself send our best respects to you and your family. Remember us to Mrs. Jackson and Miss Julia. I hope to meet you all again, if not on earth may we so live that we shall meet in that happy land where tears and partings are not known.

Let me hear from you soon. This from your friend and well wisher,

EDWARD LEWIS,
formerly, but now WILLIAM BRADY.

GEORGE UPSHER.—The third in this arrival was also a full man. Slavery had robbed him shamefully it is true; nevertheless he was a man of superior natural parts, physically and intellectually. Despite the efforts of slave-holders to keep him in the dark, he could read and write a little. His escape in the manner that he did, implied a direct protest against the conduct of Dr. Thomas W. Upsher, of Richmond, Va., whom, he alleged, deprived him of his hire, and threatened him with immediate sale. He had lived in North Carolina with the doctor about two years. As a slave, his general treatment had been favorable, except for a few months prior to his flight, which change on the part of his master led him to fear that a day of sale was nigh at hand. In fact the seventh of July had been agreed upon when he was to be in Richmond, to take his place with others in the market on sale day; his hasty and resolute move for freedom originated from this circumstance. He was well-known in Norfolk, and had served almost all his days in that city. These passengers averaged about six feet, and were of uncommonly well-developed physical structure.

The pleasure of aiding such men from the horrors of Carolina Slavery was great.

HON. L. McLANE'S PROPERTY, SOON AFTER HIS DEATH, TRAVELS VIA THE UNDERGROUND RAIL ROAD.—WILLIAM KNIGHT, ESQ., LOSES A SUPERIOR "ARTICLE."

Jim Scott, Tom Pennington, Sam Scott, Bill Scott, Abe Bacon, and Jack Wells.

An unusual degree of pleasure was felt in welcoming this party of young men, not because they were any better than others, or because they had suffered more, but simply because they were found to possess certain knowledge and experience of slave life, as it existed under the government of the chivalry; such information could not always be obtained from those whose lot had been cast among ordinary slave-holders. Consequently the Committee interviewed them closely, and in point of intellect found them to be above the average run of slaves. As they were then entered on the record, so in like manner are the notes made of them transferred to these pages.

Jim was about nineteen years of age, well grown, black, and of prepossessing appearance. The organ of hope seemed very strong in him. Jim had been numbered with the live stock of the late Hon. L. McLane, who had been called to give an account of his stewardship about two months before Jim and his companions "took out."

As to general usage, he made no particular charge against his distinguished master; he had, however, not been living under his immediate patriarchal government, but had been hired out to a farmer by the name of James Dodson, with whom he experienced life "sometimes hard and sometimes smooth," to use his own words. The reason of his leaguing with his fellow-servants to abandon the old prison-house, was traceable to the rumor, that he and some others were to appear on the stage, or rather the auction-block, in Baltimore, the coming Spring.

Tom, another member of the McLane institution, was about twenty-five years of age, of unmixed blood, and a fair specimen of a well-trained field-hand. He conceived that he had just ground to bring damages against the Hon. L. McLane for a number of years of hard service, and for being deprived of education. He had been compelled to toil for the Honorable gentleman, not only on his own place, but on the farms of others. At the time that Tom escaped, he was hired for one hundred dollars per annum (and his clothes found him), which hire McLane had withheld from him contrary to all justice and fair dealing; but as Tom was satisfied, that he could get no justice through the Maryland courts, and knew that an old and intimate friend of his master had already proclaimed, that "negroes had no rights which white men are bound to respect;" also, as his experience tended to confirm him in the belief, that the idea was practically carried out in the courts of Maryland; he thought, that it would be useless to put in a plea for justice in Maryland. He was not, however, without a feeling of some satisfaction, that his old master, in giving an account of his stewardship at the Bar of the Just One, would be made to understand the amount of his indebtedness to those whom he had oppressed. With this impression, and the prospects of equal rights and Canada, under her British Majesty's possessions, he manifested as much delight as if he was traveling with a half million of dollars in his pocket.

Sam, another likely-looking member of this party, was twenty-two years of age, and a very promising-looking young fugitive, having the appearance of being able to take education without difficulty. He had fully made up his mind, that slavery was never intended for man, and that he would never wear himself out working for the "white people for nothing." He wanted to work for himself and enjoy the benefits of education, etc.

Bill Scott, another member of the McLane party, was twenty-one years of age, "fat and slick," and fully satisfied, that Canada would agree with him in every particular. Not a word did he utter in favor of Maryland, but said much against the manner in which slaves were treated, how he had felt about the matter, etc.

Abe was also from the McLane estate. He possessed apparently more general intelligence than either of his companions. He was quite bright-witted, a ready talker, and with his prospects he was much satisfied. He was twenty-two years of age, black, good-looking, and possessed very good manners. He represented, that his distinguished master died, leaving thirteen head of slaves. His (Abe's) father, Tom's mother and the mother of the Scotts were freed by McLane. Strong hopes were entertained that before the old man's death he would make provision in his will for the freedom of all the other slaves; when he died, the contrary was found to be the fact; they were still left in chains. The immediate heirs consisted of six sons and five daughters, who moved in the first circle, were "very wealthy and aristocratic." Abe was conversant with the fact, that his master, the "Hon. L. McLane, was once Secretary under President Jackson;" that he had been "sent to England on a mission for the Government," and that he had "served two terms in Congress." Some of the servants, Abe said, were "treated pretty well, but some others could not say anything in the master's favor." Upon the whole, however, it was manifest that the McLane slaves had not been among the number who had seen severe hardships. They came from his plantation in Cecil county, Maryland, where they had been reared.

In order to defend themselves on the Underground Rail Road, they were strongly armed. Sam had a large horse pistol and a butcher knife; Jack had a revolver; Abe had a double-barrelled pistol and a large knife; Jim had a single-barrelled pistol and counted on "blowing a man down if any one touched" him. Bill also had a single-barrelled pistol, and when he started resolved to "come through or die."

Although this party was of the class said to be well fed, well clothed, and not over-worked, yet to those who heard them declare their utter detestation of slavery and their determination to use their instruments of death, even to the taking of life, rather than again be subjected to the yoke, it was evident that even the mildest form of slavery was abhorrent. They left neither old nor young masters, whom they desired to serve any longer or look up to for care and support.

Jack, who was not of the McLane party, but who came with them, had been kept in ignorance with regard to his age. He was apparently middle-aged, medium size, dark color, and of average intelligence. He accused William Knight, a farmer, of having enslaved him contrary to his will or wishes, and averred that he fled from him because he used him badly and kept mean overseers. Jack said that his master owned six farms and kept three overseers to manage them. The slaves numbered twenty-one head. The names of the overseers were given in the following order: "Alfred King, Jimmy Allen, and Thomas Brockston." In speaking of their habits, Jack said, that they were "very smart when the master was about, but as soon as he was gone they would instantly drop back." "They were all mean, but the old boss was meaner than them all," and "the overseers were 'fraider' of him than what I was," said Jack.

His master (Mr. Knight), had a wife and seven children, and was a member of the Episcopal Church, in "good and regular standing." He was rich, and, with his family, moved in good society. "His wife was too stingy to live, and if she was to die, she would die holding on to something," said Jack. Jack had once had a wife and three children, but as they belonged to a slave-holder ("Jim Price") Jack's rights were wholly ignored, and he lost them.

ARRIVAL FROM HIGHTSTOWN, 1858.

Robert Thompson (A Preacher).

Slavery exempted from the yoke no man with a colored skin no matter what his faith, talent, genius, or worth might be. The person of Christ in a black skin would scarcely have caused it to relinquish its tyrannical grasp; neither God nor man was regarded by men who dealt in the bodies and souls of their fellow-men. Robert stated to the Committee that he fled from "John R. Laten, a very harsh kind of a farmer, who drank right smart," that on the morning he "took out," while innocent of having committed any crime, suddenly in a desperate fit of passion, his master took him "by the collar," at the same time calling loudly to "John" for "ropes." This alarming assault on the part of his master made the preacher feel as though his Satanic majesty had possession of him. In such a crisis he evidently felt that preaching would do no good; he was, however, constrained to make an effort. To use his own words, he said: "I gave a sudden jerk and started off on a trot, leaving my master calling, 'stop! stop!' but I kept on running, and was soon out of sight."

The more he thought over the brutal conduct of his master the more decided he became never to serve him more, and straightway he resolved to try to reach Canada. Being in the prime of his life (thirty-nine years of age) and having the essential qualifications for traveling over the Underground Rail Road, he was just the man to endure the trials consequent upon such an undertaking.

Said Robert: "I always thought slavery hard, a very dissipated life to live. I always thought we colored people ought to work for ourselves and wives and children like other people." The Committee saw that Robert's views were in every word sound doctrine, and for further light asked him some questions respecting the treatment he had received at the hands of his mistress, not knowing but that he had received kindness from the "weaker vessel;" while enduring suffering under his master; but Robert assured them in answer to this inquiry that his mistress was a very "ill, dissipated woman," and "was not calculated to sympathize with a poor slave." Robert was next interviewed with regard to religious matters, when it was ascertained that he bore the name of being a "local preacher of the gospel of the Bethel Methodist denomination." Thus in leaving slavery he had to forsake his wife and three children, kinfolks and church, which arduous task but for the brutal conduct of the master he might have labored in vain for strength to perform.

As he looked calmly back upon the past, and saw how he and the rest of the slaves had been deprived of their just rights he could hardly realize how Providence could suffer slave-holders to do as they had been doing in trampling upon the poor and helpless slaves. Yet he had strong faith that the Almighty would punish slave-holders severely for their wickedness.

ARRIVAL FROM VIRGINIA, 1858.

Mary Frances Melvin, Eliza Henderson, and Nancy Grantham.

Mary Frances hailed from Norfolk; she had been in servitude under Mrs. Chapman, a widow lady, against whom she had no complaint to make; indeed, she testified that her mistress was very kind, although fully allied to slavery. She said that she left, not on account of bad treatment, but simply because she wanted her freedom. Her calling as a slave had been that of a dress-maker and house servant. Mary Frances was about twenty-three years of age, of mixed blood, refined in her manners and somewhat cultivated.

Eliza Henderson, who happened at the station at the same time that Frances was on hand, escaped from Richmond. She was twenty-eight years of age, medium size, quite dark color, and of pleasant countenance. Eliza alleged that one William Waverton had been wronging her by keeping her down-trodden and withholding her hire. Also, that this same Waverton had, on a late occasion, brought his heavy fist violently against her "jaws," which visitation, however "kindly" intended by her chivalrous master, produced such an unfavorable impression on the mind of Eliza that she at once determined not to yield submission to him a day longer than she could find an Underground Rail Road conductor who would take her North.

The blow that she had thus received made her almost frantic; she had however thought seriously on the question of her rights before this outrage.

In Waverton's household Eliza had become a fixture as it were, especially with regard to his children; she had won their affections completely, and she was under the impression that in some instances their influence had saved her from severe punishment; and for them she manifested kindly feelings. In speaking of her mistress she said that she was "only tolerable."

It would be useless to attempt a description of the great satisfaction and delight evinced by Eliza on reaching the Committee in Philadelphia.

Nancy Grantham also fled from near Richmond, and was fortunate in that she escaped from the prison-house at the age of nineteen. She possessed a countenance peculiarly mild, and was good-looking and interesting, and although evidently a slave her father belonged strictly to the white man's party, for she was fully half white. She was moved to escape simply to shun her master's evil designs; his brutal purposes were only frustrated by the utmost resolution. This chivalric gentleman was a husband, the father of nine children, and the owner of three hundred slaves. He belonged to a family bearing the name of Christian, and was said to be an M.D. "He was an old man, but very cruel to all his slaves." It was said that Nancy's sister was the object of his lust, but she resisted, and the result was that she was sold to New Orleans. The auction-block was not the only punishment she was called upon to endure for her fidelity to her womanhood, for resistance to her master, but before being sold she was cruelly scourged.

Nancy's sorrows first commenced in Alabama. Five years previous to her escape she was brought from a cotton plantation in Alabama, where she had been accustomed to toil in the cotton-field. In comparing and contrasting the usages of slave-holders in the two States in which she had served, she said she had "seen more flogging under old Christian" than she had been accustomed to see in Alabama; yet she concluded, that she could hardly tell which State was the worst; her cup had been full and very bitter in both States.

Nancy said, "the very day before I escaped, I was required to go to his (her master's) bed-chamber to keep the flies off of him as he lay sick, or pretended to be so. Notwithstanding, in talking with me, he said that he was coming to my pallet that night, and with an oath he declared if I made a noise he would cut my throat. I told him I would not be there. Accordingly he did go to my room, but I had gone for shelter to another room. At this his wrath waxed terrible.

Next morning I was called to account for getting out of his way, and I was beaten awfully." This outrage moved Nancy to a death-struggle for her freedom, and she succeeded by dressing herself in male attire.

After her harrowing story was told with so much earnestness and intelligence, she was asked as to the treatment she had received at the hand of Mrs. Christian (her mistress). In relation to her, Nancy said, "Mrs. Christian was afraid of him (master); if it hadn't been for that I think she would have been clever; but I was often threatened by her, and once she undertook to beat me, but I could not stand it. I had to resist, and she got the worst of it that time."

All that may now be added, is, that the number of young slave girls shamefully exposed to the base lusts of their masters, as Nancy was—truly was legion. Nancy was but one of the number who re-sisted influences apparently overpowering. All honor is due her name and memory!

She was brought away secreted on a boat, but the record is silent as to which one of the two or three Underground Rail Road cap-tains (who at that time occasionally brought passengers), helped her to escape. It was hard to be definite concerning minor matters while absorbed in the painful reflections that her tale of suffering had naturally awakened. If one had arisen from the dead the horrors of Slavery could scarcely have been more vividly pictured! But in the multitude of travelers coming under the notice of the Commit-tee, Nancy's story was soon forgotten, and new and marvellous nar-ratives were told of others who had shared the same bitter cup, who had escaped from the same hell of Slavery, who had panted for the same freedom and won the same prize.

ARRIVAL FROM RICHMOND, 1858.

Orlando J. Hunt.

When Orlando escaped from Richmond the Underground Rail Road business was not very brisk. A disaster on the road, resulting in the capture of one or two captains, tended to damp the ardor of some who wanted to come, as well as that of sympathizers. The road was not idle, however. Orlando's coming was hailed with great satisfaction. He was twenty-nine years of age, full black, possessed considerable intelligence, and was fluent in speech; fully qualified to give clear statements as to the condition of Slavery in Richmond, etc. While the Committee listened to his narrations with much interest, they only took note of how he had fared, and the character of the master he was compelled to serve. On these points the substance of his narrations may be found annexed:

"I was owned by High Holser, a hide sorter, a man said to be rich, a good Catholic, though very disagreeable; he was not cruel, but was very driving and abusive in his language towards colored people. I have been held in bondage about eighteen years by Holser, but have failed, so far, to find any good traits in his character. I purchased my mother for one hundred dollars, when she was old and past labor, too old to earn her hire and find herself; but she was taken away by death, before I had finished paying for her; twenty-five dollars only remained to be paid to finish the agreement. Owing to her unexpected death, I got rid of that much, which was of some consequence, as I was a slave myself, and had hard work to raise the money to purchase her."

Thus, finding the usages of Slavery so cruel and outlandish, he resolved to leave "old Virginny" and "took out," via the Underground Rail Road. He appeared to be of a religious turn of mind and felt that he had "a call to preach."

After his arrival in Canada, the following letter was received from him:

ST. CATHARINES, C.W., May 6th, 1858.

MY DEAR FRIEND:—WM. STILL:—Mr. Orlando J. Hunt, who has just arrived here from Richmond, Va., desires me to address to you a line in his behalf. Mr. Hunt is expecting his clothing to come from Richmond to your care, and if you have received them, he desires you to forward them immediately to St. Catharines, in my care, in the safest and most expeditious way in your power. Mr. Hunt is much pleased with this land of freedom, and I hope he may do well for himself and much good to others. He preached here in the Baptist church, last evening.

He sends his kind regards and sincere thanks to you and your family, and such friends as have favored him on his way. Very respectfully yours,

HIRAM WILSON, for ORLANDO HUNT.

ARRIVAL FROM VIRGINIA, 1858.

William Carpenter.

Escaped from the Father of the Fugitive Slave Law—Senator Mason.

It was highly pleasing to have a visit from a "chattel" belonging to the leading advocate of the infamous Fugitive Slave Bill. He was hurriedly interviewed for the sake of reliable information.

That William possessed a fair knowledge of slave life under the Senator there was no room to doubt, although incidents of extreme cruelty might not have been so common on Mason's place as on some others. While the verbal interchange of views was quite full, the hour for the starting of the Underground Rail Road train arrived too soon to admit of a full report for the record book. From the original record, however, the following statement is taken as made by William, and believed to be strictly true. We give it as it stands on the old Underground Rail Road book: "I belonged to Senator Mason. The Senator was down on colored people. He owned about eighty head—was very rich and a big man, rich enough to lose all of them. He kept terrible overseers; they would beat you with a stick the same as a dog. The overseers were poor white trash; he would give them about sixty dollars a year."

The Fugitive Slave Law and its Father are both numbered with the "Lost Cause," and the "Year of Jubilee has come."

CROSSING THE BAY IN A SKIFF.

William Thomas Cope, John Boice Grey, Henry Boice and Isaac White.

These young bondmen, whilst writhing under the tortures heaped upon them, resolved, at the cost of life, to make a desperate trial for free land; to rid themselves of their fetters, at whatever peril they might have to encounter. The land route presented less encouragement than by water; they knew but little, however, concerning either way. After much anxious reflection, they finally decided to make their Underground Rail Road exit by water. Having lived all their lives not far from the bay, they had some knowledge of small boats, skiffs in particular, but of course they were not the possessors of one. Feeling that there was no time to lose, they concluded to borrow a skiff, though they should never return it. So one Saturday evening, toward the latter part of January, the four young slaves stood on the beach near Lewes, Delaware, and cast their longing eyes in the direction of the Jersey shore. A fierce gale was blowing, and the waves were running fearfully high; not daunted, however, but as one man they resolved to take their lives in their hands and make the bold adventure.

With simple faith they entered the skiff; two of them took the oars, manfully to face uncertain dangers from the waves. But they remained steadfast, oft as they felt that they were making the last stroke with their oars, on the verge of being overwhelmed with the waves. At every new stage of danger they summoned courage by remembering that they were escaping for their lives.

Late on Sunday afternoon, the following day, they reached their much desired haven, the Jersey shore. The relief and joy were unspeakably great, yet they were strangers in a strange land. They knew not which way to steer. True, they knew that New Jersey bore the name of being a Free State; but they had reason to fear that they were in danger. In this dilemma they were discovered by the captain of an oyster boat whose sense of humanity was so strongly appealed to by their appearance that he engaged to pilot them to Philadelphia. The following account of them was recorded:

William Thomas was a yellow man, twenty-four years of age, and possessing a vigorous constitution. He accused Shepherd P. Houston of having restrained him of his liberty, and testified that said Houston was a very bad man. His vocation was that of a farmer, on a small scale; as a slave-holder he was numbered with the "small fry." Both master and mistress were members of the Methodist Church. According to William Thomas' testimony his mistress as well as his master was very hard on the slaves in various ways, especially in the matter of food and clothing. It would require a great deal of hard preaching to convince him that such Christianity was other than spurious.

John stated that David Henry Houston, a farmer, took it upon himself to exercise authority over him. Said John, "If you didn't do the work right, he got contrary, and wouldn't give you anything to eat for a whole day at a time; he said a 'nigger and a mule hadn't any feeling.'" He described his stature and circumstances somewhat thus: "Houston is a very small man; for some time his affairs had been in a bad way; he had been broke, some say he had bad luck for killing my brother. My brother was sick, but master said he wasn't sick, and he took a chunk, and beat on him, and he died a few days after." John firmly believed that his brother had been the victim of a monstrous outrage, and that he too was liable to the same treatment.

John was only nineteen years of age, spare built, chestnut color, and represented the rising mind of the slaves of the South.

Henry was what might be termed a very smart young man, considering that he had been deprived of a knowledge of reading. He was a brother of John, and said that he also had been wrongfully enslaved by David Houston, alluded to above. He fully corroborated the statement of his brother, and declared, moreover, that his sister had not long since been sold South, and that he had heard enough to fully convince him that he and his brother were to be put up for sale soon.

Of their mistress John said that she was a "pretty easy kind of a woman, only she didn't want to allow enough to eat, and wouldn't mend any clothes for us."

Isaac was twenty-two, quite black, and belonged to the "rising" young slaves of Delaware. He stated that he had been owned by a "blacksmith, a very hard man, by the name of Thomas Carper." Isaac was disgusted with his master's ignorance, and criticised him, in his crude way, to a considerable extent. Isaac had learned black-smithing under Carper. Both master and mistress were Methodists. Isaac said that he "could not recommend his mistress, as she was given to bad practices," so much so that he could hardly endure her. He also charged the blacksmith with being addicted to bad habits. Sometimes Isaac would be called upon to receive correction from his master, which would generally be dealt out with a "chunk of wood" over his "no feeling" head. On a late occasion, when Isaac was being *chunked* beyond measure, he resisted, but the persistent blacksmith did not yield until he had so far disabled Isaac that he was rendered helpless for the next two weeks. While in this state he pledged himself to freedom and Canada, and resolved to win the prize by crossing the Bay.

While these young passengers possessed brains and bravery of a rare order, at the same time they brought with them an unusual amount of the soil of Delaware; their persons and old worn-out clothing being full of it. Their appearance called loudly for imme-diate cleansing. A room—free water—free soap, and such other as-sistance as was necessary was tendered them in order to render the work as thorough as possible. This healthy process over, clean and comfortable clothing were furnished, and the change in their ap-pearance was so marked, that they might have passed as strangers, if not in the immediate corn-fields of their masters, certainly among many of their old acquaintances, unless subjected to the most care-ful inspection. Raised in the country and on farms, their masters and mistresses had never dreamed of encouraging them to conform to habits of cleanliness; washing their persons and changing their garments were not common occurrences. The coarse garment once on would be clung to without change as long as it would hold to-

gether. The filthy cabins allotted for their habitations were in themselves incentives to personal uncleanliness. In some districts this
was more apparent than in others. From some portions of Maryland
and Delaware, in particular, passengers brought lamentable evidence of a want of knowledge and improvement in this direction.
But the master, not the slave, was blameworthy. The master, as has
been intimated, found but one suit for working (and sometimes
none for Sunday), consequently if Tom was set to ditching one day
and became muddy and dirty, and the next day he was required to
haul manure, his ditching suit had to be used, and if the next day he
was called into the harvest-field, he was still obliged to wear his
barn-yard suit, and so on to the end. Frequently have such passengers been thoroughly cleansed for the first time in their lives at the
Philadelphia station. Some needed practical lessons before they understood the thoroughness necessary to cleansing. Before undertaking the operation, therefore, in order that they might be made to
feel the benefit to be derived therefrom, they would need to have
the matter brought home to them in a very gentle way, lest they
might feign to fear taking cold, not having been used to it, etc.

It was customary to say to them: "We want to give you some
clean clothing, but you need washing before putting them on. It will
make you feel like a new man to have the dirt of slavery all washed
off. Nothing that could be done for you would make you feel better
after the fatigue of travel than a thorough bath. Probably you have
not been allowed the opportunity of taking a good bath, and so have
not enjoyed one since your mother bathed you. Don't be afraid of
the water or soap—the harder you rub yourself the better you will
feel. Shall we not wash your back and neck for you? We want you to
look well while traveling on the Underground Rail Road, and not
forget from this time forth to try to take care of yourself," &c., &c.
By this course the reluctance where it existed would be overcome
and the proposition would be readily acceded to, if the water was
not too cool; on the other hand, if cool, a slight shudder might be
visible, sufficient to raise a hearty laugh. Yet, when through, the
candidate always expressed a hearty sense of satisfaction, and was
truly thankful for this attention.

ARRIVAL FROM KENT COUNTY, MD., 1858.

Asbury Irwin, Ephraim Ennis, and
Lydia Ann Johns.

The party whose narratives are here given brought grave charges against a backsliding member of the Society of Friends—a renegade Quaker. Doubtless rare instances may be found where men of the Quaker persuasion, emigrating from free and settling in slave States and among slaveholders, have deserted their freedom-loving principle and led captive by the force of bad examples, have linked hands with the oppressor against the oppressed. It is probable, however, that this is the only case that may turn up in these records to the disgrace of this body of Christians in whom dwelt in such a signal degree large sympathy for the slave and the fleeing bondman. Many fugitives were indebted to Friends who aided them in a quiet way, not allowing their left hand to know what their right hand did, and the result was that Underground Rail Road operations were always pretty safe and prosperous where the line of travel led through "Quaker settlements." We can speak with great confidence on this point especially with regard to Pennsylvania, where a goodly number might be named, if necessary, whose hearts, houses, horses, and money were always found ready and willing to assist the fugitive from the prison-house. It is with no little regret that we feel that truth requires us to connect the so-called owner of Asbury, Ephraim, and Lydia with the Quakers.

Asbury was first examined, and his story ran substantially thus: "I run away because I was used bad; three years ago I was knocked dead with an axe by my master; the blood run out of my head as if it had been poured out of a tumbler; you can see the mark plain enough—look here," (with his finger on the spot). "I left Millington, at the head of Chester in Kent County, Maryland, where I had been

328 · *William Still*

held by a farmer who called himself Michael Newbold. He was
originally from Mount Holly, New Jersey, but had been living in
Maryland over twenty years. He was called a Hickory Quaker,
and he had a real Quaker for a wife. Before he was in Maryland
five years he bought slaves, became a regular slave-holder, got
to drinking and racing horses, and was very bad—treated all
hands bad, his wife too, so that she had to leave him and go to Philadelphia to her kinsfolks. It was because he was so bad we all had to
leave," &c.

While Asbury's story appeared truthful and simple, a portion of
it was too shocking to morality and damaging to humanity to be
inserted in these pages.

Asbury was about forty years of age, a man of dark hue, size and
height about mediocrity, and mental ability quite above the average.

Ephraim was a fellow-servant and companion of Asbury. He was
a man of superior physical strength, and from all outward appearance, he possessed qualities susceptible of ready improvement. He
not only spoke of Newbold in terms of strong condemnation but of
slave-holders and slavery everywhere. The lessons he had learned
gave him ample opportunity to speak from experience and from
what he had observed in the daily practices of slave-holders; consequently, with his ordinary gifts, it was impossible for him to utter his
earnest feelings without making a deep impression.

Lydia also fled from Michael Newbold. She was a young married
woman, only twenty-two years of age, of a chestnut color and a
pleasant countenance. Her flight for liberty cost her her husband, as
she was obliged to leave him behind. What understanding was entered into between them prior to her departure we failed to note at
the time. It was very clear that she had decided never to wear the
yoke again.

ARRIVAL FROM DELAWARE, 1858.

Theophilus Collins, Andrew Jackson Boyce, Handy Burton and Robert Jackson. A Desperate, Bloody Struggle—Gun, Knife and Fire Shovel, Used by an Infuriated Master.

Judged from their outward appearance, as well as from the fact that they were from the neighboring State of Delaware, no extraordinary revelations were looked for from the above-named party. It was found, however, that one of their number, at least, had a sad tale of outrage and cruelty to relate. The facts stated are as follows:

Theophilus is twenty-four years of age, dark, height and stature hardly medium, with faculties only about average compared with ordinary fugitives from Delaware and Maryland. His appearance is in no way remarkable. His bearing is subdued and modest; yet he is not lacking in earnestness. Says Theophilus, "I was in servitude under a man named Houston, near Lewes, Delaware; he was a very mean man, he didn't allow you enough to eat, nor enough clothes to wear. He never allowed a drop of tea, or coffee, or sugar, and if you didn't eat your breakfast before day he wouldn't allow you any, but would drive you out without any. He had a wife; she was mean, too, meaner than he was. Four years ago last Fall my master cut my entrails out for going to meeting at Daniel Wesley's church one Sabbath night. Before day, Monday morning, he called me up to whip me; called me into his dining-room, locked the doors, then ordered me to pull off my shirt. I told him no, sir, I wouldn't; right away he went and got the cowhide, and gave me about twenty over my head with the butt. He tore my shirt off, after I would not pull it off; he ordered me to cross my hands. I didn't do that. After I wouldn't do that he went and got his gun. and broke the breech of that over my head. He then seized up the fire-tongs and struck me over the head ever so often. The next thing he took was the parlor shovel and he beat on me with that till he broke the handle; then he took the blade and stove it at my head with all his might. I told him that I was bound to come out of that room. He run up to the door and drawed his knife and told me if I ventured to the door he would stab me. I never made it any better or worse, but aimed straight for the door; but before I reached it he stabbed me, drawing the knife (a common pocket knife) as hard as he could rip across my stomach; right away he began stabbing me about my head," (marks were plainly to be seen). After a desperate struggle, Theophilus succeeded in getting out of the building.

"I started," said he, "at once for Georgetown, carrying a part of my entrails in my hands for the whole journey, sixteen miles. I went to my young masters, and they took me to an old colored woman, called Judah Smith, and for five days and nights I was under treatment of Dr. Henry Moore, Dr. Charles Henry Richards, and Dr. William Newall; all these attended me. I was not expected to live for a long time, but the Doctors cured me at last."

———

Andrew reported that he fled from Dr. David Houston. "I left because of my master's meanness to me; he was a very mean man to his servants," said Andrew, "and I got so tired of him I couldn't stand him any longer." Andrew was about twenty-six years of age, ordinary size; color, brown, and was entitled to his freedom, but knew not how to secure it by law, so resorted to the Underground Rail Road method.

Handy, another of this party, said that he left because the man who claimed to be his master "was so hard." The man by whom he had been wronged was known where he came from by the name of Shepherd Burton, and was in the farming business. "He was a churchman," said Handy, "but he never allowed me to go to church a half dozen times in my life."

Robert belonged to Mrs. Mary Hickman, at least she had him in her possession and reaped the benefit of his hire and enjoyed the leisure and ease thereof while he toiled. For some time prior to his leaving, this had been a thorn in his side, hard to bear; so when an opening presented itself by which he thought he could better his condition, he was ready to try the experiment. He, however, felt that, while she would not have him to look to for support, she would not be without sympathy, as she was a member of the Episcopal Church; besides she was an old-looking woman and might not need his help a great while longer.

ARRIVAL FROM MARYLAND, 1859.

Ann Maria Jackson and Her Seven Children—Mary Ann, William Henry, Frances Sabrina, Wilhelmina, John Edwin, Ebenezer Thomas, and William Albert.

The coming of the above named was duly announced by Thomas Garrett:

WILMINGTON, 11th mo., 21st, 1858.

DEAR FRIENDS—McKIM AND STILL:—I write to inform you that on the 16th of this month, we passed on four able bodied men to Pennsylvania, and they were followed last night by a woman and her six children, from three or four years of age, up to sixteen years, I believe the whole belonged to the same estate, and they were to have been sold at public sale, I was informed yesterday, but preferred seeking their own master; we had some trouble in getting those last safe along, as they could not travel far on foot, and could not safely cross any of the bridges on the canal, either on foot or in carriage. A man left here two days since, with carriage, to meet them this side of the canal, but owing to spies they did not reach him till 10 o'clock last night; this morning he returned, having seen them about one or two o'clock this morning in a second carriage, on the border of Chester county, where I think they are all safe, if they can be kept from Philadelphia. If you see them they can tell their own tales, as I have seen one of them. May He, who feeds the ravens, care for them. Yours,

THOS. GARRETT.

The fire of freedom obviously burned with no ordinary fervor in the breast of this slave mother, or she never would have ventured with the burden of seven children, to escape from the hell of Slavery.

Ann Maria was about forty years of age, good-looking, pleasant countenance, and of a chestnut color, height medium, and intellect above the average. Her bearing was humble, as might have been expected, from the fact that she emerged from the lowest depths of Delaware Slavery. During the Fall prior to her escape, she lost her husband under most trying circumstances: he died in the poorhouse, a raving maniac. Two of his children had been taken from their mother by her owner, as was usual with slave-holders, which preyed so severely on the poor father's mind that it drove him into a state of hopeless insanity. He was a "free man" in the eye of Delaware laws, yet he was not allowed to exercise the least authority over his children.

Prior to the time that the two children were taken from their mother, she had been allowed to live with her husband and children, independently of her master, by supporting herself and them with the white-wash brush, wash-tub, etc. For this privilege the mother doubtless worked with double energy, and the master, in all probability, was largely the gainer, as the children were no expense to him in their infancy; but when they began to be old enough to hire out, or bring high prices in the market, he snatched away two of the finest articles, and the powerless father was immediately rendered a fit subject for the mad-house; but the brave hearted mother looked up to God, resolved to wait patiently until in a good Providence the way might open to escape with her remaining children to Canada.

Year in and year out she had suffered to provide food and raiment for her little ones. Many times in going out to do days' work she would be compelled to leave her children, not knowing whether during her absence they would fall victims to fire, or be carried off by the master. But she possessed a well tried faith, which in her flight kept her from despondency. Under her former lot she scarcely murmured, but declared that she had never been at ease in Slavery a day after the birth of her first-born. The desire to go to some part of the world where she could have the control and comfort of her children, had always been a prevailing idea with her. "It almost broke my heart," she said, "when he came and took my children away as soon as they were big enough to hand me a drink of water. My husband was always very kind to me, and I had often wanted him to run away with me and the children, but I could not get him in the notion; he did not feel that he could, and so he stayed, and died broken-hearted, crazy. I was owned by a man named Joseph Brown; he owned property in Milford, and he had a place in Vicksburg, and some of his time he spends there, and some of the time he lives in Milford. This Fall he said he was going to take four of my oldest children and two other servants to Vicksburg. I just happened to hear of this news in time. My master was wanting to keep me in the dark about taking them, for fear that something might happen. My master is very sly; he is a tall, slim man, with a smooth face, bald head, light hair, long and sharp nose, swears very hard, and drinks. He is a widower, and is rich."

On the road the poor mother, with her travel-worn children became desperately alarmed, fearing that they were betrayed. But God had provided better things for her; her strength and hope were soon fully restored, and she was lucky enough to fall into the right hands. It was a special pleasure to aid such a mother. Her arrival in Canada was announced by Rev. H. Wilson as follows:

NIAGARA CITY, Nov. 30th, 1858.

DEAR BRO. STILL:—I am happy to inform you that Mrs. Jackson and her interesting family of seven children arrived safe and in good health and spirits at my house in St. Catharines, on Saturday evening last. With sincere pleasure I provided for them comfort quarters till this morning, when they left for Toronto. I got them conveyed there at half fare, and gave them letters of introduction to Thomas Henning, Esq., and Mrs. Dr. Willis, trusting that they will be better cared for in Toronto than they could be at St. Catharines. We have so many coming to us we think it best for some of them to pass on to other places. My wife gave them all a good supply of clothing before they left us. James Henry, an older son is, I think, not far from St. Catharine, but has not as yet reunited with the family. Faithfully and truly yours, HIRAM WILSON.

ARRIVAL FROM VIRGINIA, 1860.

*Jenny Buchanan. A Kind Master; Jenny Chastised One of His Sons
for an Insult, and as a Punishment She Was Sold—Seized for
Debt—Sold a Second Time.*

Jenny was about forty-five years of age, a dark mulatto, stature medium, manners modest and graceful; she had served only in high
life; thus she had acquired a great deal of information. She stated
that she was born a slave, under John Bower, of Rockbridge, Virginia, and that he was the owner of a large plantation, with a great
number of slaves. He was considered to be a good man to his servants, and was generally beloved by them. Suddenly, however, he
was taken ill with paralysis, which confined him to his bed. During
this illness one of the sons, a young gentleman, offered an insult to
Jenny, for which she felt justified in administering to him, a severe
chastisement. For this grave offence she was condemned to be sold
to a trader by the name of William Watts, who owned a place in
Mississippi. The conditions of sale were that she was to be taken out
of the state and never to be allowed to return. It so happened, however, before she was removed that Watts, the trader, failed in order
to cheat his creditors it was supposed. Governor McDowell, of Virginia, was one of those to whom he was largely indebted for a number of slaves which he, the Governor, had placed in his hands for
disposal, some time before the trader took the benefit. Therefore, as
the Governor was anxious to recover his loss as much as possible, he
seized on Jenny. It was through this interference that the condition
relative to her being sent out of the state was broken.

"The Governor," said Jenny, "was a very fine gentleman, as good
as I could expect of Virginia. He allowed his slaves to raise fowl and
hogs, with many privileges of one kind and another; besides he kept
them all together; but he took sick and died. There was a great

change shortly after that. The slaves were soon scattered like the wind. The Governor had nine sons and daughters.

After his death Mrs. McDowell, alias Mrs. Sally Thomas, took possession, and employed an overseer, by the name of Henry Morgan. He was a very good man in his looks, but a very rascally man; would get drunk, and sell her property to get whisky. Mrs. McDowell would let him do just as he pleased. For the slightest complaint the overseer might see fit to make against any of the slaves, she would tell him to sell them"—"Sell, Mr. Morgan." "He would treat them worse than he would any dog; would beat them over the head with great hickory sticks, the same as he would beat an ox. He would pasture cows and horses on the plantation, and keep the money. We slaves all knew it, and we told her; but our words would not go in court against a white man, and until she was told by Mr. White, and her cousin, Dr. Taylor, and Mr. Barclay, she would not believe how shamefully this overseer was cheating her. But at last she was convinced, and discharged him, and hired another by the name of John Moore. The new one, if anything, was worse than the old one, for he could do the most unblushing acts of cruelty with pleasure. He was a demon."

Finally the estate had to be settled, and the property divided. At this time it was in the hands of the oldest daughter, Mistress Sally, who had been married to Frank Thomas, the Governor of Maryland. But the Governor had discarded her for some reason or other, and according to his published account of her it might seem that he had good reason for doing so. It was understood that he gave her a divorce, so she was considered single for life. It was also understood that she was to buy in the homestead at a moderate price, with as many slaves as she might desire.

Said Jenny, "I was sold at this settlement sale, and bought in by the 'grass widow' for four hundred dollars." The place and a number of slaves were bought in on terms equally as low. After this the widow became smitten with a reverend gentleman, by the name of John Miller, who had formerly lived North; he had been a popular preacher. After a courtship, which did not last very long, they were married. This took place three years ago, prior to the writing of this narrative. After the marriage, Rev. Mr. Miller took up his abode on the old homestead, and entered upon his duties as a slave-holder in good earnest.

"How did you like him?" inquired a member of the Committee.

"I despised him," was Jenny's prompt answer.

"Why did you despise him?"

"Because he had such mean ways with him," said Jenny. She then went on to remark as follows:—"Coming there, taking so much authority over other people's servants. He was so mean that he broke up all the privileges the servants had before he came. He stopped all hands from raising chickens, pigs, etc. He don't like to see them hold up their heads above their shoulders." Didn't he preach? she was asked. "Yes, but I never heard him preach; I have heard him pray though. On Thursday nights, when he would not want the servants to go into town to meeting, he would keep up until it would be too late for them to go. He is now carrying on the farm, and follows butchering. He has not yet sold any of the slaves, but has threatened to sell all hands to the trader."

Jenny once had a husband, but he went to Canada, and that was all she could tell about him, as she had never had a letter or any direct information from him since he left. That she was childless, she regarded as a matter of great satisfaction, considering all the circumstances.

CROSSING THE BAY IN A BATTEAU.

Sharp Contest with Pursuers on Water. Fugitives Victorious.
Thomas Sipple, and His Wife, Mary Ann, Henry Burkett, and
Elizabeth, His Wife, John Purnell, and Hale Burton.

This party were slaves, living near Kunkletown, in Worcester county, Maryland, and had become restive in their fetters. Although they did not know a letter of the alphabet, they were fully persuaded that they were entitled to their freedom. In considering what way would be safest for them to adopt, they concluded that the water would be less dangerous than any other route. As the matter of freedom had been in their minds for a long time, they had frequently counted the cost, and had been laying by trifling sums of money which had fallen perchance into their hands. Among them all they had about thirty dollars. As they could not go by water without a boat, one of their number purchased an old batteau for the small sum of six dollars. The Delaware Bay lay between them and the Jersey shore, which they desired to reach. They did not calculate, however, that before leaving the Delaware shore they would have to contend with the enemy. That in crossing, they would lose sight of the land they well understood. They managed to find out the direction of the shore, and about the length of time that it might take them to reach it. Undaunted by the perils before them the party repaired to the bay, and at ten o'clock, P.M. embarked direct for the other shore.

Near Kate's Hammock, on the Delaware shore, they were attacked by five white men in a small boat. One of them seized the chain of the fugitives' boat, and peremptorily claimed it. "This is not your boat, we bought this boat and paid for it," spake one of the brave fugitives. "I am an officer, and must have it," said the white man, holding on to the chain. Being armed, the white men threatened to shoot. Manfully did the black men stand up for their rights, and declare that they did not mean to give up their boat alive. The parties speedily came to blows. One of the white men dealt a heavy blow with his oar upon the head of one of the black men, which knocked him down, and broke the oar at the same time. The blow was immediately returned by Thomas Sipple, and one of the white men was laid flat on the bottom of the boat. The white men were instantly seized with a panic, and retreated; after getting some yards off they snapped their guns at the fugitives several times, and one load of small shot was fired into them. John received two shot in the forehead, but was not dangerously hurt. George received some in the arms, Hale Burton got one about his temple, and Thomas got a few in one of his arms; but the shot being light, none of the fugitives were seriously damaged. Some of the shot will remain in them as long as life lasts. The conflict lasted for several minutes, but the victorious bondmen were only made all the more courageous by seeing the foe retreat. They rowed with a greater will than ever, and landed on a small island. Where they were, or what to do they could not tell. One whole night they passed in gloom on this sad spot. Their hearts were greatly cast down; the next morning they set out on foot to see what they could see. The young women were very sick, and the men were tried to the last extremity; however, after walking about one mile, they came across the captain of an oyster boat. They perceived that he spoke in a friendly way, and they at once asked directions with regard to Philadelphia. He gave them the desired information, and even offered to bring them to the city if they would pay him for his services. They had about twenty-five dollars in all. This they willingly gave him, and he brought them according to agreement. When they found the captain they were not far from Cape May light-house.

Taking into account the fact that it was night when they started, that their little boat was weak, combined with their lack of knowledge in relation to the imminent danger surrounding them, any intelligent man would have been justified in predicting for them a watery grave, long before the bay was half crossed. But they crossed safely. They greatly needed food, clothing, rest, and money, which they freely received, and were afterwards forwarded to John W.

Jones, Underground Rail Road agent, at Elmira. The subjoined letter giving an account of their arrival was duly received:

ELMIRA, June 6th, 1860.

FRIEND WM. STILL:—All six came safe to this place. The two men came last night, about twelve o'clock; the man and woman stopped at the depot, and went east on the next train, about eighteen miles, and did not get back till to-night, so that the two men went this morning, and the four went this evening.

O, old master don't cry for me,

For I am going to Canada where colored men are free.

P.S. What is the news in the city? Will you tell me how many you have sent over to Canada? I would like to know. They all send their love to you. I have nothing new to tell you. We are all in good health. I see there is a law passed in Maryland not to set any slaves free. They had better get the consent of the Underground Rail Road before they passed such a thing. Good night from your friend,

JOHN W. JONES.

ARRIVAL FROM DORCHESTER CO., 1860.

Harriet Tubman's Last "Trip" to Maryland.

STEPHEN ENNETS and wife, MARIA, with three children, whose names were as follows: HARRIET, aged six years; AMANDA, four years, and a babe (in the arms of its mother), three months old. The following letter from Thomas Garrett throws light upon this arrival:

WILMINGTON, 12th mo., 1st, 1860.

RESPECTED FRIEND:—WILLIAM STILL:—I write to let thee know that Harriet Tubman is again in these parts. She arrived last evening from one of her trips of mercy to God's poor, bringing two men with her as far as New Castle. I agreed to pay a man last evening, to pilot them on their way to Chester county; the wife of one of the men, with two or three children, was left some thirty miles below, and I gave Harriet ten dollars, to hire a man with carriage, to take them to Chester county. She said a man had offered for that sum, to bring them on. I shall be very uneasy about them, till I hear they are safe. There is now much more risk on the road, till they arrive here, than there has been for several months past, as we find that some poor, worthless wretches are constantly on the look out on two roads, that they cannot well avoid more especially with carriage, yet, as it is Harriet who seems to have had a special angel to guard her on her journey of mercy, I have hope. Thy Friend, THOMAS GARRETT.

N.B. We hope all will be in Chester county to-morrow.

These slaves from Maryland, were the last that Harriet Tubman piloted out of the prison-house of bondage, and these "came through great tribulation."

Stephen, the husband, had been a slave of John Kaiger, who would not allow him to live with his wife (if there was such a thing as a slave's owning a wife.) She lived eight miles distant, hired her time, maintained herself, and took care of her children (until they became of service to their owner), and paid ten dollars a year for her hire. She was owned by Algier Pearcy. Both mother and father desired to deliver their children from his grasp. They had too much intelligence to bear the heavy burdens thus imposed without feeling the pressure a grievous one.

Harriet Tubman being well acquainted in their neighborhood, and knowing of their situation, and having confidence that they would prove true, as passengers on the Underground Rail Road, engaged to pilot them within reach of Wilmington, at least to Thomas Garrett's. Thus the father and mother, with their children and a young man named John, found aid and comfort on their way, with Harriet for their "Moses." A poor woman escaping from Baltimore in a delicate state, happened to meet Harriet's party at the station, and was forwarded on with them. They were cheered with clothing, food, and material aid, and sped on to Canada. Notes taken at that time were very brief; it was evidently deemed prudent in those days, not to keep as full reports as had been the wont of the secretary, prior to 1859. The capture of John Brown's papers and letters, with names and plans in full, admonished us that such papers and correspondence as had been preserved concerning the Underground Rail Road, might perchance be captured by a pro-slavery mob. For a year or more after the Harper's Ferry battle, as many will remember, the mob spirit of the times was very violent in all the principal northern cities, as well as southern ("to save the Union.") Even in Boston, Abolition meetings were fiercely assailed by the mob. During this period, the writer omitted some of the most important particulars in the escapes and narratives of fugitives. Books and papers were sent away for a long time, and during this time the records were kept simply on loose slips of paper.

ARRIVAL FROM RICHMOND.

John William Dungy.—Brought a Pass from Ex. Gov. Gregory.

"He ought to be put in a cage and kept for a show," said Anna Brown, daughter of the hero, John Brown, at the house of the writer, where she happened to meet the above named Underground Rail Road passenger. He had then just returned from Canada, after being a Refugee four years. In the mean time through the war and the Proclamation of Father Abraham the fetters had been torn from the limbs of the slave, and the way to Richmond was open to all. John William on this occasion was on his way thither to see how his brethren together with their old oppressors looked facing each other as freemen. Miss Anna Brown was *en route* to Norfolk, where she designed to teach a school of the unfettered bondmen. The return of the Refugee was as unexpected as it was gratifying. Scarcely had the cordial greetings of the writer and his family ended and the daughter of Brown been introduced before the writer was plying his Refugee guest with a multiplicity of questions relative to his sojourn in Canada, etc. "How have you been getting along in Canada? Do you like the country?" "First-rate," said John William. "You look as though you had neither been starved, nor frozen. Have you had plenty of work, made some money, and taken care of yourself?" "Yes." "When you were on the Underground Rail Road on your way to Canada you promised that you were going to keep from all bad habits; how about the 'crittur?' do you take a little sometimes?" "No, I have not drank a drop since I left the South" replied John William with emphasis. "Good!" "I suppose you smoke and chew at any rate?" "No, neither. I never think of such a thing." "Now don't you keep late hours at night and swear occasionally?" "No, Sir. All the leisure that I have of evenings is spent over my books as a general

344 · *William Still*

thing; I have not fallen into the fashionable customs of young men."
Miss Brown, who had been an attentive listener, remarked: "HE
OUGHT TO BE PUT IN A CAGE, ETC."

He was twenty-seven years of age when he first landed in Philadelphia, in the month of February, 1860, per steamer Pennsylvania,
in which he had been stowed away in a store-room containing a lot
of rubbish and furniture; in this way he reached City Point; here a
family of Irish emigrants, very dirty, were taken on board, and orders were given that accommodations should be made for them in
the room occupied by J.W. Here was trouble, but only for a moment.
Those into whose charge he had been consigned on the boat knew
that the kettle and pot-closet had often been used for Underground
Rail Road purposes, and he was safely conducted to quarters among
the pots. The room was exceedingly limited, but he stood it bravely.
On landing he was not able to stand. It required not only his personal efforts but the help of friends to get him in a condition to walk.
No sooner had he stepped on shore, however, than he began to cry
aloud for joy. "Thank God!" rang out sonorously from his overflowing soul. Alarmed at this indication of gratitude his friends immediately told him that that would never do; that all hands would be
betrayed; that he was far from being safe in Philadelphia. He sup-
pressed his emotion. After being delivered into the hands of the
Acting Committee, where he was in more private quarters, he gave
full vent to the joy he experienced on reaching this city. He said that
he had been trying earnestly for five years to obtain his freedom.
For this special object he had saved up sixty-eight dollars and fifteen cents, all of which but the fifteen cents he willingly paid for his
passage on the boat. Fifteen cents, the balance of his entire capital,
was all that he had when he landed in Philadelphia.

Before leaving the South he was hired in the family of Ex-
Governor Gregory. Of the Governor and his wife he spoke very
highly,—said that they were kind to him and would readily favor
him whenever he solicited them to do so. He stated that after making his arrangements to start, in order that he might be away several
days before being missed, he told Mrs. Gregory that he would be
glad to spend a week with his mother, (she lived some distance in

the country). As he was not feeling very well she kindly acceded to his request, and told him to ask the Governor for a pass and some money. The Governor was busy writing, but he at once granted the prayer, wrote him a pass, gave John five dollars, adding that he was sorry that he had no more in his pocket, &c. John bowed and thanked the Governor, and soon got ready for his visit; but his route lay in a far different direction than that contemplated by the Governor and his lady. He was aiming for the Underground Rail Road. As has already been intimated, he was not owned by the Governor, but by the Ferrell heirs—five children who had moved from Virginia to Alabama years back. "Every Ferrell that lives is down on slaves; they are very severe," said John. Yet he had not suffered as many others had who belonged to them, as he had been a dining-room servant. At one time they had owned large numbers of slaves, but latterly they had been selling them off. Contrary to John's wishes his Alabama owners had notified him as well as the Governor, that in a short while he was to be taken to Alabama. This induced John to act with great promptness in leaving at the time that he did.

After passing several years in Canada as has been already noticed, he returned to Richmond and paid a visit to his old home.

He found that the governor and his wife had both departed, but two of the daughters (young ladies), still lived. They were both glad to see him; the younger especially; she told him that she was glad that he escaped, and that she "prayed for him." The elder remarked that she had always thought that he was too "good a Christian to run away." Another thing which she referred to, apparently with much feeling, was this: On his way to Canada, he wrote to the governor, from Rochester, "that he need put himself to no trouble in hunting him up, as he had made up his mind to visit Canada." She thought that John was rather "naughty," to write thus to her "papa," nevertheless, she was disposed to forgive him, after she had frankly spoken her mind.

John found Richmond, which so long had held him in chains, fully humbled, and her slave power utterly cast down. His wondering eyes gazed until he was perfectly satisfied that it was the Lord's doings, and it was marvellous in his eyes. He was more than ever resolved to get an education, and go back to Virginia, to help teach his brethren who had been so long denied the privilege. It was not long before he was at Oberlin College, a faithful student, commanding the highest respect from all the faculty for his good deportment and studious habits.

After advancing rapidly there, the way opened more fully to pursue his studies with greater facilities and less expense at a college in one of the Eastern States. He accepted the favors of friends who offered him assistance, with a view of preparing him for a mission among the freedmen, believing that he possessed in a high degree, the elements for a useful worker, preacher, organizer and teacher. As the friends alluded to, were about taking measures to start a college at Harper's Ferry, especially for the benefit of the Freedmen, they anticipated making this latitude the field of his future endeavors, at least for a time. Ere he graduated in view of the fact that the harvest in the South so urgently called for laborers, he was solicited to be an agent for the Storer College,* and subsequently to enter upon a mission under the auspices of the Free-Will Baptists, in Martinsburg, Virginia. For three or four years he labored in this field with commendable zeal and acceptably, gather-

* The appended extract from an official circular, issued by the Board of Instruction of Storer College, will throw light upon this Institution: STORER COLLEGE, HARPER'S FERRY, WEST VIRGINIA. This Institution, deriving its name from John Storer, Esq., late of Sanford, Me., who gave ten thousand dollars to aid in its establishment, is located at Harper's Ferry, West Va., and has been chartered with full powers by a special act of the Legislature. The Corporation has been regularly organized, about thirty thousand dollars in money has been obtained, a large tract of land has been purchased, ample buildings have been secured, and a Normal School has been in successful operation during the last eighteen months. The U.S. authorities have repeatedly expressed their confidence in and sympathy with this undertaking, by liberal grants of money and buildings, and the agent for the distribution of the Peabody Fund, has pledged pecuniary aid to the best of the pupils in attendance, who may be in need of such assistance. REV. J. CALDER, D.D., Pres., Harrisburg, Penna. Harper's Ferry, West Va., March 1, 1869. REV. N.C. BRACKETT, Act. Sec'y., Harper's Ferry, West Va.

ing young and old in day and Sunday-schools, and also organizing churches. By his constant labors his health became impaired; receiving a call from a church in Providence, he accepted, not without knowing, however, that his mission was to be left in faithful hands, to carry on the good work.

There is still need of efficient laborers in the Shenandoah Valley. According to the testimony of Mr. Dungy, scores of places may still be found where the children have no school privileges, and where many, both old and young, have never had the opportunity of entering a meeting-house or church since the war, as the spirit of the white Christians in these regions is greatly embittered against the colored people, owing to the abolition of Slavery; and they do not invite them to either church or school. Indeed, the churches are closed against them. At different times, Mr. Dungy has eloquently represented the condition of the colored churches of the South, in the city of Philadelphia. As a speaker, Mr. Dungy is able and interesting, of good address, remarkably graceful in his manners, and possessing much general information.

The subjoined letters received from him, while a fugitive in Canada, are characteristic of the man, and will repay a perusal.

BRANTFORD, March 3d, 1860.

MR. WM. STILL, DEAR SIR:—I have seated myself this evening to write you a few lines to inform you that I have got through my journey, and landed safely in Brantford, where I found my friend, Stepney Brown, and we expressed great joy at meeting each other, and had a great shaking of hands, and have not got done talking yet of the old times we had in Virginia.

I thank God I am enjoying vigorous health, and hope you all are well, as it is written in the first Psalm, "Blessed is the man that walketh not in the counsel of the ungodly, nor standeth in the way of sinners, nor sitteth in the seat of the scornful."

I wish you may think of me often and pray for me that I may grow a man, one of the followers of our meek and lowly Saviour. Give my love to Mrs. Still, and family, and the Rev. Mr. Gibbs, that was residing with you when I was there.

I must now inform you a little about Canada, at least as much of it as I have seen and heard. I arrived in the city of Hamilton, on the 15th February, 1860, at nine o'clock in the evening, and the weather was dreary and cold, and the cars laid over there until ten o'clock next day, and I went up into the city and saw a portion of it. I then started for Toronto, arrived there same day at 12 o'clock. There I met friends from Richmond, remained there several days; during the time we had a very extensive snow storm, and I took the opportunity of walking around the city looking at the elephants, and other great sights. I liked it very much; but upon hearing that my friend and brother Stepney Brown was in Brantford, I became disatisfied and left for Brantford on the 21st February, 1860. I have found it a very pleasant, and have been told it is the prettiest place in Canada.

It is built upon the Grand River, which is two hundred miles long, and empties into Lake Erie. It rises to a great height every spring, and great masses of ice come down, bringing bridges, saw-logs, trees, and fairly sweeps everything before it. The people who live upon the flats are in great danger of being drowned in their houses.

I got a situation immediately at the Kerby House, by the influence of my friend and brother, Stepney Brown, who I must say has been very kind to me, as also have the people of Brantford. The Kerbey House is the largest hotel in the town about 250 rooms, and a stable at the back, with a gas-house of its own. No more at present, but remain,

Yours very respectfully, JOHN WILLIAM DUNGY.

P.S. Write at your earliest convenience, and oblige your friend, J.W.D.

BRANTFORD, April 20th.

MR. STILL, DEAR SIR:—I feel myself quite lonesome this evening, and not hearing from you lately I take this opportunity to drop you a few lines. I have not much to say, brother Brown has left for the falls, and expects to return next winter. The weather is mild and warm at this time; the grass is putting up and begins to look like spring. I thank the Lord I am enjoying good health at this time. I hope this letter will find you and your family well, give my compliments to them all and Mr. Gibbs and the young lady that was at your house when I was there. Times has been hard this winter, but they are increasing for the better. I wrote to you a few days ago, I don't know whether you got my letter. I asked in my letter if Mr. Williams was on the pennsylvania, that runs from their to Richmond, Va. I should have written to him, but I did not know his number, I also named a friend of mine, Mr Plumer if he arrives their pleas to tell him to come to Brantford, where I am for there are good chances for business I think a great deal about my colored brethren in the South but I hope to be a benefit to them one of these days. We have quite a melancholy affair about one of our colored brothers who made his escape from the South those who took him up have gone back to obtain witness to convict him for murder. These witness is to be here on Monday 23 inst but the defendence of the law says they shant take him back unless they bring good witness and men of truth I will write you more about it after the trial comes of. I must say a little about myself. I want to devote myself to study if I can for the next twelve months. I expect to leave the Kirby House on the 5th of may. I have taken a barber shop which is a very good situation and one hand employed with me. I would be much oblige to you if you would give me some advice what to do. I sent you the morning herald yesterday which contained a accident which occurd on the G. trunk R.W. you will see in it that we don't have much politics here. The late destructive fire we had I thought it would have kept brantford back this summer but it is increasing slowly I have nothing more to say at this time. I hope the Lord may bless you all and take care of you in this world, and after time receive you in his everlasting kingdom through Jesus Christ our Lord. Answer this as soon as convenient. Good bye. Yours respectfully J.W. DUNGY.

BRANTFORD, C.W., JANUARY 11th, 61.

MR. WM. STILL, DEAR SIR:—I take this opportunity to drop you a few lines to let you hear from me. I am well at this time, hoping this will find you the same.

I acknowledge my great neglectness of you with great regret that I have not answered your letter before this, I hope you will excuse me as I have succeeded in getting me a wife since I wrote to you last.

My mind has been much taken up in so doing for several months past. Give my compliments to your wife and your family, and Mr. Gibbs, also hoping they are all well. Tell Mrs. Still to pray for me that I may grow in grace and the knowledge of the truth as it is in Jesus.

I often think of you all. I pray that the time may come when we will all be men in the United States. We have read here of the great disturbance in the South. My prayer is that this may be a deathblow to Slavery. Do you ever have any Underground Rail Road passengers now? Times have been very prosperous in Canada this year.

The commercial trade and traffic on the railways has been very dull for these few months back. Business on the Buffalo and Lake Huron railway has been so dull that a great number of the hands have been discharged on account of the panic in the South.

Canada yet cries, Freedom! Freedom! Freedom!

I must now say a little about my friend and brother Stepney Brown, he lived about six months at the Niagara Falls and is now going to school here in Brantford, he sends his best respects to you all. He and I often sit together at night after the labor of the day is over talking about our absent friends wishing we could see them once more.

Mr. Brown and myself have been wishing for one or two of your slavery standards and would be much obliged to you if you would send some of the latest.

Please let me hear from you as soon as possible. I must now bring my letter to a close and remain your affectionate friend, J.W. DUNGY.

P.S. May the Lord be with you. J.W. DUNGY.

Address your letter to John W. Dungy, Brantford, C.W.

"AUNT HANNAH MOORE."

In 1854 in company with her so-called Mistress (Mary Moore) Aunt Hannah arrived in Philadelphia, from Missouri, being *en route* to California, where she with her mistress was to join her master, who had gone there years before to seek his fortune. The mistress having relatives in this city tarried here a short time, not doubting that she had sufficient control over Aunt Hannah to keep her from contact with either abolitionists or those of her own color, and that she would have no difficulty in taking her with her to her journey's end. If such were her calculations she was greatly mistaken. For although Aunt Hannah was destitute of book-learning she was nevertheless a woman of thought and natural ability, and while she wisely kept her counsel from her mistress she took care to make her wants known to an abolitionist. She had passed many years under the yoke, under different owners, and now seeing a ray of hope she availed herself of the opportunity to secure her freedom. She had occasion to go to a store in the neighborhood where she was stopping, and to her unspeakable joy she found the proprietor an abolitionist and a friend who inquired into her condition and proffered her assistance. The store-keeper quickly made known her condition at the Anti-slavery Office, and in double-quick time J.M. McKim and Charles Wise as abolitionists and members of the Vigilance Committee re-paired to the stopping-place of the mistress and her slave to de-mand in the name of humanity and the laws of Pennsylvania that Aunt Hannah should be no longer held in fetters but that she should be immediately proclaimed free. In the eyes of the mistress this procedure was so extraordinary that she became very much excited and for a moment threatened them with the "broomstick," but her raving had no effect on Messrs. McKim and Wise, who did not rest contented until Aunt Hannah was safely in their hands. She had lived a slave in Moore's family in the State of Missouri about ten years and said she was treated very well, had plenty to eat, plenty to wear, and a plenty of work. It was prior to her coming into the possession of Moore that Aunt Hannah had been made to drink the bitter waters of oppression. From this point, therefore, we shall present some of the incidents of her life, from infancy, and very nearly word for word as she related them:

"Moore bought me from a man named McCaully, who owned me about a year. I fared dreadful bad under McCaully. One day in a rage he undertook to beat me with the limb of a cherry-tree; he began at me and tried in the first place to snatch my clothes off, but he did not succeed. After that he beat the cherry-tree limb all to pieces over me. The first blow struck me on the back of my neck and knocked me down; his wife was looking on, sitting on the side of the bed crying to him to lay on. After the limb was worn out he then went out to the yard and got a lath, and he come at me again and beat me with that until he broke it all to pieces. He was not satisfied then; he next went to the fence and tore off a paling, and with that he took both hands, 'cursing' me all the time as hard as he could. With an oath he would say, 'now don't you love me?' 'Oh master, I will pray for you,' I would cry, then he would 'cuss' harder than ever.' He beat me until he was tired and quit. I crept out of doors and throwed up blood; some days I was hardly able to creep. With this beating I was laid up several weeks. Another time Mistress Mc-Caully got very angry. One day she beat me as bad as he did. She was a woman who would get very mad in a minute. One day she began scolding and said the kitchen wasn't kept clean. I told her the kitchen was kept as clean as any kitchen in the place; she spoke very angry, and said she didn't go by other folks but she had rules of her own. She soon ordered me to come in to her. I went in as she ordered me; she met me with a mule-rope, and ordered me to cross my hands. I crossed my hands and she tied me to the bedstead. Here her husband said, 'my dear, now let me do the fighting.' In her mad fit she said he shouldn't do it, and told him to stand back and keep out of the way or I will give you the cowhide she said to him. He then 'sot' down in a 'cheer' and looked like a man condemned to be hung; then she whipped me with the cowhide until I sunk to the floor. He then begged her to quit. He said to his wife she has begged and begged and you have whipped her enough. She only raged 'wus;' she turned the butt end of the cowhide and struck me five or six blows over my head as hard as she could; she then throwed the cowhide down and told a little girl to untie me. The little girl was not able to do it; Mr. McCaully then untied me himself. Both times that I was beat the blood run down from my head to my feet.

"They wouldn't give you anything to eat hardly. McCaully bore the name of coming by free colored children without buying them, and selling them afterwards. One boy on the place always said that he was free but had been kidnapped from Arkansas. He could tell all about how he was kidnapped, but could not find anybody to do anything for him, so he had to content himself.

"McCaully bought me from a man by the name of Landers. While in Landers' hands I had the rheumatism and was not able to work. He was afraid I was going to die, or he would lose me, and I would not be of any service to him, so he took and traded me off for a wagon. I was something better when he traded me off; well enough to be about. My health remained bad for about four years, and I never got my health until Moore bought me. Moore took me for a debt. McCaully owed Moore for wagons. I was not born in Missouri but was born in Virginia. From my earliest memory I was owned by Conrad Hackler; he lived in Grason County. He was a very poor man, and had no other slave but me. He bought me before I was quite four years old, for one hundred dollars. Hackler bought me from a man named William Scott. I must go back by good rights to the beginning and tell all: Scott bought me first from a young man he met one day in the road, with a bundle in his arms. Scott, wishing to know of the young man what he had in his bundle, was told that he had a baby. 'What are you going to do with it?' said Scott. The young man said that he was going to take it to his sister; that its mother was dead, and it had nobody to take care of it. Scott offered the young man a horse for it, and the young man took him up. This is the way I was told that Scott came by me. I never knowed anything about my mother or father, but I have always believed that my mother was a white woman, and that I was put away to save her character; I have always thought this. Under Hackler I was treated more like a brute than a human being. I was fed like the dogs; had a trough dug out of a piece of wood for a plate. After I growed up to ten years old they made me sleep out in an old house standing off some distance from the main house where my master and mistress lived. A bed of straw and old rags was made for me in a big trough called the tan trough (a trough having been used for tanning purposes). The cats about the place came and slept with me, and was all the company I had. I had to work with the hoe in the field and help do everything in doors and out in all weathers. The place was so poor that some seasons he would not raise twenty bushels of corn and hardly three bushels of wheat. As for shoes I never knowed what it was to have a pair of shoes until I was grown up. After I growed up to be a woman my master thought nothing of taking my clothes off, and would whip me until the blood would run down to the ground. After I was twenty-five years old they did not treat me so bad; they both professed to get religion about that time; and my master said he would never lay the weight of his finger on me again. Once after that mistress wanted him to whip me, but he didn't do it, nor never whipped me any more. After awhile my master died; if they had gone according to law I would have been hired out or sold, but my mistress wanted to keep me to carry on the place for her support. So I was kept for seven or eight years after his death. It was understood between my mistress, and her children, and her friends, who all met after master died, that I was to take care of mistress, and after mistress died I should not serve anybody else. I done my best to keep my mistress from suffering. After a few years they all became dissatisfied, and moved to Missouri. They scattered, and took up government land. Without means they lived as poor people commonly live, on small farms in the woods. I still lived with my mistress. Some of the heirs got dissatisfied, and sued for their rights or a settlement; then I was sold with my child, a boy."

Thus Aunt Hannah reviewed her slave-life, showing that she had been in the hands of six different owners, and had seen great tribulation under each of them, except the last; that she had never known a mother's or a father's care; that Slavery had given her one child, but no husband as a protector or a father. The half of what she passed through in the way of suffering has scarcely been hinted at in this sketch. Fifty-seven years were passed in bondage before she reached Philadelphia. Under the good Providence through which she came in possession of her freedom, she found a kind home with a family of Abolitionists, (Mrs. Gillingham's), whose hearts had been in deep sympathy with the slave for many years. In this situation Aunt Hannah remained several years, honest, faithful, and obliging, taking care of her earnings, which were put out at interest for her by her friends. Her mind was deeply imbued with religious feeling, and an unshaken confidence in God as her only trust; she connected herself with the A.M.E. Bethel Church, of Philadelphia, where she has walked, blameless and exemplary up to this day. Probably there is not a member in that large congregation whose simple faith and whose walk and conversation are more commendable than Aunt Hannah's. Although she has passed through so many hardships she is a woman of good judgment and more than average intellect; enjoys good health, vigor, and peace of mind in her old days, with a small income just sufficient to meet her humble wants without having to live at service. After living in Philadelphia for several years, she was married to a man of about her own age, possessing all her good qualities; had served a lifetime in a highly respectable Quaker family of this city, and had so won the esteem of his kind employer that at his death he left him a comfortable house for life, so that he was not under the necessity of serving another. The name of the recipient of the good Quaker friend's bounty and Aunt Hannah's companion, was Thomas Todd. After a few years of wedded life, Aunt Hannah was called upon to be left alone again in the world by the death of her husband, whose loss was mourned by many friends, both colored and white, who knew and respected him.

WOMAN ESCAPING IN A BOX, 1857.

She Was Speechless.

In the winter of 1857 a young woman, who had just turned her majority, was boxed up in Baltimore by one who stood to her in the relation of a companion, a young man, who had the box conveyed as freight to the depot in Baltimore, consigned to Philadelphia. Nearly all one night it remained at the depot with the living agony in it, and after being turned upside down more than once, the next day about ten o'clock it reached Philadelphia. Her companion coming on in advance of the box, arranged with a hackman, George Custus, to attend to having it brought from the depot to a designated house, Mrs. Myers', 412 S. 7th street, where the resurrection was to take place.

Custus, without knowing exactly what the box contained, but suspecting from the apparent anxiety and instructions of the young man who engaged him to go after it, that it was of great importance, while the freight car still remained on the street, demanded it of the freight agent, not willing to wait the usual time for the delivery of freight. At first the freight agent declined delivering under such circumstances. The Hackman insisted by saying that he wished to despatch it in great haste, said it is all right, you know me, I have been coming here for many years every day, and will be responsible for it. The freight-master told him to "take it and go ahead with it." No sooner said than done. It was placed in a one horse wagon at the instance of Custus, and driven to Seventh and Minster streets.

The secret had been intrusted to Mrs. M. by the young companion of the woman. A feeling of horror came over the aged woman, who had been thus suddenly entrusted with such responsibility. A few doors from her lived an old friend of the same religious faith with herself, well known as a brave woman, and a friend of the slave, Mrs. Ash, the undertaker or shrouder, whom every body knew among the colored people. Mrs. Myers felt that it would not be wise to move in the matter of this resurrection without the presence of the undertaker. Accordingly, she called Mrs. Ash in. Even her own family was excluded from witnessing the scene. The two aged women chose to be alone in that fearful moment, shuddering at the thought that a corpse might meet their gaze instead of a living creature. However, they mustered courage and pried off the lid. A woman was discovered in the straw but no sign of life was perceptible. Their fears seemed fulfilled. "Surely she is dead," thought the witnesses.

"Get up, my child," spake one of the women. With scarcely life enough to move the straw covering, she, nevertheless, did now show signs of life, but to a very faint degree. She could not speak, but being assisted arose. She was straightway aided up stairs, not yet uttering a word. After a short while she said, "I feel so deadly weak." She was then asked if she would not have some water or nourishment, which she declined. Before a great while, however, she was prevailed upon to take a cup of tea. She then went to bed, and there remained all day, speaking but a very little during that time. The second day she gained strength and was able to talk much better, but not with ease. The third day she began to come to herself and talk quite freely. She tried to describe her sufferings and fears while in the box, but in vain. In the midst of her severest agonies her chief fear was, that she would be discovered and carried back to Slavery. She had a pair of scissors with her, and in order to procure fresh air she had made a hole in the box, but it was very slight. How she ever managed to breathe and maintain her existence, being in the condition of becoming a mother, it was hard to comprehend. In this instance the utmost endurance was put to the test. She was obviously nearer death than Henry Box Brown, or any of the other box or chest cases that ever came under the notice of the Committee.

In Baltimore she belonged to a wealthy and fashionable family, and had been a seamstress and ladies' servant generally. On one occasion when sent of an errand for certain articles in order to complete arrangements for the Grand Opening Ball at the Academy of

Music, she took occasion not to return, but was among the missing. Great search was made, and a large reward offered, but all to no purpose. A free colored woman, who washed for the family, was suspected of knowing something of her going, but they failing to get aught out of her, she was discharged.

Soon after the arrival of this traveler at Mrs. Myers' the Committee was sent for and learned the facts as above stated. After spending some three or four days in Mrs. Myers' family she remained in the writer's family about the same length of time, and was then forwarded to Canada.

Mrs. Myers was originally from Baltimore, and had frequently been in the habit of receiving Underground Rail Road passengers; she had always found Thomas Shipley, the faithful philanthropist, a present help in time of need. The young man well knew Mrs. Myers would act with prudence in taking his companion to her house.

George Custus, the hackman, a colored man, was cool, sensible, and reliable in the discharge of his duty, as were the other parties, therefore every thing was well managed.

With this interesting case our narratives end, except such facts of a like kind as may be connected with some of the sketches of stockholders. A large number on the record book must be omitted. This is partly owing to the fact that during the first few years of our connection with the Underground Rail Road, so little was written out in the way of narratives, that would hardly be of sufficient interest to publish; and partly from the fact that, although there are exceptional cases even among those so omitted, that would be equally as interesting as many which have been inserted, time and space will not admit of further encroachment. If in any way we have erred in the task of furnishing facts and important information touching the Underground Rail Road, it has not been in overstating the sufferings, trials, perils, and marvellous escapes of those described, but on the contrary. In many instances after hearing the most painful narratives we had neither time nor inclination to write them out, except in the briefest manner, simply sufficient to identify parties, which we did, not dreaming that the dark cloud of Slavery was so soon to give way to the bright sunlight of Freedom.

ORGANIZATION OF THE
VIGILANCE COMMITTEE.

Meeting to Form a Vigilance Committee.

As has already been intimated, others besides the Committee were deeply interested in The Road; indeed, the little aid actually rendered by the Committee, was comparatively insignificant, compared with the aid rendered by some who were not nominally members. To this latter class of friends, it seems meet that we should particularly allude. Before doing so, however, simple justice to all concerned, dictates that we should here copy the official proceedings of the first meeting and organization of the Philadelphia Vigilance Committee as it existed until the very day that the ever to be remembered Emancipation Proclamation of Abraham Lincoln, rendered the services of the organization and road no longer necessary. It reads as follows:

"PENNSYLVANIA FREEMAN," DECEMBER 9, 1852.

Pursuant to the motion published in last week's "Freeman," a meeting was held in the Anti-slavery rooms, on the evening of the 2d inst., for the purpose of organizing a Vigilance Committee.

On motion Samuel Nickless was appointed chairman, and William Still secretary. J.M. McKim then stated at some length, the object of the meeting. He said, that the friends of the fugitive slave had been for some years past, embarrassed, for the want of a properly constructed active, Vigilance Committee; that the old Committee, which used to render effective service in this field of Anti-slavery labor, had become disorganized and scattered, and that for the last two or three years, the duties of this department had been performed by individuals on their own responsibility, and sometimes in a very irregular manner; that this had been the cause of much dissatisfaction and complaint, and that the necessity for a remedy of this state of things was generally felt. Hence, the call for this meeting. It was intended now to organize a committee, which should be composed of persons of known responsibility, and who could be relied upon to act systematically and promptly, and with the least possible expenditure of money in all cases that might require their attention.

James Mott and Samuel Nickless, expressed their hearty concurrence in what had been said, as did also B.N. Goines and N.W. Depee. The opinion was also expressed by one or more of these gentlemen, that the organization to be formed should be of the simplest possible character; with no more machinery or officers than might be necessary to hold it together and keep it in proper working order. After some discussion, it was agreed first to form a general committee, with a chairman, whose business it should be to call meetings when necessity should seem to require it, and to preside at the same; and a treasurer to take charge of the funds; and second, to appoint out of this general committee, an acting committee of four persons, who should have the responsibility of attending to every case that might require their aid, as well as the exclusive authority to raise the funds necessary for their purpose. It was further agreed that it should be the duty of the chairman of the Acting Committee to keep a record of all their doings, and especially of the money received and expended on behalf of every case claiming their interposition.

The following persons were appointed on the General Vigilance Committee:

GENERAL VIGILANCE COMMITTEE.

———

Robert Purvis,	Morris Hall,
Charles H. Bustill,	Nathaniel Depee,
Samuel Nickless,	Charles Wise,

Jacob C. White,   J.M. M'Kim,
Cyrus Whitson,   Isaiah O. Wears,
J. Asher,   John D. Oliver,
J.P. Burr   Prof. C.L. Reason,
William Still,   Henry Gordon,
P. Williamson,   W.H. Riley,
B.N. Goines,

Robert Purvis was understood to be Chairman of the General Committee, having been nominated at the head of the list, and Charles Wise was appointed treasurer. The Acting Committee was thus constituted:

William Still, chairman, N.W. Depee, Passmore Williamson, J.C. White. This Committee was appointed for the term of one year.

On motion, the proceedings of this meeting were ordered to be published in the "Pennsylvania Freeman."

(Adjourned.)

William Still, Secretary. Samuel Nickless, Chairman.

—

The Committee having been thus organized, J.M. McKim, corresponding secretary and general agent of the Pennsylvania Anti-slavery Society, issued the subjoined notice, which was published shortly afterwards in the "Pennsylvania Freeman," and the colored churches throughout the city:

"We are pleased to see that we have at last, what has for some time been felt to be a desideratum in Philadelphia, a responsible and duly authorized Vigilance Committee. The duties of this department of Anti-slavery labor, have, for want of such an organization, been performed in a very loose and unsystematic manner. The names of the persons constituting the Acting Committee, are a guarantee that this will not be the case hereafter. They are—

William Still (Chairman), 31 North Fifth Street,
Nathaniel W. Depee, 334 South Street,
Jacob C. White, 100 Old York Road, and

Passmore Williamson, southwest cor. Seventh and Arch Streets.

We respectfully commend these gentlemen, and the cause in which they are engaged, to the confidence and co-operation of all the friends of the hunted fugitive. Any funds contributed to either of them, or placed in the hands of their Treasurer, Charles Wise, corner of Fifth and Market Streets, will be sure of a faithful and judicious appropriation."